Henry —

Best wishes for

great goals!

DNA
LEADERSHIP

through

GOAL-DRIVEN
MANAGEMENT

DNA
LEADERSHIP
through
GOAL-DRIVEN
MANAGEMENT

James R. Ball

THE
GOALS
INSTITUTE

DNA Leadership through Goal-Driven Management

Published in the United States by The Goals Institute, Inc. Books and other materials published may be purchased in volume for educational, business, or sales and promotional use. For information, please contact us at:

The Goals Institute, Inc.
Post Office Box 3736
Reston, VA 20195-1736
www.goalsinstitute.com
e-mail: info@goalsinstitute.com

Jacket design Young Design

Book design and typography AAH Graphics

Publisher's Cataloging-in-Publication
(Provided by Quality Books, Inc.)
Ball, James R.
    DNA leadership through goal-driven management/James R. Ball.
    p. cm.
    Includes index.
    Preassigned LCCN: 97-70642
    ISBN 1-887570-00-4
    1. Management by objectives   I. Title
    HD30.65.B35 1997   658.4'012
                                         QBI97-40496

DNA Leadership™, GOAL-DRIVEN MANAGEMENT™, Goal Power™, Gyroscopic Planning™, MOSAIC™, and The Goals Institute™ are trademarks of The Goals Institute, Inc.

Printed in the United States of America

2 3 2 8 7 4 2 3 6 2 7 4 3

For Dolly

Special notices, acknowledgements, and thanks

First, I want to thank Jennifer Kuchta, my business partner—for her encouragement, support, and her many contributions to the development, content, writing, and editing of this work. Without her help this book would not be available for you to read.

And thank you to all the people who contributed to this book, particularly: Susan Baughn and Ann Hunter for their editorial input; Julie Young for her graphic and design creativity; Steve Hunter for his book design and layout expertise; Gayle Kennedy, Greg Franzke, Jennifer Ball, and Carol Weaver for their advice on the content and organization of the materials; and Jim Kofalt, Carl Mook, and Skip Lee for their valuable feedback.

I especially want to thank Richard Bartlett for his incisive insight and suggestions in titling this book.

In addition, there are numerous sources for the many stories and examples in this work, and authors and sources have been cited and credited where possible. I greatly appreciate the input of these individuals and the work of these authors and their publishers, and I thank them.

I also want to thank my mother and my father—for believing in me, for encouraging me, and for showing me how to work hard, and how to love and to care for others.

Last, and most importantly, thank you Dolly—for supporting me and for being there with me all these years.

"Most people are intelligent.

*What separates successful organizations
and people from others is that they
find and follow methods."*

—Jim Ball

Summary Table of Contents

Part One
21st-Century Leadership

Part Two
GOAL-DRIVEN MANAGEMENT

Part Two
GOAL-DRIVEN MANAGEMENT
(continuation)

Part Three
Success summary
and executive recommendations

Detailed Table of Contents

Part One
21st-Century Leadership

Part Two
GOAL-DRIVEN MANAGEMENT

Part Three
Success summary and executive recommendations

List of Illustrations

"Methods are the masters of masters."

—Charles Maurice de Talleyrand

Introduction

Imagine this.

You have 100 trillion microscopic cells to work with. Your job is to organize them, bond them together, and motivate them to express their individuality while they work together to create a vibrant, growing, functioning human body.

How are you going to approach this challenge? What models or blueprints are available to guide you? What methods and techniques will you use to perform the tasks before you?

Now imagine this.

The cells you have to work with are not cells of humans, they *are* humans. Humans are the cells of your business. Your job is to organize them, bond them together, and motivate them to express their individuality while they work together to form a vibrant, growing, functioning human business.

These two challenges are conceptually similar. The difference is that the model and methods used to organize the cells in our bodies still work well. But the models and methods we have been using in business are out of date.

We all know that the world has changed and continues to change. Speed. Knowledge. Know-how. Creativity. Innovation. These are the watchwords. We compete in global markets and yet we must market on an individualized basis.

Several questions loom on the horizon.

How can business leaders approach their challenges in this changed and changing world? What models or blueprints are available to guide their work? What methods and techniques can they use?

Is there a control panel leaders can use for 21st-century leadership and management?

Yes, there is.

The 21st-century control panel

The 21st-century control panel is *DNA Leadership,* so named because of the correlations between the leadership approach we need and the biological principles of cell theory and DNA.

The goals of bodies are to thrive and grow. To achieve their goals, our bodies focus on building the fabric of cells and implanting internal command centers within the cells themselves—so that cells are activated on autopilot to do what they must do and to become what they must become.

Biologically, the fabric of our cells is amino acids.

The imbedded autopilot mechanism is DNA. Deoxyribonucleic acid. DNA is the transforming agent. DNA gives the orders that control the growth and functionality of each cell.

The fabric of a business is the composite of the individuals in the business, the knowledge and skills they possess, and the business culture, environment, missions, visions, and philosophies.

The embedded autopilot mechanisms in a business are the goals of the business and the goals of the individuals in it. Goals are the transforming catalyst. Goals control the growth and functioning of the individuals and the business as a whole. Goals determine what the business and the individuals in it will or will not become and accomplish.

Selecting the right goals is critical. So is aligning and linking those goals throughout the DNA fabric of the business.

But even when these steps are taken you still have not achieved true *DNA Leadership.* A key ingredient is missing.

The missing ingredient: execution.

After the right goals have been selected, the right environment and culture have been created, and desirable guiding missions, visions, and philosophies have been established, someone still has to do the work. And doing the work is no longer as easy as it used to be. Workers need to be smarter, more knowledgeable, and more creative. They must share their know-how and expertise and work better together as a team—all in our changed and changing world.

How can leaders direct and manage the work that must be done? How can leaders help those who must do the work, so that they are empowered to contribute individually, but united to work as an integrated body toward common goals?

Are there tools leaders can use for these tasks?

Yes, there are.

The tools: Two methods for *DNA Leadership*

In addition to describing what must be done to effect *DNA Leadership,* this book contains two comprehensive step-by-step *methods* that show you *how* to do it.

Most people are intelligent, but only some are successful.

What separates successful organizations and people from others is whether they find and follow methods. A method provides a set of tracks for the trains to run on. In this case, the "trains" are leadership and goal achievement.

When you find and follow a method you have a basis to improve what you are doing. You have a common frame of reference for communicating with individuals and for teaching and developing your collective skills.

To effect *DNA Leadership,* leaders must create and cascade the organization's missions, visions, and philosophies throughout. Associates must buy into these guiding precepts. When this occurs the organization is bonded together by the same DNA fabric. Once this is accomplished, the DNA fabric must be *expressed* through the establishment of goals and the creation of action plans at the company level *and at the individual level.* Then the company must be managed to achieve its collective goals.

This book contains two proprietary methods to accomplish these tasks: *MOSAIC*™ and *GOAL-DRIVEN MANAGEMENT*™.

MOSAIC is a method for regenerating DNA within an organization and for determining which areas to concentrate on when establishing goals and action plans. It derives its name from an acronym for the six levels of performance and fulfillment it describes: Mastery, Outstanding, Satisfactory, Acceptable, Intolerable, and Counterproductive. When you use the *MOSAIC* method, you end up with aligned and linked DNA fabric throughout and a systematic and balanced approach for growth.

GOAL-DRIVEN MANAGEMENT is a method for establishing and achieving specific goals. When you follow GOAL-DRIVEN MANAGEMENT, you develop specific action plans and create specific systems to achieve your goals. You implement, monitor, and improve those plans and systems to obtain optimum results in the least time.

MOSAIC and GOAL-DRIVEN MANAGEMENT are the tools of *DNA Leadership*—tools to help you lead your organization and achieve your goals—for your organization and yourself.

Benefits for businesses and organizations

Businesses and organizations can use *MOSAIC* and GOAL-DRIVEN MANAGEMENT as their central leadership and management infrastructure from top to bottom. When used properly as integral elements of a *DNA Leadership* approach, *MOSAIC* and GOAL-DRIVEN MANAGEMENT are to businesses what DNA is to the cells in your body—they direct and process all important functions. Some of the functions affected are:

Strategic and operational planning: Developing mission statements, vision-of-success statements, goals, strategic plans, and operational plans at the company level; establishing supporting goals and action plans at all levels within the company—including goals and action plans for workgroups, teams, and individuals.

Linkage and alignment: Building the important linkage and alignment required between the intended strategic direction of the company determined by top management and the actual work being performed throughout the organization on a day-to-day basis.

Accountability: Creating a series of solid connections between company missions and individual actions thus increasing accountability and assuring that workgroups and individuals work on the tasks they should be working on to contribute toward achieving company goals.

Teamwork, innovation, and best practices: Strengthening communication and teamwork; sharing expertise, know-how, and best practices throughout an organization; plus stimulating continual improvement and innovation.

Delegation and management: Delegating authority and responsibility; managing and monitoring others toward achieving agreed-upon goals; adopting sound strategies and action plans that will save time and help avoid going down dead-end streets.

Benefits for individuals

Regardless of their experience level, individuals will gain from employing the *DNA Leadership* approach and using *MOSAIC* and *GOAL-DRIVEN MANAGEMENT*.

If you are a seasoned executive, the principles in this book will provide new ideas and techniques while recharging and refocusing you, thus increasing your odds for greater success.

If you are a less experienced leader or are just starting your career, you can use the book's methods and concepts as a complete blueprint and set of tools for success.

As with any tool, nothing can be gained without the desire to learn. It takes study and practice to get good at using the techniques in these methods. But the efforts required are *in*significant when measured against the payoffs.

A better approach, not a quick fix

My goal in writing this book is to offer methods, insights, and suggestions to those seeking better approaches to leadership, management, and goal achievement.

This book is needed today. The old leadership models are tired and worn. Many firms and individuals never learned the essential principles involved in establishing and achieving goals or they have slipped away from using the fundamental principles that work. Often, organizations and individuals develop skills for "handling things," but they allow the skills for establishing plans and strategies and taking positive, concrete actions to atrophy.

We must move *from* a reactive mode where the majority of efforts are spent putting out fires and solving yesterday's problems. We must move *to* an environment where tomorrow's opportunities are pursued today. We must get back to fundamental principles that work.

The methods in this book work. They do not promise or provide a quick fix, but with diligent effort by companies and individuals serious about creating a 21st-century growth organization and achieving more and greater goals, the results can be substantial.

I wish I had read a book explaining these concepts when I began my career. I know I would have achieved more, and my businesses would have been more successful, in less time, and with fewer difficulties and less wasted effort.

You know, individuals who are very successful are not "lucky" as some people may think they are. It's that "unlucky" individuals don't know precisely what they want. They have no methods and no plans, or they have faulty methods and faulty plans. Those who are "lucky" know their goals precisely. Because they use sound methods and follow an exact plan to get them, "good luck" seems to pursue them.

In this spirit, good luck!

Part
One

21st-Century
Leadership

Part One Overview

Chapter 1, DNA Leadership, introduces a modern model leaders can use to create a culture and environment for guiding the growth of their companies into the 21st century.

Chapter 2, The vital link: Goal alignment with missions, visions, and philosophies, illustrates how to establish alignment and linkage among strategic direction, operational control, and transaction processing so that actions of associates support your company's missions, visions, values, and goals. "Cascading," "buy-in," and other techniques are described. This chapter also explains what should be included in mission, vision, and philosophy statements.

Chapter 3, Goal power, explains how you can use the fundamental principles that make goals so powerful—as leadership tools for increasing productivity and growth in your business, and as tools for improving individual development and growth.

Chapter 4, MOSAIC: A method for identifying goals for balance and growth, explains how you can use *MOSAIC* to create and regenerate DNA throughout and determine where goals should be established to optimize business and individual potential. This chapter illustrates how to define and apply six discrete levels of performance for use in coaching, mentoring, and developing individuals. A business and an individual example of how to apply *MOSAIC* are provided.

Chapter 5, Why GOAL-DRIVEN MANAGEMENT works, shows you how to apply the techniques in this book so you can be on autopilot in pursuing your goals.

1

DNA Leadership

My partner, Dan, and I were just launching our venture capital firm when we met with two individuals who had formed a new business called Cable Educational Network, Inc. During a several-hour session the individuals described their business. Near the end of the evening they got to the heart of the matter. They needed capital fast because the company was going to miss a payroll soon.

At the time we had not completed our own fund-raising efforts, so we were not prepared to invest in this new venture. But, we liked the individuals and thought the business concept had excellent potential. On the drive home Dan and I decided to help these individuals secure their seed capital. *Their* goal became *our* goal. The moment it did, everything changed.

Dan got on a plane to New York two days later to meet with an investment banking firm and other investors who had expressed an interest in the company. I began discussing the transaction with firms we knew locally to see if they might participate.

As we got closer to the deadline when the company would run out of cash, the activity heightened. Our firm was asked to serve as escrow agent for the transaction. Dan stepped in as a surrogate chief financial officer of the company. Lawyers swarmed in their conference rooms to prepare legal documents. We worked around the clock. When the smoke cleared, we completed the closing and the company was on the way to its destiny. John Hendricks, CEO, one of the individuals we had met with early on, later dropped use of the name Cable Educational Network, Inc.

Today we all recognize the name of this successful company as the Discovery Channel.

Our collective decision to pursue a definite goal with a definite purpose and a definite deadline galvanized and magnetized everyone involved. The moment we decided to help John Hendricks secure his initial capital, it was as if the train we were on instantly switched to a new set of tracks going in a new direction. We immediately began rearranging our schedules and taking actions we had not planned previously. The goal to raise the capital by the deadline became the catalyst to action, and it pulled us in the new direction.

Our experience with the Discovery Channel was like the one NASA had when President Kennedy announced: "We are going to put a man on the moon by the end of the decade." NASA had fallen behind in the space race when the Russians launched Sputnik, the world's first satellite, in 1957. In response, Kennedy met with his advisors to determine what the United States could do to regain preeminence. Several alternatives were considered. One idea was putting a man on the moon. When Kennedy seized on that goal and announced it to the American people, the goal revitalized NASA and provided the driving force for its own fulfillment.

Establishing goals simply because you want to achieve them is a good reason to set goals. But as these examples illustrate, goals are more valuable than just the end results they represent: goals are transforming catalysts that create power.

21st-century leadership

The primary task of a 21st-century leader is to move people from where they are to where they have never been before—by getting individuals to become more than they thought they could become and to accomplish more than they thought was possible.

Motivation of this kind is an inside job. The motivating catalyst must be extraordinary and it must be implanted *within* the individuals—just as President Kennedy implanted his vision to put a man on the moon into those in charge at NASA and John Hendricks implanted his dream for the Discovery Channel into Dan, me, and many others.

We know it's important to formulate a company's mission, vision, and philosophies. We know it's important, too, for individuals to implement these both in spirit and through their actions. And we know it's important for companies to innovate and grow. But how are leaders to accomplish all that? What are the best ways for leaders to create and communicate missions, visions, and philosophies *and* have individuals buy in to them and take appropriate actions to fulfill them—as though they were on a common quest? Leaders need a reliable up-to-date leadership model to follow.

Locomotive Leadership

The oldest leadership approach is authoritative. Company leaders adopt their missions, visions, and philosophies, stand before company employees, point to the top of the mountain, shout "Charge!" and go running toward the summit.

The metaphor I use for this approach is *Locomotive Leadership*. Envision a powerful locomotive pushing or pulling a three-hundred car train. The locomotive can't pull on three hundred cars all at once, but what it can do is pull on one car, get it moving, let it pull on the second car, and so on. That is why the coupling devices connecting railroad cars aren't solid; they allow a little gap so momentum can be built up and the cars can be started in movement one at a time—all going down the track one after the other following the locomotive.

Locomotive Leadership is the style of leadership that businesses adopted and perfected during the industrial age. Organization charts of companies in this era were similar to each other. At the top was the president. Next were the vice presidents for the functional areas. Below each vice president were middle managers in a one-to-one chain of command. At the bottom were the masses of worker bees.

Leadership and management were straightforward. The president decided what to do, the vice presidents decided how to do it, the middle managers oversaw the daily work, and the worker bees did what they were told—no questions asked.

The chain of command in *Locomotive Leadership* was rarely altered. Like couplings between railroad cars, linkage between individuals from top to bottom provided for a little flexibility at each level, but the basic alignment was solid and inflexible.

In many organizations, particularly smaller ones, this approach may still work—because the chain of command is short and the paths or tracks the company needs to follow are clear. But in larger, more complex, and rapidly growing organizations, this approach has serious drawbacks because individuals in the field are removed physically and structurally from the company's leaders. In global companies this approach is inappropriate.

Our need for a new leadership model in the knowledge age

In an eye blink we have zoomed *through* the information age into the knowledge age. It is not enough to capture and collect information. Now it must be the precise information you need; you must put that information into context; you must bring it to the attention of those who need it; and they must act on it now.

Companies and individuals can't just be fast; in the knowledge age they must compete at warp speed. They can no longer just be responsive to change; they must create it.

In the knowledge age companies and individuals must innovate and create their own futures, or they are going to be overtaken and consumed by circumstances.

Innovation in business used to be largely an option motivated by the desire for improved profits. Markets were supply-side driven. Demand for products and services was determinable with reasonable accuracy. The channels for the sale and distribution of products and services were established and identifiable. Markets were geographically contained. Companies could operate on a linear basis, with small incremental improvements being made each new model year to their products and services, channels of distribution, and the way they transacted business.

In the knowledge age innovation isn't an option. It's a necessity for survival and growth. Here's why:

- We have shifted from manufacturer- and service-provider-driven markets to markets that are buyer-driven and buyer-controlled.

- We have gone from fixed or determinable demand with established multi-level distribution channels to fragmented demand and disintermediated distribution.

- We have switched from static markets to markets that pulse and change dynamically.

- We have leaped from an environment where marginal enhancements and improvements in products, services, and transactional activities were admired to an environment where quantum leaps are required.

- We have transformed from architecturally structured organizations in office buildings to free-flowing virtual companies where employees operate from home or in "hoteling" environments.

- We have gone from same-day service to electronic time frames where you can get what you want any time you want it.

- We have moved from mass marketing and mass merchandising to a customized world of one-to-one production, marketing, and communication. (For two excellent books on this, see *The One to One Future—Building Customer Relationships One Customer at a*

Time and *Enterprise One to One—Tools for Competing in the Interactive Age* by Don Peppers and Martha Rogers, Ph.D.)

No one makes a single widget and sells it to a small number of steady customers anymore. The single widget company of yesterday now offers sixty-eight kinds of widgets in a rainbow of colors, and these are sold to two thousand customers in a hundred different markets in eleven countries.

DNA Leadership

The mechanical *Locomotive Leadership* model is out-of-date.

We are in the knowledge age and we need a leadership model for the 21st century. This new model must provide for the creation of a culture and a framework for motivating and guiding individuals to go from where they are to where they have never been—so that they can achieve the mission and vision of the organization in a manner that is consistent with the organization's guiding principles and values.

I call the new model *DNA Leadership*. And yes, *DNA Leadership* is a direct reference to molecular DNA.

DNA is deoxyribonucleic acid—the molecular basis of our heredity and all cell compositions in our bodies. Even though our brain decides what to do, and we have thousands of different types of cells pulsating at the speed of light, each with a different job to do, all of our cells are composed of the *same fabric* and must work together to achieve our goals, or we are not going anywhere. A flaw or a switch in the wrong position in the DNA of a single cell can stop us cold. The cells in our bodies are the ultimate expression of teamwork and buy-in to a common mission.

DNA Leadership is an approach where the leaders of the organization establish guiding missions, visions, and philosophies, and then interweave these to create the organization's *DNA fabric*. The leaders use this fabric to create an environment, a culture, and an operational framework that internally motivates and empowers individuals to do what they must do and become what they must become to make their contributions to the company's intended purposes and objectives.

Individuals brought into an organization become the organization's individual cells. As cells in the body contain their basic DNA, these individual cells in the organization contain the organization's "core DNA." Individuals bring to an organization their own code of individuality as defined by their knowledge, skills, know-how, values, and beliefs. They either align with the mission, vision, values, culture, and operational framework of the organization and therefore "fit" into it because there is a DNA match, or they don't align and don't fit and are therefore rejected because the chemistry isn't right.

DNA Leadership provides for sharing of knowledge and know-how; identification, utilization, and enhancement of best practices; innovation and creativity; continuous improvement in all processes; lean and nimble transaction processing; and optimum operational efficacy. In addition, *DNA Leadership* provides for autonomy and empowerment of individuals while fostering unity and teamwork. *DNA Leadership* is a universal concept and it can be used by all businesses, big or small, in all industries.

Cell theory principles and *DNA Leadership*

Three principles of cell theory are relevant for our discussion here: (1) all living matter is made up of cells that interact and depend on each other for survival and growth; (2) cells, the fundamental units of life, are composed of DNA, the code of genetic information; and (3) the unique *expression* of the DNA within individual cells is the transforming catalyst that determines what a cell will do and become.

The corollary principles for *DNA Leadership* are: (1) all businesses are living entities made up of individuals who interact and depend on each other for survival and growth; (2) the individual is the fundamental unit in a business and individuals are composed of "core DNA," their code of individuality as defined by their knowledge, skills, know-how, values, and beliefs; and (3) the expression of goals is the transforming catalyst within individuals, and goals will determine how individuals utilize their knowledge, skills, and know-how to do what they do and become what they become, thus determining what the business becomes and achieves.

This means that for a business to change and grow it must take one or some combination of three actions: (1) alter the cell structure of the business by altering the composition of the individuals, the manner in which they interact, or the environment or culture in which they operate; (2) alter the core DNA within the individuals by altering their guiding missions, visions, and values or their knowledge, skills, and know-how; or (3) change the DNA expression of the business by changing the goals of the business and the goals the individuals in it are pursuing.

In *DNA Leadership,* goals are the transforming agent

DNA, the transforming catalyst that directs the individual cells in our bodies to become what they must become and do what they must do is the same in every cell. The cells in our eyes are composed of the same DNA as the cells in our fingertips, but because they have different functions, they express different portions of the DNA. They therefore manifest themselves differently and become specialized to do different jobs—eye cells to see, fingertip cells to feel and to touch.

Individuals: As with cells of the body, individuals are made up of the same chemical substances, but they are different in what they pursue and become. Even when two individuals pursue the same objectives, they achieve different results and different degrees of success. Sometimes these differences are minor. But in many instances the differences between what one individual achieves and what another individual in the same field achieves

Cell theory principles and
DNA Leadership

There are three principles of cell theory: (1) all living matter is made up of cells that interact and depend on each other for survival and growth; (2) the cell is the fundamental unit of life and cells are composed of DNA, the code of genetic information; and (3) the unique *expression* of the DNA within individual cells is the transforming catalyst that determines what a cell will do and become.

These principles are applicable in business: (1) all businesses are living entities made up of individuals who interact and depend on each other for survival and growth; (2) the individual is the fundamental unit in a business and individuals are composed of "core DNA," their code of individuality as defined by their knowledge, skills, know-how, values, and beliefs; and (3) the expression of goals is the transforming catalyst within individuals, and goals will determine how individuals utilize their knowledge, skills, and know-how to do what they do and become what they become, thus determining what the business becomes and achieves.

This means that for a business to change and grow it must take one or some combination of three actions: (1) alter the cell structure of the business by altering the composition of the individuals or the manner in which they interact, or the environment or culture in which they operate; (2) alter the DNA within the individuals by altering their guiding missions, visions, and values or their knowledge, skills, and know-how; or (3) change the DNA of the business by changing the goals of the business and the goals the individuals in it are pursuing.

are substantial. What is the transforming catalyst that directs one individual to become a doctor and another to become a salesperson? What transforming catalyst causes one doctor or one salesperson to become a leader and another doctor or salesperson to achieve only mediocre results? What causes these differences?

Goals are the transforming agents that cause the differences. A doctor pursues the goal of becoming a doctor. A salesperson pursues the goal of becoming a salesperson. One doctor will perform better or worse than other doctors, and one salesperson will perform better or worse than other salespersons because of the fabric of their DNA and the goals they each pursue.

Businesses: Consider two comparable companies. Both are composed of the same basic ingredient, people. So what makes one company become a software development firm and the other become a chain of restaurants? And what makes one software development firm or one restaurant chain become more successful than another? What causes these differences?

Once again, goals are the transforming agents that cause the differences. A software firm pursues goals of becoming a software firm. A restaurant chain pursues goals of becoming a restaurant chain. One software firm or restaurant chain will perform better or worse than a competitor based on the fabric of the DNA of the businesses—as determined by the mission, vision, values, culture, and operational framework of the business—*and the goals they each pursue.*

The *DNA Leadership* fabric

The most important features of the *DNA Leadership* model are the DNA fabric itself and the ability leaders have to use the fabric as a virtual control panel for guiding the growth and development of their organizations.

The common DNA fabric that runs throughout organizations promotes autonomy and independent thinking and actions by individuals and groups. At the same time it cultivates interdependent relationships among individuals in the organization and their sense of unity when it comes to the pursuit of the

organization's mission, vision, and goals. This is similar to the way
our bodies work.

Any cell in our bodies can detect and respond to any change
at any time without getting permission or directions from other
cells. You instantly jerk your hand away from the hot stove without waiting for your brain to analyze the situation and give you
the okay.

Though they can act independently, the cells in our bodies
work together in unity and harmony toward common objectives.
When you run up the stairs your legs don't have to send a message
to your heart to pump more blood; your heart knows what you
are doing because it is moving up the stairs with you, so it starts
pumping more blood automatically.

This is the way it is in business, too. Top management can't
stay constantly in touch with changing market conditions and the
needs and sensitivities of employees, customers, and suppliers
throughout their extensive organizations. Executives must rely on
the DNA fabric within the individuals to stimulate their good
judgment in pursuing company missions and visions of success.

Nordstrom's department stores provides an example of one
aspect of the *DNA Leadership* approach. Employees are indoctri-
nated into the "Nordstrom way" by a variety of means so the
DNA fabric of Nordstrom's mission, values, and philosophies is
integrated into the very being of individuals. This minimizes the
need for rules and regulations. Nordstrom employees are told that
rule number one is: "Use good judgment in all situations." They
are told there are no other rules.

When I was a new staff member at Arthur Andersen, we
joked about how we were becoming so ingrained with the
"Andersen way" that soon we would be required to wear under-
wear with Arthur Andersen labels stitched into it. It was only later
in my career that I realized the value of my indoctrination into the
"Andersen way." To this day, the Andersen DNA—integrity,
quality, intolerance for mediocrity, uncompromising service,

attention to details, and investment in the development of good people—is in my being. Arthur Andersen's own words, "think straight, talk straight," still serve as a guiding precept in my life.

The DNA molecular model in business is defined by a company's mission statement, vision statement, philosophies, codes and practices of conduct, culture, environment, and its methods for transacting business.

The transmutation of missions, visions, philosophies, and so on from one individual to another is called "buy-in"—individuals buy in to ideas, objectives, and values so concretely that they adopt them as their own. When there is buy-in throughout an organization, the same DNA fabric of the organization is within every individual.

The hurdle in *DNA Leadership* is that for this to work, everyone must evolve from the same DNA molecular model. A company's DNA must be regenerated and ingrained into employees from the moment they are hired. Company leaders must take steps to continually refine, expand, and amplify a company's DNA through every cell in the organization. This takes more time, effort, and resources than you might imagine. It is not cheap or easy to create a culture like those that exist at companies like Arthur Andersen, Nordstrom, General Electric, and Disney. And it is not cheap or easy to maintain such a culture once it is created. Persistance and constant vigilance are required. Little details are important. But the investment is worthwhile and the long-term payoffs are substantial.

DNA Leadership through buy-in

If business leaders want employees to pursue an agreed-upon mission and vision for their companies, then the leaders must create an environment that stimulates and encourages buy-in at the individual level.

The way to establish buy-in is to create a sense of ownership on behalf of the individuals buying in. There are two ways to create a true sense of ownership. You can incorporate some of the individual into what you are creating, or you can incorporate some of what you are creating into the individual. For *DNA Leadership* there has to be a DNA transfer, either *from* the individual to the company or from the company *to* the individual.

Take mission statements, for example. The easiest way to get individuals to buy into a mission statement is to get them involved in the process of creating it. This provides a forum for their input and warms them to the ideas of others in a natural and acceptable manner. No one hands them a statement and says, "Here, follow this." Instead, they put their mark on the words themselves and acquire pride of authorship and ownership during the process. The mission statement includes their DNA, so to speak.

But not everyone can be involved in drafting or fine-tuning company mission, vision, and philosophy statements and goals. How can individuals acquire a sense of ownership?

The answer is deceptively simple. Individuals must create and own their *own* mission, vision, and philosophy statements and goals—which embody the core DNA from company statements and goals.

If individuals have their own mission, vision, and philosophy statements—statements they were involved in creating, with guidance from the corporate DNA department—then there is a good chance they will buy into them and pursue them.

If individuals have their own goals, goals they were involved in creating—again with guidance from the corporate DNA people—then there is a good chance they will buy into them and pursue them as well.

As simple as it sounds, the way to cascade corporate mission, vision, and philosophy statements, and goals to every level in the company is to have divisions, units, teams, and individuals develop their own mission, vision, and philosophy statements, and goals—by beginning with the corporate versions and making appropriate modifications. The chart below shows how the flow might look graphically.

Cascading Effect

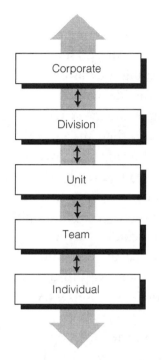

The cascading process: How it works

The "cascading" concept is not new. Many companies, some very large, do what is illustrated. In many large organizations each division or unit has its own mission, vision, and philosophy statements, its own goals and action plans, and its own adaptations of methods, systems, and procedures. The cascading process is necessary not because the executives running the company couldn't adopt sound missions, visions, goals, and so on, but because the cascading process provides for buy-in and "DNA transfer" from one cell to another one step at a time.

The cascading process begins at the corporate level. Company leaders adopt fundamental mission, vision, and value statements. They establish strategic parameters and overall objectives for three-, five-, or ten-year periods. These are cascaded down to subsidiary companies or divisions, which then define supporting missions, objectives, goals, and plans at their level. Then missions, visions, and plans are cascaded within the divisions to units, workgroups, and teams, which in turn cascade the missions, visions, goals, and plans to individuals. Throughout the process there is continual linkage and alignment. The resulting effect is that the goals, plans, and actions of individuals are in line with the overall corporate mission, vision, objectives, and plans.

The process of specifying and aligning objectives, goals, and plans at the various levels within a company, including the individual level, requires time and effort. But this cascading is essential to ensure individuals and workgroups are making their required contributions to the desired corporate goals in a manner consistent with the company's overall beliefs, philosophies, and values.

The benefits of internal linkage and alignment are performance, results, and value. Organizations with this kind of linkage are stronger and more capable than other organizations because they are, in effect, "DNA bonded"—that is, they come from the same seed, the same mission.

Achieving alignment through the creation and management of *doer-centered* goals

An objective of *DNA Leadership* is to integrate each individual in an organization into an overall *self-managed, self-directed, self-motivated,* and *self-improving system. DNA Leadership* requires leaders to influence and manage the goal selection and action planning processes in their organizations.

Like DNA expression, goals are the transforming catalyst for all growth and development. Goals therefore are extremely important and they have great power. The power of goals is discussed in *Chapter 3*.

An integral aspect of the *GOAL-DRIVEN MANAGEMENT* method discussed in *Part Two* of this book is to create a participatory environment where goals and plans are considered and established by the "doers" in the organization.

In a participatory environment, managers and supervisors do not set goals or develop plans for their associates. Instead, managers first inform associates about the purposes, values, and objectives of the organization. Then managers clarify the roles the associates play and the contributions they are expected to make in order for overall company goals to be achieved. Next, managers teach associates *how* to set and pursue goals and *how* to develop and use systems to drive daily progress. Finally, managers work with associates to establish their individual goals, plans, and systems. When this is completed, the manager becomes a coach and support team member to help associates achieve their goals.

The intent is to create a process that helps individuals achieve desired goals. This includes teaching them the right skills, helping them develop and follow the right plans, and showing them how to employ the best methods and procedures. The objective is for managers to help others set goals and then help them achieve them. For this to occur, the managers themselves must be good at setting and pursuing goals.

When using *DNA Leadership,* it is essential for individuals doing the work to help select or shape the goals they are pursuing, the plans they are following, and the tools and methods they are using. Managers must help doers see what they are doing by helping them clarify their goals and analyze their work processes. Then the individuals themselves can assess their personal alignment with corporate missions and objectives.

The *doer-centered* approach to *DNA Leadership through* GOAL-DRIVEN MANAGEMENT is necessary because our world is dynamic and intense with changes. Management cannot control or monitor individuals sufficiently through external influences; the only alternative is to control and influence the DNA fiber for results and goals.

When DNA fiber is properly transferred into goals, the result is true empowerment, true *DNA Leadership*.

This is an inside-out, rather than an outside-in approach. It represents a fundamental shift in the way we have historically thought and acted towards goals and the way we have motivated individuals to take action to achieve goals.

To effect an inside-out *DNA Leadership* approach, organizations need a method of providing for the engineering and regeneration of desirable DNA throughout. Then there will be alignment and congruency among corporate missions, visions, and values, and the goals, plans, and actions of business units, teams, and individuals. Our methods to achieve such alignment and congruency are *MOSAIC* and *GOAL-DRIVEN MANAGEMENT*. These are explained briefly below—and more completely in *Chapter 4* and *Part Two* of this book, respectively.

The *MOSAIC* and *GOAL-DRIVEN MANAGEMENT* methods

MOSAIC is a method for regenerating corporate DNA through the creation and cascading of missions, visions, and philosophies throughout an organization. *MOSAIC* provides specific tools for dividing a business, a business unit, the responsibilities of a team, or the roles and responsibilities of individuals into discrete functional parts and for establishing specific criteria for use in measuring and guiding performance. *MOSAIC* also is used for identifying opportunities where goals can be established for balanced growth and improvement.

GOAL-DRIVEN MANAGEMENT is a method for selecting specific goals, the DNA-transforming catalyst, and creating and implementing specific action plans to achieve desired performance levels. There are five keys in *GOAL-DRIVEN MANAGEMENT* and each of these provides success strategies, tactics, and implementation action steps to ensure goal achievement.

MOSAIC and *GOAL-DRIVEN MANAGEMENT* can be used separately and they will provide many benefits and results. However, these methods are intended to be used together to create, regenerate, and transfer an organization's DNA fabric throughout the organization and to drive actions which achieve the organization's intended purposes and results. The principles, strategies, tools, techniques, and action steps to accomplish this are contained in the remainder of this book.

2

The vital link:
Goal alignment with
missions, visions, and
philosophies

I met Pete Egoscue. Pete is the man who helped Jack Nicklaus
fix his back without surgery so Nicklaus could go on playing and
winning golf tournaments. Pete showed me a technique he
described in his book, *The Egoscue Method of Health Through
Motion*, which I use to relieve back pain whenever my bad back
creeps up. The method is simple. I lie with my back flush to the
floor with both legs up at right angles resting on a chair so they
also are bent at perfect right angles at the knees. No matter how
much pain my back has been in, in a half hour the pain is gone and
usually I am fast asleep.

This technique allows my body and spinal structure to return
to what Pete refers to as "perfect alignment." Pete told me that
one of the biggest sources of back pain is poor posture. It causes
our normal perfect alignment to go out of sync. Without perfect
alignment your energy, effectiveness, and in turn, your results
deteriorate rapidly. And in the case of Jack Nicklaus, he is in pain
and can't golf.

The concept of alignment also applies to your goals. Are they
aligned with your intended purposes, beliefs, and objectives? Goal

power is increased when you achieve goal alignment, and it is diminished when you do not.

Goal alignment in business

Alignment of business goals means agreement among the business's mission, vision, values, goals, plans, and actions—from the overall company perspective all the way to the individual perspective. Alignment in a business also means "unity"—when everyone is working harmoniously as a unit toward the same common objectives and purposes. When a business is in perfect alignment, the company is DNA-bonded and there is a clear line of sight between the company's mission, vision, and values, and the goals, plans, and actions of individuals.

Personal alignment

Alignment of personal goals means agreement among your roles, responsibilities, beliefs, plans, goals, and actions. You are in alignment when there is congruency among these factors. Are you pursuing goals that help you fulfill your desires and purposes? Are you selecting goals that help you achieve *what* you want to achieve *when* you want to achieve it? Are you pursuing goals *you* want to be pursuing? Are your goals harmonious with your roles and responsibilities? Are your actions consistent with your values and beliefs?

Alignment requires linkage to actual implementation

For business mission, vision, and philosophy statements to have value they must be communicated and bought into throughout the entire organization. Then they must be transformed into specific goals, action plans, processes, procedures, and finally tangible *actions* at the individual level. In other words, there must be DNA linkage and alignment among mission, vision, and philosophy statements and goals at the company level; and goals, action plans, actions, and results at the individual level. This linkage and alignment must be in place day-in and day-out so actions are continually in alignment from top to bottom and throughout an organization.

Regardless of how much effort executives spend developing their mission and vision statements and plans, these efforts are for naught if individuals don't make their required contributions to the achievement of specific goals.

In some cultures the figure carved at the bottom of the totem pole is afforded the greatest ranking and prestige. This is because the weight of the totem pole must be borne by those at the bottom. This concept applies in business—if employees at the lowest level don't do their part, then the organization is structurally weakened and vulnerable.

Recently I read an article featuring the president of a growing chain of retail stores. The president was quoted as saying he believed a key to the company's success was its attention to detail in day-to-day activities at the stores.

One weekend I went into one of these stores to purchase a laser printer for my daughter in college. Not only could I not find anyone to wait on me, when I asked the manager where the shopping carts were, he looked up from his papers and said, "They must be out in the parking lot." Then he went back to his figures.

I purchased a printer that day—at a competitor's store. There is a breakdown between what the president of this chain intends and what the store manager and employees are doing to implement his intentions. The company's mission statement, philosophies, and objectives are *not* linked and aligned with the actual actions employees are taking in the stores. The people at the store level don't possess the same DNA as the president. As a result, this company does not "walk its talk."

Alignment establishes linkage among three elements

Companies can be considered in alignment when there is linkage aligning three elements: (1) the strategic direction of the company; (2) the operational control of the company; and, (3) the transactional processing of the company.

Strategic direction of a company is established by the owners and senior management members. Strategic direction is documented in the company's mission, vision, values, and philosophy statements and in the company's business plan.

Operational control of a company is established by management personnel at various levels and is represented by a company's management practices, operating processes and procedures, personnel processes and policies, cultural idiosyncracies, goals, operating plans, and budgets.

Transactional processing activities are affected by the individuals in a company based on their personal missions, visions, values, goals, *and actions*. Companies do not process transactions or take actions; people do.

How mission, vision, and philosophy statements interrelate to goals and action plans

We don't know what we don't know about ourselves and our businesses. And until we make an effort to find out, we don't know what we think about what we are doing, how we are doing, and where we are going.

One of the greatest values of developing mission, vision, and philosophy statements is that you are forced to reflect on what you believe to be important and evaluate what you have accomplished and want to accomplish.

Leaders must consider the purposes and objectives of their

businesses and their business philosophies when evaluating historical results and developing future strategies.

By going through the process of developing mission, vision, and philosophy statements, you begin to see yourself and your business clearly. This clarity helps create buy-in as it lets you see where you or your business may have shortcomings or be "out of balance." It helps you focus on opportunities for growth and development. It provides a foundation from which to choose your goals and your strategies to pursue them.

Thinking through and deciding upon mission and vision statements is like having a shipmate climb to the bird's nest above the topsail to get a visual confirmation of the ship's heading. "Land ho!" he shouts and points when it is visually clear to him which way the ship should be piloted.

Alignment among company statements

Companies develop a number of statements to document their purposes, objectives, values, goals, and planned actions.

For this discussion I have defined six statements, each representing a management tool that should be DNA aligned with each of the other tools. The six tools are illustrated in the graphic on the next page; they are mission statements, vision statements, philosophy statements, goal statements, action plans, and systems and procedures. In practice, individuals and organizations define and use these tools to suit their circumstances and needs. Thus, there are many versions or models of these tools in use, and often there are overlaps among them.

Mission statements

Business mission statements address the question: Why does our business exist? Mission statements pronounce a *purpose* and reason for being in business. A mission statement defines the roles and *responsibilities* the business has to its customers, employees,

Six Key Management Tools

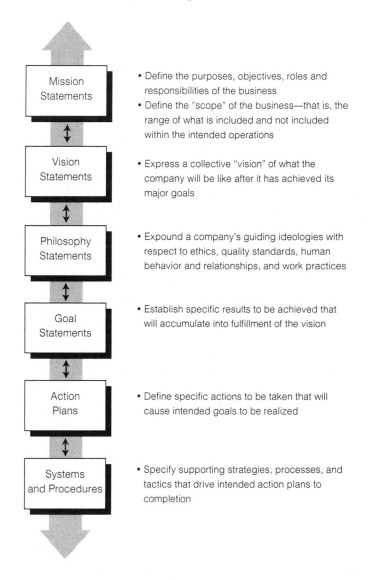

Mission Statements
- Define the purposes, objectives, roles and responsibilities of the business
- Define the "scope" of the business—that is, the range of what is included and not included within the intended operations

Vision Statements
- Express a collective "vision" of what the company will be like after it has achieved its major goals

Philosophy Statements
- Expound a company's guiding ideologies with respect to ethics, quality standards, human behavior and relationships, and work practices

Goal Statements
- Establish specific results to be achieved that will accumulate into fulfillment of the vision

Action Plans
- Define specific actions to be taken that will cause intended goals to be realized

Systems and Procedures
- Specify supporting strategies, processes, and tactics that drive intended action plans to completion

suppliers, and the communities in which it operates. A mission statement also establishes the *scope* of the business by providing guidance for what is and is not intended to be within the operating parameters of the business. The mission statement thus serves as a lighthouse for guiding business activities, allocating corporate resources, and establishing specific goals and plans to achieve them.

Purpose addresses the questions of *who* and *what* in terms of the needs the company intends to serve. Whose needs will the company meet? What are those needs in terms of the products and services the company will provide? Johnson & Johnson, the healthcare products firm, defines its "who" as doctors, nurses, and patients, mothers and fathers, and others who use the company's products. Johnson & Johnson's "what" are the healthcare products the company sells.

Responsibilities addresses the questions of *who* and *what* in terms of the responsibilities a company has to itself and others. Who is the company responsible to and what are the company's responsibilities? One of Johnson & Johnson's self-proclaimed responsibilities is to provide "clean, orderly, and safe working conditions"; a community responsibility is to "encourage civic improvements and better health and education."

Scope addresses the questions of *where* and *what* in terms of markets, products and services, operating practices, and other variables that define what the company is or is not about. What markets will the company serve? Where will the company sell its products? Local markets, national markets, or global markets? What products will be offered?

The stated mission of a business may evolve and be refined periodically, but in general, the mission statement of an organization has a longer-term, if not a limitless, perspective.

Vision statements

Vision statements address this question: What is our business going to be like five or ten years from now? Vision statements are sometimes called "visions of success." Vision statements may be long-term or near-term. They are updated and revised as time passes, results are achieved, and circumstances change.

Vision statements create in words a vision of what the company will look like as of a future date or a description of what the company will have achieved when it has accomplished its major goals by the stated date. A vision statement mobilizes an organization and brings individuals to action toward specified common goals.

The vision of a company covers *What?*, *When?*, and *Where?* What are we going to accomplish? When and where are we going to accomplish it? Are we going to put a man on the moon by the end of the decade? Are we going to send a rocket to circle Mars? Are we going to have 2,000 facilities by the year 2000 or are we shooting for 1,500 by the end of next year?

Sometimes information like this is included in statements companies make available to the public. General Electric's "vision of success" of becoming a Six Sigma quality company by the year 2000 is widely known. (Six Sigma is a term used to specify the highest level of performance—performance that is virtually error free. See the *Glossary* for more details.)

Some companies are specific and may state goals such as "10% annual sales growth" or "20% rate of return" in the body of their vision statements.

Philosophy statements

Philosophy statements are sometimes called statements of belief or codes of conduct. They address the question: What values, principles, and practices do we intend to follow and abide by in our business? Philosophy statements expound a company's guiding ideologies with respect to ethics, quality standards, human behavior and relationships, work practices, and similar aspects that reflect the core character of a company and its leaders.

Goal statements

Goal statements document specific tangible end results intended to be achieved. Goal statements are covered in *Chapters 7, 8, 9, and 10.*

Action plans

Action plans define the specific actions to be taken so that desired goals are achieved. Action plans represent the *cause* elements to accomplish the desired effects. Action plans are covered in *Chapters 11, 12, 13,* and *14.*

Systems and procedures

Systems and procedures establish the operating, managerial, transactional, and other processes and procedures the company will follow to offer and provide its products and services. Systems and procedures address questions of *How?* For example, how will the company sell? Will it sell wholesale or retail? Will it establish distributors, a franchise organization, an agency field force, or will it open stores in major metropolitan malls? Systems and procedures are covered in *Chapters 21, 22,* and *23.*

What companies include in their mission, vision, and philosophy statements

There is no one way to prepare business statements and there are no rules as to purpose, form, and content. The nature and composition of business statements depend on the individuals and the kind of company they intend to build.

We can learn from what others have done. Two good books to read are *The Mission Statement Book—301 Corporate Mission Statements from America's Top Companies,* by Jeffrey Abrahams, and *Say It & Live It—The 50 Corporate Mission Statements That Hit The Mark,* by Patricia Jones and Larry Kahaner. While I don't think all of the mission statements in these books are stellar examples, they do provide valuable food for thought.

Because mission, vision, and philosophy statements are tools, the overriding considerations when crafting a business statement are its intended purposes and uses.

Businesses usually do not have just one solitary mission,

vision, or philosophy. Even though some companies have single-sentence statements, it is rarely possible to summarize all important aspects of a business into a nice, neat twenty-five-words-or-less package.

Some components of what we might call the mission of a company often are found, not in a company's mission statement, but in its statement of corporate philosophy or its vision statement. There is also a gray area between mission statements and vision statements. Some companies combine aspects of each into statements called "corporate purposes and objectives." Mission, vision, and philosophy statements tend to evolve and become refined over time.

A technique some companies use is to prepare sound-bites of portions of their business statements. These are short, snappy statements that capture and embody the essence of one or more elements of the company's mission, vision, or philosophies into memorable phrases that can radiate to all levels of personnel.

Some examples of corporate sound-bites are:

- *Every guest leaves satisfied* (Marriott)

- *Total Customer Satisfaction* (Motorola)

- *The Document Company* (Xerox)

- *Beer is our core business and always will be* (Anheuser-Busch)

- *Our purpose is to provide unlimited opportunity to women* (Mary Kay Cosmetics)

There is nothing static or sacred about what to do or not to do in the process. Do what makes sense. Keep it simple. See *Chapter 4* for illustrative mission, vision, and philosophy statements for the Jones Insurance Agency.

Statements of individuals

As discussed earlier, to establish a common DNA fabric through-out an organization, individuals should establish their own mission, vision, and philosophy statements and their own goals and action plans in support of corporate objectives and purposes. Statements for individuals are functionally the same as those described for businesses. See *Chapter 4* for examples of mission and vision statements for an individual, Holly.

Why some people struggle preparing mission, vision, and philosophy statements

I have been in many meetings where the company leaders gathered to develop mission, vision, or philosophy statements. Some of the participants were unclear as to what we were trying to accomplish, what we wanted to end up with, or how we were going to go about doing what we had come to do.

The facts that some people have difficulty preparing business statements and that many people don't know how to begin or complete the process shouldn't be surprising. Most individuals have had little exposure or training in this area. This is not a skill we were supposed to have learned in ninth grade. It wasn't taught in junior high school or anywhere else.

But our lack of training in the development of mission, vision, and philosophy statements does not diminish their importance as tools for guiding growth and development and for beginning the goal-setting process. We should make the effort to develop these statements. There can be substantial payoffs when they are properly prepared.

Chapter 4 provides more information on mission and vision statements along with examples of components of these statements for a business and an individual.

3

Goal power

Just as a magnet exerts a magnetic field that attracts iron, when we place goals in front of ourselves, instantly we are drawn in their direction by an imperceptible force—goal power. This principle is exciting because it means you can alter your results by altering your goals.

This magnetizing phenomenon is not applicable only to big goals like raising capital for the Discovery Channel or sending a man to the moon. It is a universal truth that applies to goals in all shapes and sizes. Whether it is a business or personal goal, big or small, the moment you establish a goal, the goal pulls you and your resources toward it.

I am not talking about some abstract kind of pseudo-energy—the energy created by establishing a goal is *real* energy created at the biological level in your brain and other cells. Power is released when you fix goals in your mind as definite wants you intend to obtain. Goals create a pulling power that becomes a part of the means for achieving the goals. The greater your goals and your desires to have them, and the clearer you can see the path to obtaining them, the greater the power they exert.

The significance of this is that merely establishing a definite goal you intend to pursue is a step toward achieving the goal itself. You don't have to know how you are going to achieve a goal before you start making progress towards it. All that is required is that you make a definite decision—establish a goal. Magnetic attraction goes to work at once.

The principles of goal power and magnetic attraction

Goal Power: Power is defined in physics as the measure of the amount of work that can be accomplished per unit of time; that is, the results we can achieve in a day, week, month, year, or lifetime. A truck that can carry a given load a certain distance in *one* hour has twice the power of a truck that can carry the same load the same distance in *two* hours. Goals create power—because goals concentrate our resources and efforts to enable us to achieve greater results in less time.

Magnetic Attraction: Firmly established goals create a magnetic-like attraction that draws us to them. A business will grow in the direction of its goals and become defined by the goals it pursues. By selecting which personal goals to pursue, we alter the directions of our individual growth and what we become.

When you establish a goal you create a specific target. This focusing of your attention becomes an integral part of the *means* to hitting the target.

The primary stimulus for your actions is the mental tension you create in your mind when you become aware of the gap between where you are and where you want to be. Once you become aware of this gap you subconsciously and consciously will begin to find ways to bridge it.

How the gap of discontent creates change

The gap between actuality and desire is "discontent." Through discontent, all progress is made. Business leaders and businesses that become content have begun their demise. Businesses and individuals must innovate and change to survive and prosper.

Ralph S. Larsen, Chairman and Chief Executive Officer of

Johnson & Johnson, put it this way in his letter to shareholders in a recent annual report: "One of our biggest priorities is to continue to prepare the entire organization to deal with rapid, and often unpredictable, technological and market changes. Rather than fearing change, we want our people to welcome it, to embrace it, and to turn the ability to handle change into an important competitive advantage."

The way we create change is to become discontented with where we are and the goals we are pursuing and to establish new goals that will pull us in new directions.

One of the challenges businesses face is contentment with existing results and goals that are below the potential of the organization and the individuals in it. A common technique is to adopt goals that have been created by adding five or ten percent to last year's results. This is dangerous because it avoids the question of "What's possible?"

In a *Fortune* magazine article, Douglas Ivester, Coca-Cola's president and chief operating officer, said he urges everyone at Coke to forsake traditional arbitrary goal-setting such as "The market's expanding 5%, so we'll shoot for 6%." Instead, Ivester promotes "destination planning," which requires asking and answering three questions at every level in the organization: "What's possible for your business? What are the barriers to achieving that? How can we remove the barriers?"

Unfortunately, it is easier to *not* ask and answer these questions than it is to ask and answer them. Real *DNA Leadership* is required to pursue a "What's possible?" approach throughout an organization.

Goals are the means to our self-fulfillment

We are born with great capabilities, but we will not achieve our potential until we call upon ourselves to fulfill it. We will "rise to the occasion" when it presents itself. To assure self-fulfillment, we must provide the occasions to rise to.

The differences between what one person and another achieves depend more on goal choices than on abilities. If you could look inside people using a magic x-ray, you would see that the profound differences between very successful people and others are the goals they pursue. Individuals with similar talents, intelligence, and abilities will achieve different results because they select and pursue different goals.

The same is true for businesses. Each goal choice the executives, managers, and employees of a business make affects what the business is or is not becoming. There is no escaping this—even little choices are important because their cumulative effect over time will have an impact.

What is often overlooked is this: the nature and direction of your evolution changes the *instant* you change your goals. Once you choose a goal, immediately you are on a new path headed toward a different destination. A management team that decides to narrow its company's product lines to focus on a narrower market niche alters what the company is becoming the moment they make their decision. A single choice can alter your business, your life, and your destiny. Like DNA expression in our cells, our goal choices express our individuality.

As the song says: "We seal our fate with the choices we make."

Goals provide our vitality

Goals provide our vitality. Without goals we lose our drive and our energy. Our enthusiasm disappears. We stagnate. Worst of all, we lose our way—because without goals we have lost our purpose and desire for life. When people have nothing to live for, they begin to wither and die. When businesses lose sight of their missions and purposes, they, too, begin to die.

Goals provide reasons and purposes for being. With goals our energies rekindle, our pace quickens, and we have renewed zeal. With goals we can see where we are headed, and we are determined to get there. Goals breathe life into our beings.

Goals stimulate and guide our growth

Goals are the ultimate tool for motivating, managing, and maximizing growth—personal growth and the growth and development of the businesses or organizations we work in, manage, or perhaps own. Goals cause growth. No goals, no growth.

Nothing alive in nature is static—not a tree, not a flower, not the cells in your body. Changes occur daily—to you, to your family, and to your business—whether you direct the changes or not. Are you using the best tool you have, goals, to cause the changes *you* desire? Have *you* chosen goals to stimulate your growth toward the results you want? Are you just existing, or do you have goals that are causing you to grow?

Think about your business. Are you using the best tool available, goals, to stimulate and guide the growth of your business? Is your business just drifting or have you established goals that are driving your business to become what you want? Are the people in your company using goals to direct their growth and to achieve the goals you want your company to achieve, or are they coasting?

During a program I asked the thirty managers present what their business goals were for the next quarter. Only one individual could identify a specific goal he intended to pursue. All the others said their only goal was to "handle the day-to-day workload." Imagine how much better off this company would be if each individual pursued just one challenging goal each quarter.

Without goals, we are destined to remain as we are, *at best*. There is an expression: "If you keep on doing what you have been doing, you will keep on getting the results you have been getting." Unfortunately, this is *not* true. If you keep on doing what you have been doing, you are going to fall behind—because somebody else is going to innovate and change and pass you by. You continually need new goals to grow and develop and to help you keep up with the rest of the world.

Who is deciding your goals?

Since we alter what we and our businesses become through our goal selections, there is another principle we must heed: the principle of goal selection. The person who selects the goals is the person with the greatest power and influence.

The principle of goal selection

The person who selects the goals is the person with the greatest power and influence. To the extent that Rudy selects goals or influences the goal selections for Carol, Rudy exerts control and influence over Carol. If our objective is to have self-control, we must be the ones to decide our goals. If business leaders want to control the destiny of their companies, they must influence the selection process for the goals for their businesses.

A related element is making sure you select the best goals possible. A successful businessman who grew up on a farm claims the most valuable lesson he learned was not to skimp on seeds. "Always buy the best seed you can," he says. It is the same with goals. Always establish the best goals you can. What some business leaders overlook is goals are seeds—you and your business can become only what you plant.

Goals make us greater than we were before we had them

The greatest value of goals is that they enable us to become greater than we were before we had them—not greater because the goal was achieved, but greater because of what we had to become to achieve it.

Dick, a friend of mine, announced his goal of running in a marathon scheduled in six months. He had never run in a marathon, so during the six months prior to the race he adopted a disciplined running schedule to build up his strength and stamina. When the day came, he ran twenty-six miles non-stop and completed the event.

The fact that Dick completed the marathon and achieved his goal is good, but the additional benefits he gained are better. Dick is healthier, more energetic, stronger, and physically better looking than he was before he set his goal. He looks younger. As a result of his goal, he achieved other results along the way.

Did it matter that Dick selected a marathon as his goal? Suppose he had selected a goal of running twenty miles instead of the twenty-six in the marathon. While he may not have become quite as strong and healthy as he did when he trained for the marathon, he would have gotten stronger and healthier than he was before he had any goal at all.

When using goals to motivate and manage growth, the key variable is whether or not you have to stretch to achieve them. If you can achieve your goals without having to develop new skills and expertise, the goals have no growth power.

This same concept applies in business. I know a company with a goal of growing at 20% per year while the industry it is in is growing at 10%. It doesn't matter if the company's growth goal is 18%, 20%, or 22%—each of these is a stretch goal. The company has to become stronger to achieve a goal of this magnitude than it would if a 10% growth goal was pursued. The long-term value to the company is what happens to its people in the process—they have to become better at business than their competitors. And *that* is the real benefit.

A commercial equipment manufacturing company established the goal of clearing credit applications and shipping orders within a week of receipt. Historically it had taken six to eight weeks to get an order out the door. Reducing the processing time by more than 80% was a formidable task, but in several months it was achieved. There was great value in achieving the goal. Customers were happier. Sales increased. Profits went up. But, the greater value was that the company *had* to get better to achieve its goal. Everyone had to be quicker on their feet. Steps in the processes were eliminated. The company became more operationally effective. In other words, the company became greater than it was before it adopted the goal.

The dividing line that separates successful firms and the people in them from everyone else is how they establish and pursue their goals. When you get better at establishing and achieving goals, you not only realize greater results, but you also *get better* at realizing the results.

True or false?
On a scale of 1 to 10, goals are a 10

Often during *GOAL-DRIVEN MANAGEMENT* programs, I will ask the participants how important they think goals are on a scale of 1 to 10. I have them rate goals in comparison to everything else—such as family, money, career, and their health.

I don't know why, but most participants rate goals as an 8 or 9. Occasionally there will be several 10s, but not always.

After polling the audience for their ratings, I'll ask for a volunteer to test his or her ratings. I've described below how Matt, a regional manager in a large corporation, responded.

Are goals a ten? A conversation with Matt . . .

Jim: Matt, what was your rating for the importance of goals?

Matt: Eight.

Jim: Is eight your highest rating for anything?

Matt: No, I'd rate my family a ten.

Jim: Of course. Do you have children?

Matt: Yes, a little girl, Zoe.

Jim: Great. So you'd rate Zoe a ten. I would agree with that. How old is she?

Matt: Four.

Jim: Wonderful. What kinds of things do you want for Zoe?

Matt: A good education.

Jim: College?

Matt: Yes.

Jim: What else?

Matt: I want her to be safe from crime and to be healthy.

Jim: Let's just discuss a college education. Zoe's education is a goal, right?

Matt: Yes.

Jim: On a scale of one to ten, how important is it for you to be able to send Zoe to college?
(Matt paused several moments, then smiled.)

Matt: A ten.

Jim: And what about Zoe's health? That's a goal, too. How do you rate it?

Matt: Ten.

Jim: Her safety, that's another goal. How about it?

Matt: Ten.

Matt got the point. In reality, everything we rate a ten is a ten because of a goal we have with respect to it.

If Matt says Zoe's education is a ten, but he takes no action to read to her, help her with homework when she goes to school, and save for her college education, then what he *says* is inconsistent with what he *does*. A ten is a ten because of what you *actually* do, not because of what you think you should do.

Without a *goal* that is a ten, nothing is a ten. We may think of things as tens, but unless you have a ten goal built into it, it isn't a ten. That means goals are not sevens or eights. Goals are tens. This is a critical principle: the principle of importance.

The principle of importance

There is nothing more important than our goals because the goals we are actually pursuing provide a true and correct indication of the relative values of importance we place on those things with which our goals are associated.

Take the president of a company who says, "Our people are our most important asset." His people are a ten, right? For this president to live up to his statement, he should see to it that ten-rated goals and action plans are established and implemented for the training, development, and growth of his employees.

Goals are a part of everything we desire or care about. When something is truly a ten, there is a ten-rated goal nearby, and next to the ten-rated goal is an action plan being implemented.

This means setting and achieving goals are more important activities than most people think they are—for both personal and business situations.

Goals are a leader's greatest tool and greatest responsibility

There is nothing more important for business leaders to do than select the goals their businesses will or will not pursue—for their

---

The principle of leadership

A leader's capacity and ability to lead are directly dependent upon the leader's capacity and ability to select and communicate goals that others will pursue.

---

goal selections determine what their businesses will or will not become.

What could be more important?

A leader stands before his or her company much like Michelangelo stood before an eighteen-foot block of marble five centuries ago. Michelangelo had to look inside and see the statue of David before his hands could create it.

Similarly, a leader must look inside the company and see what the company can and should become. Then the leader must relate that vision to everyone so they can see it too, and build it with their hands. *DNA Leadership* depends upon the leader's capacity and ability to select goals and get people to buy into them.

As *Fortune* magazine reported, when Roger Smith retired as chief executive of General Motors he said, ". . . I sure wish I'd done a better job of communicating with GM people. I'd do that differently a second time around and make sure they shared and understood my vision for the company. Then they would have known why I was tearing the place up, taking out whole divisions, changing our whole production structure. If people understand the *why*, they'll work at it. Like I said I never got it all across. There we were, charging up the hill right on schedule and I looked behind me and saw that many people were still at the bottom deciding whether to come along." Keep in mind, Mr. Smith was successful. I don't think he was lamenting here; rather, he was describing what he could have done to have accomplished more.

Leaders have various approaches for creating and communicating their vision and for rallying employees to it. Some are like General Patton, who had his tank painted red so his troops couldn't miss him out in front. Others have a subdued approach. I know effective company presidents who lead their companies as quiet, behind-the-scenes visionaries. But in each instance, the vision of their company is clear, and they have done whatever they needed to do, in their own style and manner, to motivate their employees to pursue their goals for the company.

When you participate in selecting and committing to the goals you or others will pursue, you are plotting the course for what you and your business will become, *and* you are initiating the means to get there.

Walt Disney put it very well: "Of all the things I've done, the most vital is coordinating the talents of those who work for us *and pointing them toward a certain goal.*"

Goals drive teamwork

Another power of goals is the connecting and communicating power they have in coordinating team efforts. The principle of teamwork requires that everyone on the team know, understand, and agree on the goals and the game plan.

The principle of teamwork

The first requirement for creating the power of teamwork is to have everyone on the team know, clearly understand, and agree upon the *exact same set of goals* and the *exact same game plan* to achieve them on the *exact same timetable*.

This principle applies in all situations where team efforts are involved. To effect *DNA Leadership* every member of a team should buy into and agree to pursue exactly the same set of goals following the same game plan on the same timetable. Otherwise, it is every man and woman for himself or herself at the snap of the ball. And who knows what results that will achieve?

Try this 3-minute test
at your next team or group meeting

Convene your management team or your work team and ask each person to write down the five most important goals for the group for the next twelve months. Don't tell them about the exercise in advance, and don't let them ask questions or discuss the task. Just have them write down the goals for the group and prioritize them one through five.

After each member has prepared a list, start with one individual and list his or her five goals on a flip chart. Then ask others to read their lists. Put hash marks beside the goals that match and add any new goals identified. Do this until everyone has provided input.

While many will share goals, it is unlikely there will be unanimous agreement as to your group's top five goals for next year and their order of importance. Also, there likely will be several "side" goals away from the main goals identified. In one group of executives, eleven individuals had a total of nine "top five" goals and only six of the individuals agreed on one of the goals as being number one.

If you were the owner of a national football franchise, what would you guess your team's odds are for scoring, if at each snap of the ball only six of the players run the same play? It's silly to even think about winning with an approach like that, isn't it?

Goals create *Goal Power*

Imagine two comparable individuals: one with specific goals and concrete plans to achieve them; the other with some idea of what he or she wants to become, but nothing specific defined, and no formal plan. If you had to bet which one would achieve the most success, where would you place your bet? I'd bet on the individual with the goals—because those goals create *Goal Power*.

But sometimes we forget we have the ability to select *big goals*, develop plans to achieve them, implement those plans, and realize the goals.

I presented the GOAL-DRIVEN MANAGEMENT method to a group of executives at a large construction company. When I ended the program, I asked all participants to comment on how they would use the principles. When I got to someone who had seemed more reflective than the others during the day, he said, "My gosh, we have always done so well. It never dawned on me *how much better* we can do if we just improve our approach to setting and pursuing goals."

The principle of fulfillment

The goals of a business establish the means and the limits of the fulfillment of that business. A business and the people in it cannot and will not achieve their full potential unless the leaders of the business establish goals that require the business and the people in it to develop their full abilities and capabilities. A business will not grow beyond its goals.

Our personal goals establish the means and the limits of our self-fulfillment. We cannot and will not achieve our full potential unless we establish goals that require us to develop our full abilities. We will not grow beyond our goals.

This gentleman had realized that even though his group's results were excellent, he and his associates were performing below their potential. They were not approaching their capacity; they were just doing enough to be better than everyone else. The principle of fulfillment requires a business to establish goals for growth, because a business will not grow beyond its goals.

When you understand the potential you can reach by setting and pursuing goals, as the gentleman at the construction company did, that is *Goal Power*. It is within everyone's capacity to do more and achieve greater results by getting better at establishing and achieving goals.

4

MOSAIC™:
A method for identifying goals for balance and growth

Mosaic is an art form that traces its beginnings to the ancient Greeks who arranged pebbles in cement floors to decorate them. Later the pebbles were replaced by dazzling pieces of cut glass that were precisely placed to create breathtaking murals on the walls and ceilings of great cathedrals.

I chose the name *MOSAIC* for the methodology I created for transferring DNA throughout an organization and for identifying areas to concentrate on when establishing goals for two reasons.

First, my methodology requires that you define discrete levels for evaluating performance and *MOSAIC* is an excellent acronym for the six levels in the methodology: M stands for Mastery, O stands for Outstanding, S stands for Satisfactory, A stands for Acceptable, I stands for Intolerable, and C stands for Counterproductive.

Second, there are many parallels and commonalities among the mosaic art form, the *MOSAIC* methodology, and the processes businesses and individuals go through to select their goals and determine what they will become.

Composition: Mosaics are composed of many unique parts, and the pieces you select and their placement determine the picture you create. Until the artist selects and places each piece of glass or stone, he doesn't know for sure what the final mosaic is going to be. Our businesses and our lives are similarly composed of many unique parts, and the goals and actions that we choose determine what we and our businesses can and will become. Until you determine and develop each of the parts in your business or your life by selecting goals, you don't know exactly what you are creating or what you will end up with. *MOSAIC* drives the identification of areas to concentrate on when setting goals so that you can determine how you will express yourself and what you will accomplish and become rather than leaving things to chance.

Mosaic art and *MOSAIC* graphic comparisons

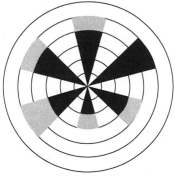

Mosaic art form   *MOSAIC* graphic display

Big picture and balance: You can't get up close to a mosaic and appreciate its whole or evaluate its balance. To get the big picture you must step back and view all the little pieces at once. Similarly, you can't evaluate where you are and where you want to be in business or in life by being close to and assessing only one or a few elements. To see the big picture and to determine whether you are in balance, you have to step back and look at the composite of the parts. *MOSAIC* requires the creation of composite graphical displays that identify out-of-balance conditions and provide a big picture of where you are in comparison to where you want to be.

DNA transfer and regeneration: Interestingly, the early Greek creators of mosaics, both intentionally and coincidentally, implanted many of their cultural idiosyncrasies in Russia and other countries by defining and adopting standardized decorating schemes and training other artisans in their use. Similarly, the best way to transfer culture throughout an organization is to implant philosophies, missions, visions, and goals at the DNA level among the individuals within the organization and then create common standards for measuring and monitoring performance. *MOSAIC* uses a cascading approach to accomplish this regeneration and to create alignment throughout a company, and it establishes six standard levels of performance for use in guiding business and individual development and growth.

Hands-on creation: Mosaics are very much a hands-on art form. They require the personal involvement of the artist in creating the design, preparing the surface, and placing the stones and glass. This results in a mosaic that embodies the essence of the artist. Similarly, if you are going to become what you can become, then it is up to you to decide what that is and take actions to achieve it. It is the same in business. If a business is to fulfill its potential, then it is up to the individuals in charge to achieve it. *MOSAIC* requires hands-on user involvement in specifying performance criteria and in assessing where you are and where you want to be.

MOSAIC begins where the wagon wheel concept leaves off

You have probably come across the "wagon wheel" concept for planning a business or your life. Draw a wheel with a spoke for each business or life component. Label the center of the wheel zero and the outside ten. Plot your present position on each spoke with a dot. Connect the dots to see how out of balance you are.

This is not a bad exercise if your objective is to stimulate your thinking. But I don't know anyone who uses the wagon wheel concept as a tool for managing business or individual growth and development.

The wagon wheel falls short for several reasons.

First, the calibration of the spokes from zero to ten is subjective. There are no concrete references or benchmark definitions for making the current and desired performance assessments. Everyone understands what zero means, but what is a ten, *exactly*? And what's the difference between a five and a six?

Second, the explanations I have seen or heard of the wagon wheel exercise leave a lot unexplained after you have connected the dots to reveal your out-of-balance wheel. It is as if you now realize you have a wheel with short spokes, and then you somehow magically are supposed to set new goals and continue on your journey. Well, what are you supposed to do about the wheel, and where are the tools and instructions to fix it? Where is the solid linkage to your goals? What steps should you take after you have drawn your wheel? It is important to have a method to identify where you are. But it is *more* important to have a method for determining specifically where you want to be and then for determining how to get there.

Third, it is not clear how you should use the wagon wheel as an ongoing tool. There are thousands of individuals who have plotted their spokes and drawn their wheels in learning exercises and then have never referred to their drawings again. Knowledge is valuable only if you apply it.

MOSAIC is a systematic approach for assessing current progress and for planning and guiding growth and development. *MOSAIC* builds on the wagon wheel and incorporates numerous essential enhancements and innovations. Instead of providing you

Wagon wheel and *MOSAIC* graphic comparisons

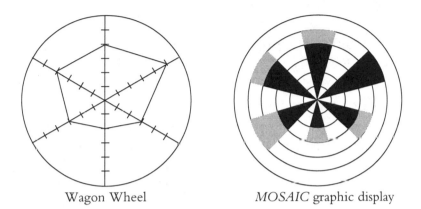

Wagon Wheel   *MOSAIC* graphic display

with an out-of-balance wagon wheel you never refer to, *MOSAIC* is intended to be a modern high-performance tool you will use to guide your business and individual growth and development on an ongoing basis.

Uses and features of *MOSAIC*

Businesses can use *MOSAIC* to identify where goals should be established to balance operating functions. The process helps identify and focus resources on opportunities for growth and improvement. *MOSAIC* also is used to guide the goals and actions of individuals to help them make their intended contributions toward corporate objectives.

    MOSAIC is a tool to use in employee performance reviews and employee coaching. Since *MOSAIC* drives the creation of *specific* performance criteria, it takes the guesswork and subjectivity out of performance appraisals. *MOSAIC* provides quantitative data analyses and graphical displays so individuals can literally *see* their performance and progress on a Where am I now? versus a Where do I want to be? comparative basis.

    Individuals can use *MOSAIC* to self-manage their personal performance and development and to identify goals that are congruent with personal values and desires.

The *MOSAIC* method has nine core attributes:

1. Reflective process: *MOSAIC* is a reflective process using a question-and-answer approach that requires you to *think*—to think about what you believe to be important and not important; to think about your purposes, objectives, and values; to think about where you are, what is possible, and where you want to be; and to think about the best ways to achieve the results you want.

2. Balanced approach: *MOSAIC* provides for a "balanced" approach. Each component of a business and each role or responsibility of an individual is considered.

3. Specific performance criteria: *MOSAIC* requires the establishment and documentation of specific performance criteria. These criteria can be used to measure, evaluate, and manage progress toward missions, visions, and goals, and targeted results such as return on investment.

4. Graphical data analysis: *MOSAIC* provides for creating graphical displays depicting assessments of how well companies, workgroups, or individuals are fulfilling their objectives and purposes.

5. Constant change and innovation: *MOSAIC* drives continual performance improvement by using the performance criteria and graphical displays as reference points for determining goals and plans.

6. Alignment: *MOSAIC* provides for the alignment of goals and actions within an organization from top to bottom and for the monitoring and maintaining of alignment once it is established.

7. Communication and cooperation: *MOSAIC* provides bases for communication, cooperation, and teamwork across organizations.

8. Identification of what's possible: *MOSAIC* identifies and clarifies the gap between where we are and what's possible so we may establish goals and plans to achieve our potential and the potential for our businesses.

9. Iterative approach: *MOSAIC* uses an iterative approach. Businesses and individuals are mosaics of diverse elements. They do not have just one mission, one vision, and one goal; rather they have many missions, visions, and goals. For this reason we repeatedly cycle back and forth in our analyses while constantly narrowing to better and better results. This way we don't waste time trying to perfect one element that can only be developed on an interdependent basis with other elements.

The six levels of *MOSAIC*

The most important part of the *MOSAIC* method is developing the six discrete levels of performance. For business applications, these six levels should be defined for every business component; for individual applications they should be defined for every role or responsibility.

Defining the six performance levels is critical because it forces you to think through and specify the benchmarks you will use to evaluate your progress and to determine what you can accomplish and become. Our minds are biological computers that require exacting instructions to function. Vagaries, generalities, and loose performance standards are hindrances to growth and development.

As Mark Twain said, "There is a big difference between lightning and a lightning bug." Similarly, there's a big difference between acceptable performance and outstanding performance, and the more accurately you define the performance level you want to achieve, the more success you will have in getting there.

The six levels of performance can be remembered by the acronym M•O•S•A•I•C with M standing for Mastery, O for Out-

MOSAIC Performance Grid

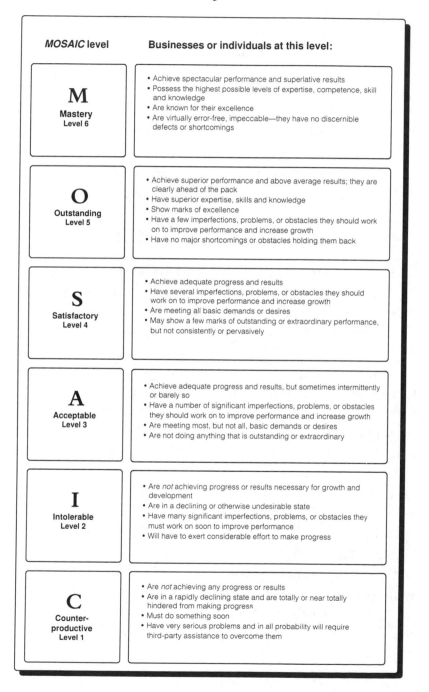

MOSAIC level	Businesses or individuals at this level:
M Mastery Level 6	• Achieve spectacular performance and superlative results • Possess the highest possible levels of expertise, competence, skill and knowledge • Are known for their excellence • Are virtually error-free, impeccable—they have no discernible defects or shortcomings
O Outstanding Level 5	• Achieve superior performance and above average results; they are clearly ahead of the pack • Have superior expertise, skills and knowledge • Show marks of excellence • Have a few imperfections, problems, or obstacles they should work on to improve performance and increase growth • Have no major shortcomings or obstacles holding them back
S Satisfactory Level 4	• Achieve adequate progress and results • Have several imperfections, problems, or obstacles they should work on to improve performance and increase growth • Are meeting all basic demands or desires • May show a few marks of outstanding or extraordinary performance, but not consistently or pervasively
A Acceptable Level 3	• Achieve adequate progress and results, but sometimes intermittently or barely so • Have a number of significant imperfections, problems, or obstacles they should work on to improve performance and increase growth • Are meeting most, but not all, basic demands or desires • Are not doing anything that is outstanding or extraordinary
I Intolerable Level 2	• Are *not* achieving progress or results necessary for growth and development • Are in a declining or otherwise undesirable state • Have many significant imperfections, problems, or obstacles they must work on soon to improve performance • Will have to exert considerable effort to make progress
C Counter-productive Level 1	• Are *not* achieving any progress or results • Are in a rapidly declining state and are totally or near totally hindered from making progress • Must do something soon • Have very serious problems and in all probability will require third-party assistance to overcome them

standing, S for Satisfactory, A for Acceptable, I for Intolerable, and C for Counterproductive.

The *MOSAIC Performance Grid* on page 54 provides definitions and guidelines for each level of performance and results. These are guidelines only. You should modify or sharpen the definitions to meet your needs. Illustrations of completed *MOSAIC Performance Grids* for a business and an individual are presented later in this chapter.

MOSAIC implementation steps

MOSAIC has five implementation steps, applicable for both business and individual use. These five steps are listed below and are illustrated in the flowchart on page 56.

1. Develop mission, vision, and philosophy statements
2. Develop *MOSAIC* performance criteria
3. Assess current performance levels
4. Determine desired performance levels
5. Establish goals and action plans

Because there are subtle differences between business and individual applications of *MOSAIC*, rather than explain the five implementation steps generically, the remainder of this chapter walks you through the *MOSAIC* process in two separate examples—first a business example, and then an individual example. The business example provided is for a small business to simplify the explanations of the *MOSAIC* process. The same implementation concepts would be applicable to a business of any size.

How to use *MOSAIC*
in business applications

The Jones Insurance Agency is a small business engaged in the sale of life insurance and equity investment products. There are eight individuals in the business: Mr. Jones, the owner; two senior asso-

MOSAIC

Implementation Action Steps

and connectivity *to* GOAL-DRIVEN MANAGEMENT

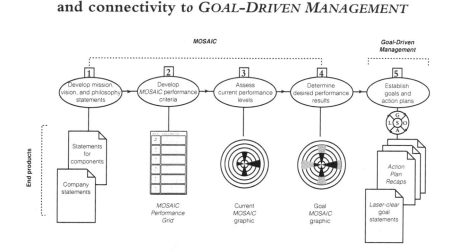

ciates; three additional associates; and two administrative staff members. Mr. Jones and the two senior associates make up the company's Executive Committee.

Step 1:
Develop mission, vision, and philosophy statements

The first step in implementing *MOSAIC* is to develop mission, vision, and philosophy statements. Many companies have completed these statements in one form or another. *Chapter 2* provides information on what should be included in the statements.

A company shouldn't finalize its vision statements without comparing them to the goals being selected during the goal planning activities described in *Part Two* of this book. Goals and visions must be aligned. Vision statements, therefore, should be developed in a back and forth manner as goals are selected and refined. Also, the *MOSAIC Performance Grid* required in Step 2 below should be used as a reference in selecting goals. This requires that the *MOSAIC Performance Grid* be completed, at least in draft form, *before* vision statements are finalized.

A business should develop mission, vision, and philosophy statements for all significant business components both at the company level and at the operating level. It is desirable and beneficial to cascade mission, vision, and philosophy statements down to workgroups and individuals. The comments below are provided for a firm or organization preparing these statements for the first time.

Jones Insurance Agency. To prepare the mission, vision, and philosophy statements for his company, Mr. Jones began by sitting down and sketching out his thoughts on paper. He and the Executive Committee then met to review his draft statements.

The group decided to develop mission, vision, and philosophy statements at the overall company level and also for each of the four major components of the company's business: (1) Sales, (2) Customer Service and Support, (3) Agent Recruiting and Development, and (4) Finance and Administration. Rather than developing long, detailed statements nobody would refer to, they agreed to keep it simple and to the point.

During the ensuing discussion they brainstormed ideas and developed points to be included in each of the statements at the company level and for each of the four business components. Mr. Jones had these typed up, and during a follow-up meeting the Executive Committee polished the words and adopted final versions of the statements. These were presented to all other associates during one of the company's regular weekly meetings. The overall statements and the illustrative statements for two of the company's components, Sales, and Customer Service and Support, are shown on the next two pages.

Step 2:
Develop *MOSAIC* performance criteria

The next step is to develop six levels of specific performance

---

Jones Insurance Agency

Step 1: Mission, Vision, and Philosophy—Overall Company Statements

Our *mission* is to market and provide the best and most suitable life insurance and long-term equity investment products and services available to the owners and employees of small- and medium-sized businesses employing ten or more persons.

Our *vision of success* is to have 2,000 "Premiere Level" clients within five years.

Our *philosophy* is to operate with the highest personal and professional standards.

---

criteria for each component of your business using the definitions in the *MOSAIC Performance Grid* on page 54 as guidelines.

Defining the *MOSAIC* levels in text can be challenging. Most individuals haven't previously thought through the specific definitions this step requires. It will take some time and soul-searching to explore the possibilities. But this is a valuable process because it forces you to think through and spell out your value judgments and priorities.

Jones Insurance Agency. Now that Mr. Jones has mission, vision, and philosophy statements for his company, he next must develop specific descriptions of the *MOSAIC* performance levels.

Mr. Jones again meets with his Executive Committee to address the task. During the meeting the group brainstorms and discusses the six levels of performance for each component of the business, and they document their results on four *MOSAIC Performance Grids*—one for each business component. For the Customer Service and Support component of the Jones Insurance Agency, the group decides to use two columns in the grid to differentiate quantitative and qualitative data. This is an optional choice on

---

Jones Insurance Agency

*Step 1: Supporting mission, vision,
and philosophy statements—
Sales and Customer Service and Support*

Sales

Our sales *mission* is to grow through the development of our agency network and a client base balanced in terms of demographic components and insurance and equity products.

Our *vision of success* is to have 2,000 "Premiere Level" clients in five years and to maintain a minimum annual revenue growth rate of 15% per year.

Our *philosophies* are to be professional in all aspects, do what's right for the customer in all circumstances, invest heavily in the personal development of our agents, and not to tolerate mediocrity in any aspect.

Customer Service and Support

Our *mission* is to provide the highest quality services and products we can possibly provide commensurate with the financial means and needs of our customers.

Our *vision of success* at the end of three years is 100% customer satisfaction and to have a one-hour response time to customer requests.

Our *philosophies* are to be professional, friendly, and courteous in all aspects, do what's right for the customer in all circumstances, and to strive to maintain reasonable and fair prices.

---

their part. Depending on the circumstances, one column per component will usually suffice.

The final *MOSAIC Performance Grid* the Executive Committee adopted for the Customer Service and Support component of the business is illustrated on the next page.

The data in the Jones Insurance Agency *MOSAIC Performance Grid* are illustrative. Another agency might develop a different grid with different items emphasized. The point of the example is to illustrate the *MOSAIC gradations*. The Executive Committee's differentiation of the *MOSAIC* levels is the key to this process. Since they took the time to define *each level* of performance for *each component* of the business, it will be easy for them to assess where the business is currently and where they want it to

Jones Insurance Agency
Step 2: *MOSAIC Performance Grid*
Customer Service and Support

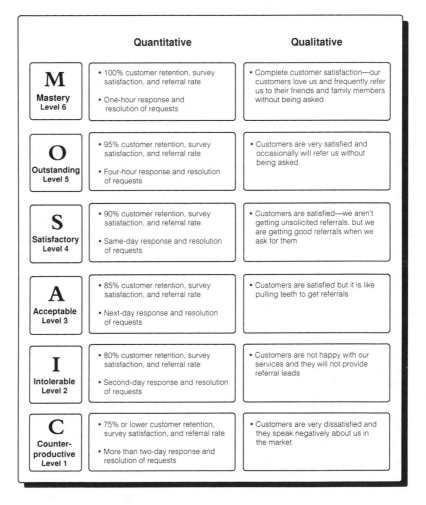

	Quantitative	Qualitative
M Mastery Level 6	• 100% customer retention, survey satisfaction, and referral rate • One-hour response and resolution of requests	• Complete customer satisfaction—our customers love us and frequently refer us to their friends and family members without being asked
O Outstanding Level 5	• 95% customer retention, survey satisfaction, and referral rate • Four-hour response and resolution of requests	• Customers are very satisfied and occasionally will refer us without being asked
S Satisfactory Level 4	• 90% customer retention, survey satisfaction, and referral rate • Same-day response and resolution of requests	• Customers are satisfied—we aren't getting unsolicited referrals, but we are getting good referrals when we ask for them
A Acceptable Level 3	• 85% customer retention, survey satisfaction, and referral rate • Next-day response and resolution of requests	• Customers are satisfied but it is like pulling teeth to get referrals
I Intolerable Level 2	• 80% customer retention, survey satisfaction, and referral rate • Second-day response and resolution of requests	• Customers are not happy with our services and they will not provide referral leads
C Counter-productive Level 1	• 75% or lower customer retention, survey satisfaction, and referral rate • More than two-day response and resolution of requests	• Customers are very dissatisfied and they speak negatively about us in the market

be one or three years from now. If the Executive Committee did not have specific data like those illustrated, they would be planning the future of the business on an *un*substantiated basis, and they most likely would be using incorrect assumptions and conclusions.

Since Mr. Jones now has adopted and documented specific performance criteria for Customer Service and Support, it is easy for him to communicate with his associates about the service levels he wants and the tasks necessary to provide such service. It is also easy to evaluate his agency's customer service performance. Rather than having only a "feel" for the situation, he can objectively evaluate progress by referring to the *MOSAIC Performance Grid*.

Step 3:
Assess current performance levels

The third step in the *MOSAIC* process is to assess current performance levels. This is accomplished by reviewing your completed *MOSAIC Performance Grids*, determining the company's current level of performance for each component, and then creating a *Current MOSAIC* graphic depicting your assessments.

This step is important because it vividly identifies out of balance conditions as well as the areas the company should concentrate on when developing goals and action plans.

The *MOSAIC* graphical display is presented like a wheel with spokes exploding outward through six concentric circles that represent the six *MOSAIC* criteria. Each outreaching spoke of the wheel represents a specific business component. There should be one spoke for each component.

The "reach" or length of each spoke is drawn in one color (black for our illustration) as far out on the concentric circles as is appropriate to reflect your assessment of criteria being met currently.

A business would be considered out of balance if the spokes are different lengths. When this situation exists, steps should be taken to establish goals and plans to move the company to a more balanced posture.

Jones Insurance Agency. To complete his *Current MOSAIC* graphic, all Mr. Jones has to do is review his *MOSAIC Performance Grids* and decide where his business is currently. Let's say Mr. Jones meets with his Executive Committee and their evaluations of current performance are as follows: Sales, Acceptable; Customer Service and Support, Satisfactory; Agent Recruiting and Development, Acceptable; Finance and Administration, Intolerable. Illustrated below is the resultant *Current MOSAIC* graphic for the Jones Insurance Agency.

Jones Insurance Agency
Step 3: *Current MOSAIC*

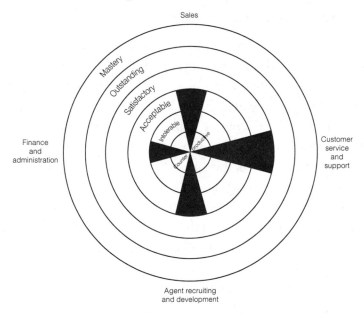

Step 4:
Determine desired performance levels

The fourth step is to determine desired performance levels. You accomplish this by reviewing your *Current MOSAIC* graphic and your *MOSAIC Performance Grids* to identify business components that are out of balance; components where the current performance level is less than that desired; and components that contain opportunities for growth and improvement. Next, for each component determine your desired level of performance for the next year or whatever period you are planning. And then create a *Goal MOSAIC* graphic depicting your desired levels of performance.

Jones Insurance Agency. As the *Current MOSAIC* indicates, the Jones Insurance Agency has an unbalanced business. Finance and administration, as represented by the shortest spoke, is the weakest area of the company. Clearly Mr. Jones has to address this and other areas to grow his business and improve its results.

After reviewing the above information with his Executive Committee, Mr. Jones decides that his desired objective for all business components is Outstanding. A summary of the company's current performance and the performance desired by Mr. Jones is presented in the table at the top of the next page.

Mr. Jones is now ready to prepare his *Goal MOSAIC* graphic. This is accomplished by extending the spokes in his *Current MOSAIC* in a different color (gray for our illustration) further out on the concentric circles to reflect the performance levels to be pursued during the current planning cycle, such as next year. For the Jones Insurance Agency, this means extending all spokes to the Outstanding level as shown by the *Goal MOSAIC* graphic on the next page.

Jones Insurance Agency
Step 4: Performance Assessment

	Current assessment	Desired objective
Sales	Acceptable	Outstanding
Customer service and support	Satisfactory	Outstanding
Agent recruiting and development	Acceptable	Outstanding
Finance and administration	Intolerable	Outstanding

Jones Insurance Agency
Step 4: *Goal MOSAIC*

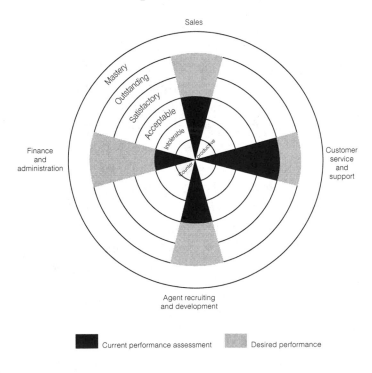

Step 5:
Establish goals and action plans

The final step is to establish goals and action plans. This is accomplished by reviewing the *Goal MOSAIC* to identify the gaps between where you are and where you want to be. These gaps would be addressed by developing specific goals and action plans using the GOAL-DRIVEN MANAGEMENT method that is presented in *Part Two* of this book.

Jones Insurance Agency. Mr. Jones and his associates have their work cut out for them. They need to develop specific goals and action plans in each area of the company to achieve their desired objectives. To accomplish this the Executive Committee meets and begins the process described in *Part Two* of this book.

Also, as a part of their overall plan in the Agent Recruiting and Development Area, they decide to adopt a program where all associates will use the *MOSAIC* and GOAL-DRIVEN MANAGEMENT methods to develop their individual mission, vision, and philosophy statements and their own *Personal Performance Plans* which will include a summary of their individual goals and action plans to achieve them.

The *Personal Performance Plans* for individuals will be developed in concert with the establishment of the company's goals and action plans. These plans will be used by Mr. Jones and his associates to guide their development and growth and also to monitor their progress and performance.

How to use *MOSAIC*
in individual applications

Holly is a single, young professional just out of college beginning her career.

Since the Jones Insurance Agency example was solely *business* oriented, Holly's example illustrates how *MOSAIC* is used for *individual and personal* components. It does not cover the career aspects of Holly's life.

Actually, Holly's *MOSAIC Performance Grid* and *MOSAIC* graphical displays presented later would be expanded to include her roles and responsibilities in her career, or as an alternative, Holly might develop separate and distinct *MOSAIC* analyses for these aspects of her life.

Individuals use the same five steps in the *MOSAIC* method as do businesses, but with a *personal* orientation. Each step is discussed below.

Step 1:
Develop mission, vision, and philosophy statements

The first step is to develop your own personal mission, vision, and philosophy statements.

Mission statements

Begin by identifying your current roles and responsibilities to yourself and to others. Next, identify any additional roles or responsibilities you intend to add. Draft a mini-mission statement for each of your major roles and responsibilities. The composite of these becomes your mission statement.

Each of us will approach this task a little differently, but regardless of your approach, you should consider these three questions when defining your mission for each of your present *and desired* roles and responsibilities:

1. What do you want to *become?*
2. What do you want to *accomplish?*
3. What is your *purpose?* In other words, who or what do you want to *help* or *serve* and how do you want to help or serve them or it?

Don't be troubled if your initial aspirations are not as high as you would like them to be when answering these questions. In particular, don't be concerned if you can't come up with a fulfilling answer to the question: What is your purpose?

While some individuals think they know exactly why they are here and what they want to achieve and become, for many of us our judgments and decisions evolve as we have experiences and continue to learn and grow. But you have to start someplace, and it is better to take a stab at answering the above questions to begin the process and then raise your sights as you go along, than it is to do nothing and wait for a revelation to move you to action.

Holly. Holly began the process of developing her mission statement by defining six areas in her life as listed below. As mentioned previously, Holly's career responsibilities have not been included in this example. "Social" below refers to Holly's roles and responsibilities in the world community, not the sociable part of her life. Here are the six areas Holly defined:

1. Spiritual

2. Family

3. Social

4. Mental

5. Physical

6. Financial

The next step Holly took was to develop mini-mission statements for each area of her life. These are illustrated at the top of the next page for three areas: Mental, Physical, and Financial.

Vision statements

You should have a mini-vision statement for each role or area in your life and the composite of these is your vision statement. Your mini-vision statements should express a cumulative "vision" of what you will have become and what you will have accomplished after you have fulfilled your mission and achieved your major goals as of some specified future date.

Holly
Step 1: Personal Mission Statements
(three areas of Holly's life)

Mental

My mission is to continue to learn and grow mentally
by providing myself a diversity of learning experiences
and exposures that continually challenge and
recharge me.

Physical

My mission is to develop and maintain my body so I
am physically strong and healthy with continuous
energy and stamina.

Financial

My mission is to provide for my current and future
financial needs so I have resources for emergencies
and so I will not be dependent upon others for
financial support.

By definition, you can't develop final vision statements until
you have substantially completed your goal selection and goal
planning activities as described in *Part Two* of this book. For this
reason, your vision statements should be developed in a back and
forth manner as your goals are selected and refined.

You should use the *MOSAIC Performance Grid* required in
Step 2 below as a reference in selecting your goals. This requires
that you complete, or at least outline, your *MOSAIC Performance
Grid before* you draft your vision statements.

Philosophy statements. *Chapter 2* provides information on
philosophy statements. Please note, however, that personal philosophy statements represent a huge subject area with many aspects
beyond the intended scope and purposes of this book.

Step 2:
Develop *MOSAIC* performance criteria

The next step is to define the six *MOSAIC* levels of performance for *each* area of your life. As mentioned earlier, this can be a challenging task since most individuals have not previously considered the possibilities. But this step is essential because it makes you think through and spell out your value judgments, beliefs, and priorities.

Holly. Holly approached this step by preparing a *MOSAIC Performance Grid* for each area of her life. Holly's grids are shown on page 70 for three categories: Mental, Physical, and Financial.

Now that Holly has completed her *MOSAIC Performance Grids*, she has greater insight into her own value judgments and priorities.

Individuals should develop their own personal *MOSAIC Performance Grids*. You may have different definitions than those in Holly's grid because of your preferences, lifestyle, and values. For example, you may want to add cultural exposures in the mental development column, or you may want to modify the physical development column to reflect that you are a vegetarian.

The power and value of this process is realized only when you take the time to complete your own personal grid so that each cell contains your personal definitions in specific and concrete terms. This isn't a ten-minute exercise. To get the greatest value, a few hours of concentrated thought are required so that your thinking progresses beyond superficial evaluations.

Initially, you may find it difficult to think out of your current mental box in identifying the outstanding and mastery levels you can pursue. A great technique is to begin with this question: If there were no obstacles in your way—not money, not time, not skills, experience, knowledge, or resources of any kind—what would you pursue? Another question to consider is the one Dr. Robert Schuller suggests: "What would you pursue if it was impossible for you to fail?"

Holly
Step 2: *MOSAIC Performance Grid*
Mental, Physical, and Financial areas

		Mental	Physical	Financial
M	**Mastery** Level 6	• Same as outstanding, plus going on a retreat for several weeks each year in mind-stimulating exposures such as extended courses, travel to new locations	• Designing and eating a perfect diet of specifically selected foods to promote health and welfare while maintaining an ongoing exercise program which has been designed to optimize my health	• Financially independent, investments and savings are adequate to provide for future financial needs, financial future does not depend upon current income
O	**Outstanding** Level 5	• Reading twenty books a year, attending many seminars during the year, taking a course on a new subject	• Eating the right foods all of the time while maintaining an ongoing exercise program five days a week	• Current income significantly exceeds current spending levels and substantial amounts of savings and investments have been accumulated
S	**Satisfactory** Level 4	• Reading ten to twelve books and attending several seminars each year	• Eating the right foods nearly all the time while on a solid exercise program three to four days a week	• Current income is in excess of current spending and savings and wealth are being accumulated
A	**Acceptable** Level 3	• Reading a book now and then	• Eating the right foods most of the time and getting a little exercise two to three days a week	• Current income meets spending levels and a viable plan exists to begin saving
I	**Intolerable** Level 2	• Not doing anything to learn new skills or gain new experiences	• Eating the wrong foods much of the time and having little or no exercise	• Current spending exceeds current income, a solution is not in sight, assets and savings are dwindling
C	**Counter-productive** Level 1	• Having exposures to negative and limitation thinking individuals	• Eating all the wrong foods all the time and being totally lethargic and sedentary	• Assets diminished, needs exceed income significantly, personal indebtedness rising rapidly

Step 3:
Assess current performance levels

The third step is to assess your current performance levels by evaluating where you are on your *MOSAIC Performance Grids* and by preparing your *MOSAIC* graphic to illustrate your assessment.

Holly. To complete her *Current MOSAIC* graphic, Holly reviewed her *MOSAIC Performance Grids* and decided that her present levels of performance and fulfillment are Spiritual, Satisfactory; Family, Outstanding; Social, Acceptable; Financial, Intolerable; Mental, Acceptable; and Physical, Satisfactory. Shown below is Holly's graphic with these assessments.

Holly
Step 3: *Current MOSAIC*

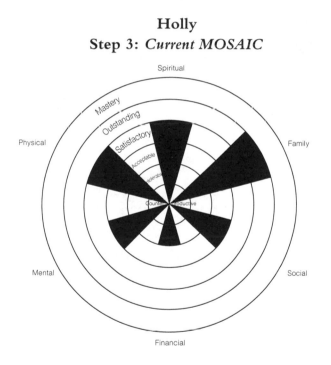

Step 4:
Determine desired performance levels

The next step is to determine your desired levels of performance. First review your *MOSAIC Performance Grids* and your

Current MOSAIC graphic to identify areas where you want to improve and grow. Then decide the performance levels you want to reach in the upcoming year (or whatever period you are planning). Finally, create a *Goal MOSAIC* to illustrate your decisions.

Holly. After reviewing her *Current MOSAIC* graphic and her *MOSAIC Performance Grids*, Holly can see that her life is *not* in balance. To address this she has decided that her objectives for the next year are to reach the following *MOSAIC* levels: Spiritual, Outstanding; Family, Outstanding; Social, Satisfactory; Financial, Acceptable; Mental, Outstanding; and Physical, Outstanding. It will take a lot of effort for Holly to make the advances she desires, but now that college is behind her she is looking forward to these new challenges.

A summary of Holly's current and desired performance assessments is presented below. Note that Holly is not trying to end up with a perfectly balanced *MOSAIC* with every aspect of her life at the Outstanding level by the end of the year. Rather than trying to make quantum leaps in all areas in just one year, Holly has decided to concentrate her efforts on the areas indicated.

Holly
Step 4: Performance Assessment

	Current assessment	Desired objective
Spiritual	Satisfactory	Outstanding
Family	Outstanding	Outstanding
Social	Acceptable	Satisfactory
Financial	Intolerable	Acceptable
Mental	Acceptable	Outstanding
Physical	Satisfactory	Outstanding

Holly
Step 4: *Goal MOSAIC*

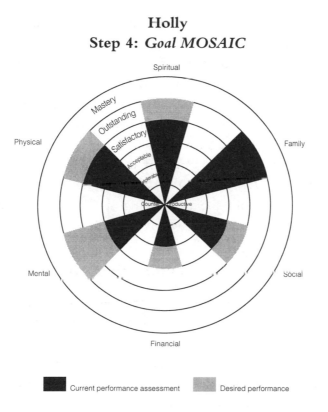

◼ Current performance assessment   ▨ Desired performance

Holly is now ready to prepare her *Goal MOSAIC* graphic. She does this by extending the spokes on her *Current MOSAIC* to reflect her desired levels of performance. Her resultant graphic is shown above.

As Holly's *Goal MOSAIC* shows, she is presently way out of balance in the financial area of her life. This is not a surprise to her since she is just starting her career, but it is an area she wants to pay attention to when she establishes her goals and action plans.

Step 5:
Establish goals and action plans

The final step is to establish goals and action plans. Review your *Goal MOSAIC* to identify the gaps between where you are and where you want to be. Then follow the *GOAL-DRIVEN*

MANAGEMENT method in *Part Two* of this book to develop goals and action plans in each area of your life.

Holly. Before proceeding to develop her goals and action plans, Holly decided to summarize her overall plans so she could evaluate the big picture of what she intends to accomplish. Holly's summary for the Mental, Physical, and Financial areas of her life is presented on the next page.

Now Holly is ready to move on to *Part Two* of this book and utilize the *GOAL-DRIVEN MANAGEMENT* method for establishing specific goals and for developing specific action plans to achieve them.

Implementation notes and other considerations

MOSAIC is an effective tool for identifying goals and action plans to pursue, but its usefulness depends upon attention to detail and discipline in implementation.

The most critical part of the process is establishing definitions of criteria for evaluating performance and fulfillment of missions and visions. As mentioned several times, it is *not* easy to develop these criteria, but they are tremendously valuable once they have been established.

The saying, "You cannot enter the same stream twice," is apropos. Once you can literally see where you are in comparison to where you could be, you will never be the same—because you will be aware of the gap and be pulled toward closing it.

When we ask individuals in our seminars what they want to be remembered for, it is heartening to learn their answers. Most people want to be remembered for the good they have done for others or for the love they have given to others.

There often is a disconnect, however, between what individuals want to be remembered for and the goals and actions they have been pursuing. When you look at the *Current MOSAIC* graphics of some individuals, they do not rate themselves very far

Holly's overall plan
(three areas)

Mental

Mission: My mission is to continue to learn and grow mentally by providing myself a diversity of learning experiences and exposures that continually challenge and recharge me.

Current assessment: Currently I am at an acceptable level in this area, but I need to develop and grow to achieve my potential.

Overall plan: My overall plan is to focus on this area and develop a specific plan to take some courses and learn some new skills.

Physical

Mission: My mission is to develop and maintain my body so I am physically strong and healthy with continuous energy and stamina.

Current assessment: I have fallen behind on my exercise and diet programs, and while I may be in the satisfactory range, this is not where I want to be.

Overall plan: My overall plan is to design a diet plan that provides the nourishment I need and accommodates my schedule, plus I am going to develop a standard weekly exercise program.

Financial

Mission: My mission is to provide for my current and future financial needs so I have resources for emergencies and so I will not be dependent on others for financial support.

Current assessment: I have gotten way behind in this area and am near the intolerable level.

Overall plan: I need some help in this area and intend to take a course and seek some assistance so that I can get on a budget that matches my income and spending levels.

out on the spokes for the areas they want to be remembered for. That is, they may currently rate themselves at only Level 2 or 3 when it comes to family and social responsibilities, yet these purportedly are their most important priorities. In such cases, the *MOSAIC* process points this out. Now aware of this *incongruence,* these individuals can focus more time and effort on setting and pursuing specific goals in these areas.

How to apply *MOSAIC* in larger organizations

The illustrations for the Jones Insurance Agency and Holly were kept simple to facilitate explanation of the *MOSAIC* method and how it is applied in the creation of *MOSAIC Performance Grids* and graphical displays of performance assessments.

Please do not let these uncomplicated examples cause you to underestimate the robustness and capabilities of *MOSAIC.* The method is *extremely flexible* and provides for scaling up or down to meet your needs—whether you are using the method for a large multinational organization, a division location, a project team, or on an individual basis.

In the earlier example for the Jones Insurance Agency, each of the four functional areas of the business were treated as individual components in the analyses. Accordingly, Mr. Jones prepared *MOSAIC Performance Grids* for each component and each component was presented as a separate spoke in the graphical analyses.

If the business were larger, Mr. Jones may have desired to subdivide each of the components into subcomponents. For example, Mr. Jones could subdivide Agent recruiting and development into four components: (1) Recruiting, (2) Training, (3) Performance management, and (4) Personnel administration. Separate *Performance Grids* could be prepared for each of these four subcomponents or they could be treated as columns on an overall *Performance Grid* for Agent recruiting and development. As to the graphical displays, each of the four subcomponents could be presented as either a slice of the Agent recruiting and development spoke (one spoke subdivided into four sections) or as separate spokes on the overall company *MOSAIC* graphical display. An alternative would be to leave the total company graphical display as is and create a separate *MOSAIC* graphical display for the further analyses of the Agent recruiting and development component; this display would have four spokes: (1) Recruiting; (2) Training; (3) Performance management; and (4) Personnel administration.

Here is another variation of cascading and subdividing. Consider the *MOSAIC Performance Grids* and graphical displays that each agent will prepare in conjunction with their *Personal Performance Plans*. Each agent will have his or her respective *Performance Grid* and graphical display. These could be rolled up to the company level by having a master *MOSAIC* graphical display with one spoke for each agent. Each of these spokes would represent a composite of the agent's overall performance assessments. This would be a useful tool for Mr. Jones. An adaptation of this would be to have each spoke for each agent subdivided into slices with each slice representing an area of performance for the agents.

The most important things to keep in mind are that the definition of performance levels is the key to the success of using *MOSAIC* and the method should be adapted to your situation and circumstances.

5

Why *GOAL-DRIVEN MANAGEMENT* works

Ever hear of Jean Foucault, the French physicist?

Without him we wouldn't have satellites or space travel. In 1852 he invented the device that enables the positioning and navigation of all satellites and space craft: the gyroscope.

I had a gyroscope when I was a kid. It was a spinning toy top inside a metal frame. As long as the inner wheel continued to spin rapidly, the gyroscope remained balanced on its pointed end.

Gyroscopic compasses, "gyros" as they are called, have been used for nearly a century to guide ships, airplanes, satellites, and spacecraft such as the Space Shuttle. Gyros are the brains of autopilot mechanisms on aircraft.

Today, no successful navigator would think of beginning a voyage without the best information and without using the best available technology, such as the NAVSTAR Global Positioning System. It consists of twenty-one gyroscopically positioned satellites circling the globe in six orbital planes 11,000 miles above the earth. It provides exact navigational information, allowing users to know their position within ten feet, their velocity within inches per second, and the time of day within a millionth of a second. Now *that* is precision.

Just as no navigator should use anything but the best technology available to get this kind of precision, no successful business executive should try to lead and guide a business without using the best approach available. In business, the best approach is to have guiding mission, vision, and philosophy statements that are aligned with and supported by goals, action plans, and systems that drive results—*DNA Leadership*.

The *MOSAIC* methodology, discussed in *Chapter 4*, addresses the development of mission, vision, and philosophy statements. GOAL-DRIVEN MANAGEMENT is a method for developing goals, action plans, and systems. Used together, these two methods provide what I refer to as *Gyroscopic Planning*™—an approach that will get you precisely where you want to go, exactly when you want to get there, on autopilot.

GOAL-DRIVEN MANAGEMENT'S core principles

GOAL-DRIVEN MANAGEMENT is based upon proven fundamental principles. Interestingly, many of the principles in this book have a comparable principle in science. Where I have been able to draw a comparison between the principles in this book and those in science, I have done so to aid in the explanation of the principles pertaining to setting and pursuing goals. Sometimes we forget we are part of the Earth. It is good to be reminded that we are subject to the laws and principles of science and nature.

Three core principles serve as the foundation for all other principles and techniques in GOAL-DRIVEN MANAGEMENT.

1. The principle of cause and effect: This principle is similar to Newton's first and third laws of motion. Newton's first law is that there will be no change in the motion of a body unless it is acted upon by an external force. If you want to change the results you have been getting, you need to change the actions you have been taking. Newton's third law asserts that for every action of force there is an equal and opposite reaction of force. This implies that you must take steps to cause the exact results you seek. No effort, no result. Wrong efforts, wrong results. Right effort, right results.

You will not get the effects you want unless you create the causes to produce them. The way to get the results you want is to create them.

2. The principle of inertia and momentum: The world is full of distractions that diminish our focus and diffuse our energies. To maximize power and effectiveness you must create a path to follow and stay on it. In business that path is composed of systems and procedures. For individuals that path is composed of habits. Your systems and habits determine what your business and you will achieve and become. To the extent that you alter and improve your goal-setting and goal-achieving systems and habits, you will improve the results you can realize.

3. The principle of concentration and focus: This principle is similar to Newton's second law of motion, which says that acceleration and power are proportional to the mass of the body. Here, mass does not necessarily mean size; rather mass is referring to the density or gravitational weight as measured by the inertia of the body being measured—that is, the amount of material *concentrated* in it. In other words, when you increase the concentration,

---

Three core principles

1. *Cause and effect:* We live in a world of cause and effect. This means effort, that is, *work*, is required to produce results. We must act to get results.

2. *Inertia and momentum:* Inertia is the tendency of a body at rest to remain at rest and a body in motion to continue in motion in the same path. Momentum is the power of a moving body. Our success in achieving our goals is dependent upon the plans and systems we create to drive actions and sustain momentum.

3. *Concentration and focus:* Concentration and focus on a few goals are required to produce power; diffused efforts and a lack of focus diminish power.

you increase the mass; and when you increase the mass, you increase the acceleration and power.

Applied to goals, this means concentration on a few goals and a few actions is required to magnify the power you can apply to achieve them. This greater power is essential when pursuing large goals. It also increases your odds for success for all goals you focus on. Conversely, a failure to concentrate your power will diffuse your energies and jeopardize completion of your goals, and it will limit your chances for success in achieving the bigger goals you have established.

GOAL-DRIVEN MANAGEMENT does not offer a magic potion or quick fix to goal achievement, but the techniques work when applied with deliberate effort in a concentrated manner. When you convert those efforts into systems and life-long habits, you get long-term results.

Put yourself on autopilot

The objective of GOAL-DRIVEN MANAGEMENT is to put you and your business on autopilot on the best courses of action toward the exact goals you desire.

The objective is not just to get on a course of action toward your goals; it is to get on the *best* possible course of action. The objective is not to pursue goals in general; it is to pursue the *exact* goals you want to achieve.

Goals are not achieved by just considering goals, stating them, or writing them down. Goals must become so internalized and integrated into your thoughts that you move toward your goals *automatically* without thinking about them.

When athletes and artisans are performing or creating, they don't stop and think, "How do I do this?" They just flawlessly execute. A surgeon does not ponder how to perform a routine procedure—she just does it. A pitcher does not take several minutes to consider how to grasp the ball during his windup—he just winds up and fires the ball.

The *GOAL-DRIVEN MANAGEMENT* method can be similarly internalized and applied with similar professional results. Time and effort are required, but with practice and repetition the techniques can become as natural as a fast-ball windup.

Once the *GOAL-DRIVEN MANAGEMENT* techniques are internalized, the executives, managers, and associates in the business will find themselves setting and successfully pursuing a larger quantity of more substantial goals than previously. In the process, the quality of the work force will improve, the business will grow, operational performance and teamwork will be enhanced, and sales and profits will increase.

As you internalize the techniques in *GOAL-DRIVEN MANAGEMENT* and acquire them as your own, you will find yourself becoming more confident and continually better at selecting and achieving bigger goals. Concurrently, your overall performance and capabilities will increase.

Use repetition to exchange old habits for new, improved habits

Repetition is the only way to learn any new skill on a permanent basis. To learn how to walk you had to try again and again. To learn how to drive you had to try again and again. To get good at setting and achieving goals, you must consciously repeat and use the techniques again and again until they are internalized. You will get good at using the techniques only after you have used them over and over.

Some businesses and individuals will find that they have been learning and repeating ineffective approaches to setting and achieving goals. This is an obstacle that can be overcome. Essentially, they have old habits they must discard in exchange for new ones. For example, many individuals do not write their goals down. Others write their goals, but they do not write them out completely. In *GOAL-DRIVEN MANAGEMENT* you should write major goals in *laser-clear* goal statements specifying all aspects of the goal. Periodically you should review them to sharpen your focus on them and imprint them into your subconscious mind. It takes a little effort before these techniques becomes habits, but once they are habits, they will be lifelong servants and reward you well.

At a breakfast meeting with three sales executives I asked the individuals what *processes* they used to establish and manage achievement of their goals. The silence following my question was telling. "That's a darn good question," one of the individuals finally said. "I have never thought about how I go about it." The other two individuals agreed. They, too, had never given any thought to determining the best techniques to use for establishing and achieving goals.

Think about it for a moment. What processes have you been learning *and repeating* with respect to setting goals and developing action plans to achieve them? Where did you learn how to select and achieve your goals? How do you go about it? When do you establish your goals and how do you manage your progress towards them? Can you remember anyone ever sitting down with you and explaining a comprehensive *process* for setting and pursuing goals? Did your goal-setting habits come from someone who knows how to set goals? Did anyone ever explain what they do to achieve their goals so you could model their approach?

Like the three individuals I had breakfast with, most people haven't taken the time to reflect on and evaluate what they are doing and should be doing to set and achieve their goals. In addition, most individuals have not had the exposures necessary to develop good goal-setting and achieving habits. The good news is that this book provides a foundation for exchanging old habits for new ones that work better and are more reliable.

A big advantage of
GOAL-DRIVEN MANAGEMENT
is that it is a step-by-step *method*

F.W. Nichol wrote years ago: "Almost all men are intelligent, it is method that they lack." The successes individuals and organizations achieve or do not achieve result largely from the methods they employ or do not employ.

GOAL-DRIVEN MANAGEMENT is a method—a method that can improve the results you have been getting by providing a systematic approach to setting and achieving goals.

In *Forbes ASAP* magazine Tom Peters wrote an article subtitled: "The model for tomorrow's brain-based organization is today's professional service outfit"—that is, professional services firms. "Real professional services firms are pioneering here [using knowledge]," Peters says.

Mr. Peters believes big professional services firms have many advantages and ideal approaches because they are so *project focused* and so *results oriented*. I wholeheartedly agree. I am biased because I was with Arthur Andersen for so many years, but I am also biased because I know that behind the scenes of these great firms are methods that work.

I learned the importance of using methods at Arthur Andersen where a system was created around a methodology for every facet of the business. Information consulting services were delivered using an approach called Method I. Audit examinations were performed following a method called Transaction Flow Auditing. We had a method for providing performance evaluations.

I had the good fortune to participate on the development teams that created or refined many of the methods above. I also created a number of other methods on my own. When I was partner in charge of an office at Andersen, I created a method for marketing professional services that worked well. I also created a

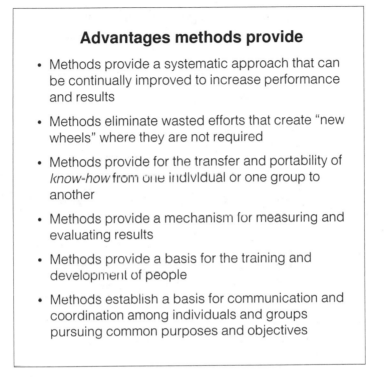

Advantages methods provide

- Methods provide a systematic approach that can be continually improved to increase performance and results

- Methods eliminate wasted efforts that create "new wheels" where they are not required

- Methods provide for the transfer and portability of *know-how* from one individual or one group to another

- Methods provide a mechanism for measuring and evaluating results

- Methods provide a basis for the training and development of people

- Methods establish a basis for communication and coordination among individuals and groups pursuing common purposes and objectives

system for providing performance reviews that I call the *Performance Grid Method* (discussed in *Chapter 4*).

My experiences with methods at Andersen, coupled with my experiences in launching and developing new companies in my venture capital business, provided the foundation and building blocks for the *DNA Leadership* approach and its supporting methodologies: *MOSAIC* and GOAL-DRIVEN MANAGEMENT.

Although I didn't call it GOAL-DRIVEN MANAGEMENT at the time, I used the principles of the GOAL-DRIVEN MANAGEMENT method at Andersen when I grew professionally from staff member to partner in charge of an office. I followed the principles when I oversaw work on more than one hundred different client situations during my career at Andersen. We also used the GOAL-DRIVEN MANAGEMENT concepts at Venture America, the venture capital firm I co-founded and served as managing partner for twelve years. We followed the principles in supporting the growth and development of the twenty-three businesses we helped finance and launch.

I have followed the *GOAL-DRIVEN MANAGEMENT* method for my own personal growth and for the launch and development of my businesses. Through our executive training business I have shared these concepts with many firms and organizations. At George Mason University I created and taught a management course entitled *Developing an Entrepreneurial Mindset,* which was based on the principles of *MOSAIC* and *GOAL-DRIVEN MANAGEMENT.*

Methods result in *transferable and manageable* "know-how"

Methods result in know-how. They provide a basis to train people and to standardize and improve performance. When people no longer have to refer to the documentation for the method to accomplish a given task, it is know-how that carries them through. Know-how is a strength of individuals, and it is one of the core assets of most organizations.

When businesses and other organizations know how to do what they do better than anybody else, they really have something. What successful companies do best is create and consistently use methods and systems.

FedEx and UPS don't deliver our packages on time by accident. Mars, Inc. doesn't stamp that little "m" on its M & M's® by good luck. Disney World doesn't maintain squeaky clean facilities by happenstance. (See *The best kept secret of successful companies* in *Chapter 21* for how they put the M on the M&M's.)

Behind every great outcome, such as getting a package overnight, making perfect candies every time, or having surgically clean rest rooms, is a systematic series of procedures that someone or some group of individuals designed, implemented, and refined.

The better the method and the more refinements to it, the better the results.

Why *GOAL-DRIVEN MANAGEMENT* is a superior approach

In addition to being a method, *GOAL-DRIVEN MANAGEMENT* is a superior approach for setting and achieving goals because it is based on principles learned through a wide array of experiences involving many industries, businesses, and personal situations. The overall approach is documented in writing and illustrated. Thus, the method can be analyzed, improved, altered, and customized by individual users.

GOAL-DRIVEN MANAGEMENT is a portable and flexible methodology. The methods and procedures can be taught to anyone and applied and adapted to any situation: business or personal; team or individual; complex or simple.

The two core questions addressed by the *GOAL-DRIVEN MANAGEMENT* method are: What should we (I) do? How should we (I) do it?

When organizations and individuals are able to answer these questions with confidence, then they have something. They have *goal power.*

Getting organized

To maximize success we need a good system for managing our goals and our plans to achieve them. We need a guidance system to keep us focused and on course.

Where *are* we supposed to keep details about our goals? When and how are we supposed to record them?

And how should we compile and organize our strategies to achieve our goals into workable action plans we will actually follow and implement? Where are we supposed to keep these?

Many people use organizers to manage their time. But most people don't have or use a *comprehensive* system for establishing and recording goals and strategies and action plans to achieve them. What's more, they don't have a system for monitoring and managing plans once they have been established. A *Goals Journal*, discussed in *Chapter 8*, and an *Action Plan Workbook*, discussed in *Chapter 13*, serve these functions.

Developing a plan to plan

One of the first actions to take when you are ready to select your goals and develop plans to achieve them is to establish a specific plan with related systems and procedures to follow.

Set aside a specific time to plan each day, week, month, and year. I plan each of my tomorrows at the end of the day before I leave the office. On Fridays I plan the upcoming week. On the last Friday of a month I plan the next month. In October and November I plan the next year. My goal is to have all the essential elements of my next year's annual plan done by Thanksgiving.

Experiment with *GOAL-DRIVEN MANAGEMENT* and adapt the methodology to your personal situation

All of the techniques in *GOAL-DRIVEN MANAGEMENT* are straightforward and easy to understand—but they are not effortless to implement, particularly the first time around. The more experience you acquire with the techniques, the easier and more powerful it becomes to use them.

For example, very few businesses and individuals are accustomed to writing out comprehensive step-by-step plans for pursuing their major goals. But a written plan, at least in summary form, is an important key to achieving goals, and it is an integral part of the *GOAL-DRIVEN MANAGEMENT* method. Developing and using written plans may come easily and naturally for some individuals. It is not easy for everyone. Practice and experimentation are required.

An executive implementing GOAL-DRIVEN MANAGEMENT for the first time told me he did not believe me when I told him how easy it would be to update his action plans the second time around. "I honestly thought you were lying to me," he said when I visited with him recently. "But now I'm a believer." In fact, he is more than a believer—he has become somewhat of an evangelist, and his results show it.

The initial hurdle companies and individuals will have to overcome is that it is easier *not* to use the techniques than it is to use them. It is always easier to remain static than it is to change.

More businesses and people can endure mediocrity and failure than can endure success. Only the superb companies and outstanding individuals will fully implement the concepts of GOAL-DRIVEN MANAGEMENT. But only with full implementation will firms and individuals reap the total range of benefits.

You can't learn to ride a bicycle without getting on and trying it yourself. So try the techniques in the GOAL-DRIVEN MANAGEMENT method. Fine tune them into your own approach as you learn more and gain more experience.

This book is not the end all. It is not where you finish. It is where you begin.

*"The objective in life is to choose the right
goals, and then to cause to occur that which
must take place to achieve them."*

—Author unknown

Part
Two

GOAL-DRIVEN MANAGEMENT

Part Two Overview

Part Two contains the Five keys to GOAL-DRIVEN MANAGEMENT: G, GET a goal; O, OUTLINE a plan; A, ACT on your plan; L, LEARN from your progress; and S, SYSTEMATIZE your efforts.

Master blueprint: On the opposite page is a step-by-step master blueprint of the *Implementation action steps* for each key. The flowcharts are miniature reproductions of the flowcharts contained in *Chapters 10, 14, 17, 20,* and *23.*

Chapter 6, Five keys to GOAL-DRIVEN MANAGEMENT, provides an overview to acquaint you with the five keys.

Standard chapters: For each of the five keys, there are three "standard chapters." I recommend that you approach each of the five keys in order by first reading the *Fundamental principles,* next reading the *Success strategies, tools, and techniques,* and then reading the *Implementation action steps.*

Chapters 7, 11, 15, 18, **and** *21, Fundamental principles*: These chapters explain the core principles on which the methodology, success strategies, and implementation steps are based.

Chapters 8, 12, 16, 19, **and** *22, Success strategies, tools, and techniques:* These chapters explain and illustrate strategies, tools, and techniques you can apply and benefit from immediately.

Chapters 10, 14, 17, 20, **and** *23, Implementation action steps:* These chapters provide implementation action steps in narrative form and in flowcharts so you have a step-by-step program for implementing each of the five keys.

Special chapters: *Chapter 9, Ten elements every goal should have* **and** *Chapter 13, Use Action Plan Recaps to simplify planning and share know-how,* provide additional tools to make implementation easy.

Five Keys

TO

GOAL-DRIVEN MANAGEMENT™

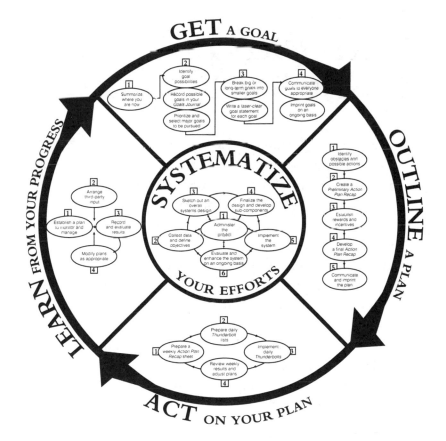

6

Five keys to *GOAL-DRIVEN MANAGEMENT*

This past summer I purchased a power washer, a machine that looks like a lawn mower with a high pressure hose coming out of the top—a washing machine for the outside of your house. In no time I had it out of the box, onto the driveway, and filled with gas and oil. I pulled on the cord a couple of times expecting it to kick over instantly. Nothing.

So, I jerked on the cord with all the fury in me. After twenty minutes I stood panting, sweating, and calling the machine and its manufacturer several choice names. The defiant block of steel sat there silently.

Dolly, my wife, appeared from nowhere with a glass of ice water. "This is a hunk of junk," I blurted out. "I've been pulling on this thing and it won't budge. Must be something wrong with the carburetor or the spark plug."

Dolly listened and then popped this amazing question: "Did you read the instructions?"

Did I read the instructions? Well, of course not. Why would I read the instructions? I knew how to oil and gas the machine and start it . . . . Didn't I?

And that is just the point. I *thought* I knew how to start the power washer, but in actuality I didn't. There was one small detail

I was not aware of. No matter how hard I snapped the cord or retraced my steps, I was not going to solve my problem by continuing the approach I had used successfully in the past for starting new pieces of yard equipment.

While I went back to pulling my guts out, Dolly retrieved the instructions from the plastic parts bag and began reading them to herself, loud enough for me to hear. As she read each instruction I would comment with "did that," "yes," or "right."

Then Dolly read these words which were inside a box on the second page of the instructions: "*Important.* Do not forget to fill the water pump casing with oil as well as the crankcase. This is required for the machine to be able to create sufficient pressure to start."

IMPORTANT

Do not forget to fill the water pump casing with oil as well as the crankcase. This is required for the machine to be able to create sufficient pressure to start.

Put oil into two holes on the same machine? Hmmmm. Never heard anything like that before. I leaned over and looked down at the power washer. There it was—*another* bright yellow oil cap—right where the arrow on the diagram in the instructions said it would be. Funny, I hadn't noticed it before.

"So that's why this came with two pints of oil," I said. Begrudgingly, I removed the yellow cap, filled the casing with oil, and pulled on the cord. Darn thing fired up instantly.

Lessons to be learned

I've shared my power washer experience with you to make two points. The first one is that we must know what *all* the required pieces are and use them if we want results in achieving our goals. There are five keys in the GOAL-DRIVEN MANAGEMENT method. Each and every one of them is required. No matter how hard I tried, I couldn't start the power washer without adding the second pint of oil. Similarly, we must use all five keys if we want to achieve our goals.

The second point is this: We don't know what we don't know, and most people think they know more about establishing and achieving goals than they actually do. What I didn't know about the power washer was keeping me from starting it, yet I stubbornly persisted in the way I always had in the past because I thought I knew all I needed to know. But I was wrong.

It is similar for goals. We don't necessarily know everything we need to know about setting and pursuing goals. Unfortunately, what we don't know *can* hurt us—by limiting or inhibiting our success in achieving the results we seek.

This book is metaphorically the instructions in the plastic bag. My objective is to provide information in a straightforward manner to help you establish and achieve your goals. Many individuals have told me that as they begin to learn more about establishing and achieving goals, they also begin to realize how little they know in comparison to how much there is to know. This book contains all the pieces of the puzzle and tells you how to place them together to achieve your goals.

IMPORTANT

There are five keys to GOAL-DRIVEN MANAGEMENT. Do not forget to use all five keys. This is required to get the maximum benefit from this book.

The five keys

There are five keys to the *GOAL-DRIVEN MANAGEMENT* method. They are easy to remember by the word G•O•A•L•S. Each letter stands for one of the keys.

G stands for **G**ET a goal
O stands for **O**UTLINE a plan
A stands for **A**CT on your plan
L stands for **L**EARN from your progress
S stands for **S**YSTEMATIZE your efforts

Unlock your goal power

Think of having your goals in a strongbox secured with an unusual lock requiring five different keys. Each key turns a chamber in the lock and partly opens it, but all five keys are required before the lock will snap open and release your goals to you. That's what you need to unlock goal power—all five keys.

The five keys you need to open the lock are G, O, A, L, and S. Nearly everyone knows something about the first key, *GET a goal*. However, most people don't know everything they need to know. Many people have misconceptions of what it takes to really get a goal.

Running through the first four keys, from *GET a goal*, to *OUTLINE a plan*, to *ACT on your plan*, to *LEARN from your progress*, individuals tend to know less and less about each successive key, yet each key is required for success in achieving goals.

The fifth key is *SYSTEMATIZE your efforts*. Only a fraction of the population grasps what it means to systematize efforts directed toward a specific goal. However, this final key is interrelated to all other keys. It is the one that springs open the lock.

Five Keys Required

The potential power that could be gained from the collective use of the five keys is not realized by most people and most organizations as they proceed from G to O, to A, to L, and to S—because they do not fully utilize all five keys. Individuals and organizations that understand and use all five keys achieve more of their goals more consistently than those who do not. They also achieve bigger goals.

While there is some power in using one or two of the five keys individually, to get real goal power, all five keys must be used all the time.

The *GOAL-DRIVEN MANAGEMENT* method is illustrated by the overall flowchart on page 93 and is summarized in the paragraphs that follow. As you read the remainder of this book you will receive comprehensive information on each key.

The graphic below provides a simplified overview of the five G•O•A•L•S keys. This graphic will be used at the beginning of each chapter in the remainder of *Part Two* to orient you to where you are in the methodology.

GET a goal

GET *a goal* in the GOAL-DRIVEN MANAGEMENT method means *purpose-driven* goal selection. This entails more than simply selecting goals or writing them down. It means that goals should be selected and prioritized in a thoughtful and deliberate manner. That way your efforts are directed toward achieving those goals that are the most important and that are congruent with your beliefs and values. It also means integrating your goals so deeply into your thinking that you literally set yourself on autopilot toward their achievement. This requires establishing specific goals and imprinting them into your subconscious mind.

OUTLINE a plan

OUTLINE *a plan* means developing a plan that is *action-driven* toward your selected goals. To do this, you must first think through the essential action steps required to achieve your goals. Then you have to outline, sequence, and organize those action steps into a summary action plan. You will use that action plan to guide and manage your efforts for achieving your goals.

An essential aspect of the GOAL-DRIVEN MANAGEMENT method is to have a written action plan for each major goal being pursued. This method provides several techniques to simplify this process. One of these is an *Action Plan Recap* sheet, which is easy to prepare and use. It is explained in *Chapter 13.*

ACT on your plan

ACT *on your plan* means that for goals to be achieved, *results-driven* actions must be taken to realize them. This is obvious, but taking the required actions to achieve our goals is easier said than done. We live in a fast-paced world with many distractions.

The overall approach is to break action steps into manageable segments you can focus on and then act on so you make progress toward your desired goals on an ongoing basis. In *GOAL-DRIVEN MANAGEMENT,* strive to make progress *daily.*

LEARN from your progress

LEARN from your progress means that if you take the time to evaluate the actions you have been applying and learn from them, then you become *improvement-driven* and no matter what results those individual actions may have produced, you are making progress. *Improvement-driven* learning requires that you measure and monitor where you are in relation to where you want to be, and what you have accomplished in relation to what you intended.

It is not enough to learn from mistakes; it is just as important to evaluate what is working right and determine how it can be improved. This requires first that you have objective information you can use to avoid fooling yourself, and then that you review and evaluate the information you have.

SYSTEMATIZE your efforts

SYSTEMATIZE your efforts means that long-term benefits from the *GOAL-DRIVEN MANAGEMENT* method will be achieved only if the core elements of the process are *habit-driven.* That is, they must be applied systematically on a consistent and sustaining basis. For example, in *Chapter 8* techniques are provided for writing *laser-clear* goal statements, and in *Chapter 13* techniques are provided for developing plans for goals using *Action Plan Recap* sheets. These techniques, or your adapted form of them, must become habits. The way to create these habits is to decide on the system you will follow until the related activities are ingrained and automatic.

Behind each significant goal you pursue there will be an underlying core of "must do" actions required to achieve long-term results. "Must do" actions are those actions that absolutely must be taken before results can be realized. In many sales situations, for example, salespersons must set appointments and must make sales presentations to have customers buy their products or services. These "must do" actions are done best if they are performed following an orderly and well-conceived method or system. Making sure that methods are in place for each "must do" action is an integral part of GOAL-DRIVEN MANAGEMENT.

In summary . . .

Remember, the five keys to GOAL-DRIVEN MANAGEMENT are:

GET a goal which is *purpose-driven*

OUTLINE a plan which is *action-driven*

ACT on your plan with steps that are *results-driven*

LEARN from your progress so your learning is
improvement-driven

SYSTEMATIZE your efforts so you become *habit-driven*

Use all of these keys together to create *goal power* for achieving your goals and you will become *goal-driven*.

7

GET a goal—
Fundamental principles

The first key in *GOAL-DRIVEN MANAGEMENT* is G. G stands for *GET a goal*. The fundamental principles pertaining to getting a goal are discussed in this chapter under these headings:

- Goals have power only if you really "GET" them

- Goals are wants you *intend* to pursue

- There are significant differences between *cause* goals and *end-result* goals

- You must concentrate on only a few goals, or you run the risk of achieving no goals

- You don't need to know your lifetime goals at the outset

- Changes in business require changes in goals

- Big goals produce big power

- We all need inspiring goals

- Limitation thinking keeps you from choosing big goals

- There are three boxes in life: Which one are you in?

- Choose goals that are congruent with your DNA as defined by your values, desires, and beliefs

- Goals have interdependent relationships with other goals

Goals have power
only if you really "GET" them

Although *GET a goal* sounds logical enough, there is more to getting a goal than most people imagine. There is a difference between selecting a goal and writing it down and really getting a goal.

When you truly get a goal, you are goal-driven. In other words, the goal gets *you*—it has a magnetizing power and you are pulled toward it automatically. When you are in the grip of your goals, you pursue them passionately with fire in your belly. This intense commitment and drive is necessary to achieve many business and personal goals, particularly big goals, for there always will be obstacles, setbacks, and delays. Therefore, you must rely on your persistence and internal drive to sustain your efforts until your goals are realized.

There are many techniques you can use to get your goals and increase your drive to achieve them. These are discussed in this chapter and in *Chapters 8, 9, and 10.*

Goals are wants you *intend* to pursue

We all have wants and dreams. But until your wants and dreams become fixed in your mind as wants you *intend* to pursue, they are not goals. This is important. As you select and firmly commit to pursuing your goals, you are forever altering what you will become as well as what your business will become.

The ingredient that makes a "goal" a real goal is intent to pursue. If you think you'd like to bring out a new line of products, but don't have any specific plans or intentions, then this isn't a goal. It is wishful thinking or musing to yourself, but it isn't a goal.

But, if you think, "let's bring out a new line of products," and then set a time frame for developing the products and initiate plans to commence the effort—then *that* is a goal. You are serious. You intend to achieve your goal.

It is easy to fool yourself into believing you are goal-driven when you may not be pursuing goals. Talking about your goals or talking about *possibly* pursuing goals is not pursuing goals. How many times have you heard yourself or someone say, "I'm going to get organized" or "I'm going to get in shape" and then not take action to get organized or in shape? Or how many times have you heard executives comment that they are going to "start being more responsive to customer needs" and then continue doing what they had been doing without changing a thing?

Uncommitted "possible pursuit" of goals is a problem. It lets you program yourself and others at the subconscious level into believing goals aren't as important as you say they are. But your subconscious mind can't be fooled. You should take goal-setting and goal-achieving seriously. If you don't require a firm and serious approach of yourself and others, you set the stage for accepting as the norm goal discussions without results—talk without walk. Discussions without results are detrimental.

There are significant differences between *cause* goals and *end-result* goals

Most of the goals we talk about are *end-result* goals.

A business *end-result* goal might be to create a newsletter by September 1. You can't *do* a newsletter. Contributing actions are required. Someone has to create the layout, develop the copy, and sketch the drawings. Only after these action steps are taken will the newsletter be completed. The supporting action steps *cause* the newsletter, the *end-result* goal, to be completed.

A personal *end-result* goal might be to lose ten pounds over the next three months. Losing ten pounds is not something you can *do*. What you can do is take actions to cause your ten-pound weight loss. For example, you can take a course to learn more about nutrition and exercise, and then you can take steps to alter your diet and to exercise.

As these examples illustrate, there are two kinds of goals: *end-result* goals and *cause* goals. The principles of cause and effect were discussed in *Chapter 5*, but let me reiterate that for every *effect* or end result desired, there must be a corresponding *cause* driving its realization.

End-result goals are the goals we want to achieve, but they generally are not doable per se. You can't push a button and enter a new global market or improve the quality of your products; contributing steps are required. *Cause* goals are supporting goals that are doable. When they are completed they collectively result in the achievement of *end-result* goals.

Cause and effect corollary:

Focus on the cause

In the bigger picture, *cause* goals are more important than *end-result* goals once *end-result* goals have been established.

Once you have established your desired *end-result* goals, you should turn your attention and focus to your *cause* goals if you want to achieve results.

What you must guard against is allowing your attention to *end-result* goals to overshadow your attention to the means to achieve them.

Years ago I wrote *The Entrepreneur's Tool Kit,* a guide for planning businesses, and described the business planning process we used in our venture capital business, which I called *backwards business planning.* Using this approach entrepreneurs plan their businesses by beginning with a vision of what they want their businesses to look like five or ten years down the road. Then they work backwards from there to identify the actions and interim accomplishments required to get there from where they are now. Through this technique we can identify the *cause* goals that accomplish our *end-result* goals.

I also covered the backwards business planning concept in my book, *Soar . . . If You Dare*, where I described the domino effect for achieving goals. The domino effect occurs when we design a series of action steps that creates a chain reaction or "domino effect." This results in the achievement of our goals. The action step "dominos" are *cause* goals. They are doable.

Cause goals are discussed more in *Chapters 11, 12*, and *13*, which describe how to outline a plan to achieve your goals. The action steps in these plans are *cause* goals.

You must concentrate on only a few goals, or you run the risk of achieving no goals

When a magnifying glass focuses sunlight toward a spot on paper, the paper ignites. Until this energy concentration occurs, nothing happens. We are the same. Our power of concentration is released when we gather our physical and mental resources and focus them on a common objective.

The principle of concentration and focus is discussed in *Chapter 5*. Unfortunately, most people live their lives without benefiting from the power of concentration. Peter Drucker, the business sage, observed this years ago when he wrote: "Concentration is the key . . . no other principle is violated as consistently as the basic principle of concentration . . . our motto seems to be let's do a little bit of everything."

When you try to pursue too many goals at the same time, you run the risk of not achieving any of them. For successful achievement, your daily efforts and attention must be narrowed and focused on one or two goals at a time.

This means consciously limiting the number of goals you pursue. While it is difficult, limiting goals often means *eliminating* goals. It is hard to turn your back on a dream, but this must be done if your other dreams are to be fulfilled. If you don't do this, you run the risk of spreading your efforts so thin that you accomplish nothing.

The principle of concentration is also applicable in business. A business cannot attack a market on numerous fronts, for example. Better results will be achieved if the business leaders identify market segments where resources can be focused to drive through results. An excellent book on concentration of marketing efforts is *Focus*, by Al Ries. Ries provides plenty of examples where companies were successful because they narrowed their marketing goals and where other companies did not fare as well because they targeted too many goals and tried to be too many things to too many people.

For example, Ries relates a comparison between The Coca-Cola Company, which focused on beverages, and PepsiCo, Inc., which divided its efforts among its beverage, snack, and restaurant businesses. Although PepsiCo was the bigger company when Ries wrote his book, The Coca-Cola Company's stock was valued at more than twice that of PepsiCo, Inc. Ries suggested a solution to Pepsi: "Spin off Pizza Hut, Taco Bell, and the other PepsiCo restaurants into a separate company." Interestingly, that is what the PepsiCo, Inc. directors voted to do in January 1997.

In addition to concentrating our focus on a few goals, we should adopt an approach that provides for balance among our *continuing* goals and our *thrusting* goals and balance among our *short-term*, *intermediate*, and *long-term* goals.

Balance *continuing* and *thrusting* goals

Continuing goals are established goals you are already pursuing. Action steps are required to achieve *continuing* goals, but the ongoing effort is already systematized and not considered extreme or extraordinary. Two examples of *continuing* goals are: continue to call on existing accounts once each month; and, continue to maintain a zero accident level in the plant. We all have many *continuing* goals, and we should evaluate the effort, resources, and sacrifices these goals require when contemplating additional goals.

Thrusting goals are new goals requiring extra effort and drive to achieve. Two examples of *thrusting* goals are: create a new customer service plan to improve relationships, quality, and response time; and, expand the company's sales efforts into Asia. Each of these goals requires special effort, energy, and sacrifices.

Peter asked me how many *thrusting* goals I thought he should have for his six-person advertising agency. He was considering five *thrusting* goals: (1) install a new computer system; (2) set up a division for Internet advertising; (3) hire sales agents in a nearby town and set up operations there; (4) begin a program to revitalize relationships with existing customers; and (5) start a training program to improve the sales skills of associates.

I told Peter that much depended upon the capacity and resources he could dedicate to these goals, but my gut instinct was to tackle no more than two of these goals during the next quarter. Provided those two goals were successfully underway and more-or-less *continuing* goals by the end of the quarter, then I recommended beginning one additional goal during each of the next three quarters, assuming continuing progress and satisfaction with results.

Peter asked me how many *thrusting* goals I was pursuing.

"One." I said. "To get this book completed. And when that's done I have my next two *thrusting* goals all lined up."

While I am in favor of pursuing *thrusting* goals, I am cautious about how many I will pursue at any one time.

A big business, of course, can and should pursue many *thrusting* goals at once. The Coca-Cola Company, for example, reported progress on more than twelve *thrusting* goals in a recent

interim report. An example of one of Coca-Cola's *thrusting* goals
was opening another major facility in Central Asia.

Balancing short-term, intermediate, and long-term goals

In addition to balance among goal types and *thrusting* and *continuing* goals as described above, it is important to have balance
among our short-term, intermediate, and long-term goals. You
should have some of each. A short-term goal is one you can
accomplish in less than a month; an intermediate goal will take
more than a month but less than a year; and a long-term goal will
take one or more years to achieve.

Short-term goals are essential. We all need to know we are
accomplishing something worthwhile every day and every week.
If we don't make short-term progress, we won't make any progress. In most instances our short-term goals are simply bite-sized
components of our intermediate and long-term goals. Two examples of short-term goals are to hold a clearance sale next month
and to present a proposal to a new client in two weeks.

Intermediate goals direct our plans and actions throughout
the year. They provide stability and enable us to expend our energies and resources in an effective manner that is consistent with
our overall desires and objectives. Two examples of intermediate
goals are to release a new line of products in the third quarter and
to institute a summer intern program for graduate students.

Long-term goals are those guiding goals on the horizon we
continually see and work towards. They provide a framework for
all other goal selections. In many cases our intermediate and short-
term goals are *cause* goals or interim goals for our long-term goals.
An example of a long-term business goal is to achieve annual sales
of $100 million in five years. An example of a long-term goal for
a new law firm associate is to make partner in six years.

You don't need to know
your lifetime goals at the outset

I have met many individuals who do not have big goals to pursue. They are frustrated because they want big goals and don't know how to create them. "Nothing really turns me on" and "I can't really get excited about anything" are typical comments.

My advice is don't worry about a big dream in the sky if you don't have one and are having trouble finding one. But take time to identify stretch goals you can pursue now to get yourself moving in a positive direction.

While a small number of people know early in life exactly what goals they want to achieve, most people don't. Most of us go through an evolutionary process. The examples below from national magazines and newspapers point out different approaches people take.

Someone who always knew what he wanted is T.J. Rodgers, CEO of Cypress Semiconductor. "I made the commitment that I would be CEO of my own company by the time I was 35," Rodgers says. He believes he had a huge advantage going through college because he knew he was going to own his own company.

Theodore W. Waitt, CEO of Gateway 2000, knew his big goal early on, too. He says: "I just always knew I was going to have my own company and be my own boss someday."

But for every person I've come across like Rodgers and Waitt, I've found dozens more who have had changing and evolving goals along the way.

Erika Williams, CEO of Cincinnati Microwave, says that earlier in her career she was having fun and making money, but she didn't have a long-term goal driving her. When she went back and earned her MBA, she got the "idea that she wanted to be a CEO." It was when she locked on to this goal that she started asking herself which positions and exposures would get her to her goal in a reasonable time frame.

Russell Simmons, founder of Def Jam Records and Def Comedy Jam says: "I never envisioned any of this . . . . I wanted to protect and develop my artists, and the record company grew out of my passion for their interests."

Another great example of an individual whose goals evolved is Ted Turner, founder of CNN, who made this statement in a speech to the Chief Executive Officers Club: "When I started out I had no idea that I'd travel as far as I have and it really has been a Disneyland and Dorothy in the Wizard of Oz kind of journey."

I, too, continue to have evolving goals. At each stage of my life, my goals seemed like big goals. In hindsight, some of them now look commonplace, but they weren't at the time. Early in life I just wanted to make it through college. Then I just wanted a decent paying job. At Arthur Andersen my goals evolved from making senior, to manager, and then partner. Finally, I wanted to be in charge of an office. Next I wanted to start my own business, then a second business, and a third. In between I wanted to teach at the college level and write several books. I tell people that I still am trying to figure out what I ultimately want to be when I grow up—and this is true in the sense that I fully expect more goals to enter my life that I don't even know about yet.

Does this mean I have not used goals as a tool for growth? No! I have always had goals and I have always used them for personal growth. But I've never been hit by a thunderbolt that revealed exactly what my purpose in life is. It may hit me someday, but until it does I'm going to keep putting one new goal after another in front of me and see how it turns out.

Changes in business require changes in goals

Businesses must continually evolve to respond and adapt to changing conditions in changing markets. This requires rethinking goals and plans and changing them periodically to reflect current conditions and perceived opportunities.

Many companies have to reinvent themselves to continue their success. General Electric Company has been a products company during its entire history. But John F. Welch Jr., CEO, recently announced the company's initiatives and plans to shift toward becoming more of a full-service company. Welch is reinventing General Electric. Similarly, Andy Grove, CEO of Intel, has redefined and is transforming his company—from being a maker of chips to being an out-in-front leader in its industry. Major shifts like these require many new and different stretch goals.

In an article in *Chief Executive* magazine, Robert W. Lear, former CEO of F.&M. Schaefer and Chairman of *Chief Executive's* advisory board, reminded us of the important little line: "It is not the big fish that eat the little fish; it is the fast ones that eat the slow ones."

The pace of business has picked up enormously. Twenty-first-century businesses must be quick and nimble in responding to changes and in creating changes and innovations. Executives must be fast on their feet to abandon goals that are no longer appropriate while adopting new goals that will grow the company in the direction intended.

Unfortunately, a few executives respond to change and innovation like the dog that chases every car going down the street. They manage on a "topic du jour" basis. Somewhere between changing courses every time we hear something new and never changing at all is a happy balance. Our job is to figure it out and apply it in our own circumstances. Except in caked and clogged organizations, when something must be done to break the crust, I do not believe in change for the sake of change unless the change is intended to create an improvement. Change is an important ingredient for success and an essential element of the change process is changing our goals.

Big goals produce big power

To unleash your potential and the potential of those who work in your business choose big goals.

Consider the headline on a recent cover of *Fortune* magazine: *Intel, Andy Grove's Amazing Profit Machine and his plan for five more years of explosive growth.* Mr. Grove is not planning on just five more years of growth, he is planning on *explosive* growth. Notice how differently that one word, explosive, makes you feel about Intel and Mr. Grove.

When business leaders choose big goals they summon the big power in their organizations. When they choose little goals they don't summon anything.

When we choose big goals we see our big power. When we choose little goals we see our little power.

Years ago, when I was in the Jaycees our chapter was having difficulty recruiting new members and keeping members involved. These problems disappeared when we abandoned our minor goals and adopted a big goal of purchasing a mobile intensive care unit for our community. This was an enormous goal for our chapter, and it challenged and inspired us. In three months we raised the money and bought the unit. Along the way we attracted new members who wanted to be part of a good thing. Our membership roster was full, and our chapter was stronger and better. We walked away with many awards at the state competition. By *substantially* increasing our goal, we increased our enthusiasm and created the energies we needed to get in gear and act.

The Jaycee example shows how one *relatively* big goal can change the direction of an organization—in this case an organization of a hundred volunteers. Selecting big goals has a positive effect on organizations. Having big goals causes us to act big. When you act big, others around you think big and act big as well, and they will think big of you and you will think big of them.

Two books I recommend are *The Magic of Thinking Big* by Dr. David J. Schwartz and *Release Your Brakes!* by James W. Newman.

One way to appreciate the power of big goals is to consider the principles of resonance and sympathetic response. The drive, energy, and activity levels of individuals toward goals varies in direct response to the nature and size of the goal—resonance. The drive, energy, and activities of one individual or group of individuals will affect the drive, energy, and activities of other individuals or groups of individuals—sympathetic response.

The principles of resonance and sympathetic response

Resonance: The drive, energy, and activity levels of individuals toward goals varies in direct response to the nature and size of the goal itself.

Sympathetic response: The drive, energy, and activities of one individual or group of individuals will affect the drive, energy, and activities of other individuals or groups of individuals.

The principles of resonance and sympathetic response imply that the bigger the goal, the bigger the response. As more individuals respond and increase the intensity of their responses, the bigger are the goals that can be achieved.

The principles operate continuously in science. In the fields of acoustics and sound, vibrations of an enormous amplitude can be created and sustained by a relatively small, periodic stimulus of the same natural vibration. This sympathetic vibration allows a small tuning fork vibrating twenty feet from a larger one to cause the larger one to vibrate.

In a similar manner, when the drive of one individual to achieve a large goal is implanted into the DNA of an organization, then the resonance and power of the entire organization to achieve the goal can become enormous.

Consider Mr. Grove's remarks in the *Fortune* article mentioned earlier: "We get the market growth we earn—by our development efforts, our investments, and our proselytization. That's absolutely in our psyche now. . . . We are driven . . . ." Those are the remarks of a man who is driven to achieve big goals and who is transferring his own DNA to others in his company. *That is DNA Leadership.*

The absence of big, inspiring goals is one of the problems today in business, the public sector, and our educational system. Individuals are not being challenged to fulfill their potential. Individuals or firms seldom fail because they try to accomplish too much—they fail because they don't try to accomplish enough. Contrary to the well-known claim, they don't "burn out"; they cool off and die out.

Businesses cannot and will not grow beyond the goals their leaders establish. One of the biggest mistakes leaders can make is to select goals that are too small or too easily reached. A business with small goals will not be able to attract and retain the brightest people with the greatest potential. Talented people need challenges constantly before them. They gravitate to opportunities and challenges consistent with their abilities.

A difference between men and women who run big companies and those who run small ones is that the individuals running big companies think differently. The difference is thinking big. At General Electric, Intel, Coca-Cola, and other successful companies, their mantra is the pursuit of big goals. General Electric refers to their big goals as "stretch" goals—goals the company has to stretch to achieve. Executives at Coca-Cola like to think in terms of "What's possible?" Other companies use such terms as BHAG, which was defined in the book *Built To Last,* by Messrs. Collins and Porras, as "Big, Hairy, Audacious Goals."

Most people will rise to the occasion when they are presented with a goal worthy of their pursuit. Unfortunately, more often than not, individuals are given tasks to perform that are *substantially* below their capacity. The expression, "you can't tempt a king with a penny," is applicable to goals and tapping into the potential of people and organizations. Goals really do make us greater than we were before we had the goals.

The selection of big goals is the most important distinction between businesses and individuals who are wildly successful and those who are not. If your desire is to have extraordinary results in your business, you must begin with extraordinary goals.

And, if you want extraordinary results on a personal basis, you must begin with extraordinary personal goals. In *Built to Last* there is a discussion between two Nordstrom employees (Nordies) where one asks the other how to become a Pacesetter. "Simple," says the other Nordie, "you set very high sales goals, and then you exceed them."

So always choose BIG.

By big, though, I don't mean so big your goals are impossible to achieve. As discussed in *Chapter 9,* goals should be demanding, but also achievable. It is not necessary that we know how we will accomplish all aspects of our goals when we select them, but we must see them as possibilities.

Please note that while I am a firm believer in big goals, I do not mean to imply by the discussion above that big business is the only way to go. To the contrary, I love small businesses, particularly those that are well run. But even a small business must continue to improve and grow or it won't be able to compete. Then it will be out of business. Small businesses need big goals, too.

We all need inspiring goals

Here is a quick exercise to see if your goals have *goal power.* Take a few minutes this evening and write out your two or three most significant goals. These can be business or personal goals. The only criterion is they must be your most important goals currently.

Now take a few minutes, find a quiet place in the house where you can be alone, and read your goals aloud to yourself.

Then ask yourself this question: Do these goals inspire me?

If your goals inspire you, great. But if they don't, think about this: Our gift of life provides us the right and also the responsibility for pursuing at least a few inspiring goals all of the time. We won't be growing and achieving our potential unless we do.

If your goals aren't inspiring to you, raise your sights and raise the bar. Select some bigger, more challenging goals—maybe in areas of your life where you have never thought about having big goals before.

Leaders are able to inspire others because they themselves are inspired by the goals they have selected to pursue. If you are in a leadership position and your goals do not inspire you, you will not be able to inspire others to pursue them on your behalf. You may think you can fake enthusiasm for a goal, but no one will be fooled. So get some big goals that you can really get excited about. Don't just seek growth, make it explosive.

Limitation thinking
keeps you from choosing big goals

Limitation thinking operates like the invisible electric fences buried in the ground that keep dogs in a yard. When dogs with a metallic collar clip stray near the concealed fence, they get a jolt and jerk back. In time, the fence doesn't even have to carry a charge to work. One or two jolts and a dog never forgets.

People are the same. Once we perceive a limitation, we remember it at the subconscious level unwaveringly and it is nearly impossible for us to go beyond it. It is *nearly* impossible, but not impossible.

Limitation thinking is a major obstacle to selecting and pursuing big goals. It is not ability, not education, not age, not race, or anything else: it is limitation thinking.

An investor in my firm's initial venture capital fund told me that our first investment was "a black hole." "That business isn't going to go anywhere and you'll just pour more and more money into it," the investor said. This is a version of limitation thinking which I call the Demon of Doubt and Despair.

As a result of this investor's doubting, my partner and I thought long and hard about whether we should continue to invest in the company. We nearly decided to stop. However, we concluded the investor did not have the knowledge, belief, or passion for the company that we had, so he probably had a limited view of the company's future. Thank goodness we chose not to follow his advice and continued to invest in the company. That so-called "black hole" was the Discovery Channel, which I told you about in *Chapter 1*.

Limitation thinking can also affect personal performance. For example, I coached a young man in the financial services industry and determined that he was not approaching people over thirty because at twenty-five he thought he was too young to sell to older individuals. The limiting thought that people over thirty would not buy services from him was an error; the limitation was only in his mind and I told him so. I explained how I liked doing business with bright young people like him, who were ready, willing, and able to provide the services I desired. He listened carefully and believed me. The limiting thought now slain, he went out the next week and sold two policies to people over thirty—resulting in a bigger week's sales than he had up to then been producing in a month!

In this case the limiting thought was easy to neutralize, but it can be difficult to overcome negative or limitation thinking that has been programmed for several years.

A common mistake many business leaders make is to think too small. Yes, some entrepreneurs have tried to grow too fast and have gotten themselves and their businesses into difficulties as a result. But the bigger and more damaging mistake, I believe, is not to attempt enough. The greater risk in business and life is *not* in reaching for the stars; it is in *not* reaching. Business leaders who aim below the possible targets limit the potential of their company, the people working in it, and themselves.

There are three boxes in life: Which one are you in?

Limitation thinking damages our personal careers just as it damages businesses.

Rick Pamplin teaches screenwriting on the West Coast. In one of Rick's lectures on fulfilling a goal to have a career in Hollywood, I heard him refer to the "three boxes of life." He called them Box A, Box B, and Box C. Regardless of the vocation we are pursuing, Rick believes we are always living in one of these three boxes, and the actions we should be taking depend largely on which box we find ourselves in.

Box A is a big, beautiful box. It is sunshine yellow and glows with warmth. In Box A you are doing exactly what you want to be doing. If you want to be an actor or screenwriter, you are acting or writing screenplays. In Box A, you are following your bliss.

Box B is a nice sized box that is bright and shiny, but it is not as big, bright, and shiny as Box A. In Box B you are doing some

Three boxes in life

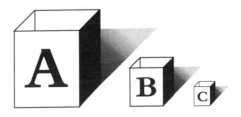

of what you want to be doing, and you are working toward being in Box A. If you want to be an actor or screenwriter, perhaps you are doing freelance or part-time work in these areas while taking additional courses and holding down another job to make ends meet. If you are in Box B, you are not where you want to be yet, but you have a plan to get there and you are working your plan.

Box C is a small, dingy colored box. In Box C you may be making a living, but you are not, as Les Brown puts it, "living your making." You don't have any plan or hopes of getting to where you want to be. If you want to be an actor or screenwriter, you are *not* acting or writing screenplays, you are *not* taking courses to study these professions, and you are *not* working for a company in the motion-picture business. What you *are* doing is burning daylight spending each day of your life doing something you really don't want to be doing.

The A–B–C box metaphor is a good one for each of us to consider as we prepare our personal mission statements and evaluate the goals we intend to pursue in each area or role of our lives.

If you find yourself in Box A, doing what you want to be doing to fulfill yourself, then great, there is nothing more to do. Just stay on course and continue improving and growing by defining more and more stretch goals.

If you find yourself in Box B working a plan to get into Box A, make sure you are following a good plan with solid stretch goals and an aggressive timetable to get into Box A. Box B is an acceptable position to be in as long as you are making progress towards Box A.

If you find yourself in Box C, then you must not waste a single moment. Immediately leap toward Box A. Using Rick Pamplin's example, if you deep down inside want to be an actor and you are not acting or learning about acting, then take whatever actions you must to get yourself immediately on track toward becoming an actor.

I have related this metaphor to many people. Once in a while someone will ask me if it isn't risky to leap abruptly from Box C to Box A. The answer is no, if you really are in Box C. The risk is not in leaping from Box C to Box A; the risk is in *not* leaping.

A principle in constant operation here is the principle of gravitational pull. Gravitational pull is the measure of the attractive force one body has on another.

The principle of gravitational pull

Gravitational pull is the measure of the attractive force one body has on another. The greater the mass and closeness of the bodies, the greater the attractive force between them. You will be pulled toward goals that *you perceive* to have the greatest gravitational pull on you because of their size and closeness as measured by your ability to reach them.

The principle of gravitational pull means you will begin to move toward a goal only when you first believe you can *and will* achieve it. If you have limiting thoughts and do not believe you can achieve a goal, then it is very *un*likely you will achieve it. You move to where you are mentally. If you are mentally more where you are than where you want to be, you are going to remain where you are. But if you are mentally where you want to be, then that is what you will achieve.

We sabotage our own goals unconsciously. We think of ourselves as too young, too old, lacking the right education, background, or skills, or as being deficient in some other manner. Others sabotage our goals, too. Careless comments like "oh really," or a frown saying, "are you serious?" have let the air out of more big goals than I care to think about.

The only true limitations that exist in your life are those you allow to exist in your mind. You need to go around them, through them, or over them; whatever is necessary to avoid limiting thoughts.

Choose goals that are congruent with your DNA as defined by your values, desires, and beliefs

To get the results you want in business and in life there must be DNA congruency among your stated goals, your values, your underlying desires, and your core beliefs.

We cannot, should not, and will not pursue goals that are incongruent with our value systems.

The engine of desire

We achieve those goals that are congruent with our desires. If you have a big goal, you must have a corresponding big desire. Big desires in business come from bold visions established by bold leaders with a belief in what their companies can become.

Our primary desires are self-preservation, personal safety, food, and shelter. Once these are satisfied our remaining desires boil down to loving others, being loved, financial security, acceptance, recognition, and power.

Congruency between goals and beliefs

Henry Ford and others are credited with the phrase: "Whether you think you can, or think you can't, you're right."

This is true when it comes to goals. If you don't believe you can achieve the goal, it is hard to imagine why or how you could. If you don't believe you can, you're right.

This does not mean you cannot change your beliefs. You can. But effort is required. You can even change your limitation thinking if you make a sufficient effort to do so. To change your beliefs you must obtain new knowledge, information, and experiences—by reading, studying, talking with others, and by altering the circumstances and environments you are in.

Years ago I assigned Norm the task of creating a consulting approach for finding opportunities to enhance profits in certain types of businesses. After a week, Norm told me he wanted off the project. "I'm just not creative," he said. "I can't create a consulting approach out of thin air."

Rather than let him off the assignment, I asked Norm to interview the presidents of twenty-five companies in the businesses we were interested in and ask them how they went about finding ways to increase revenues and reduce costs. "I can do that," Norm said.

Three weeks later Norm came in with a report recommending six approaches for improving our profitability consulting practice. Norm did what I wanted him to do in the first place, and he did it well.

What was surprising is that even after he had "unknowingly" created the new approaches we were looking for, Norm still denied the possibility that he was creative. He said if he was creative, he would have been the one to suggest interviewing the company presidents. Creativity takes many forms. Norm's comment shows how deep and incorrect our belief systems can be.

Believing in yourself and what you are trying to accomplish is essential. Salespersons who believe in their products will have an easier time selling them than salespersons who don't. All who have a goal of getting a promotion will have a hard time convincing their superiors they deserve a promotion if they don't believe they deserve it themselves.

A side issue related to your belief in your goals is whether you are pursuing goals because you *want* to pursue them or because you *have* to pursue them. We achieve goals we want to achieve. There is a risk that you will not achieve those goals you have to, but don't necessarily want to, pursue.

A goal *you want* to pursue is a goal *you* have selected because of a personal desire that is consistent with what you believe about yourself, your abilities, and your value systems.

Goals have interdependent relationships with other goals

Many goals have interdependent relationships with one another. Sometimes we must achieve Goal B before we can achieve Goal A. This is important to note so action plans can take the interrelationships into account.

A business with a stretch goal in the sales area may have difficulty achieving it until progress is made on goals to improve customer service and satisfaction. An individual with a personal goal to go on a vacation may first have to achieve certain financial goals before the personal goal is possible.

The *MOSAIC* method discussed in *Chapter 4* is ideal for identifying the big picture and the interrelationships among the various goals in your business or your life.

8

GET a goal—
Success strategies, tools,
and techniques

The success strategies, tools, and techniques for getting a goal are discussed in this chapter under the following headings:

- Begin from where you are

- Answer the question: *why?*

- Establish goals beyond those you are pursuing

- Use a *Goals Journal* to record and keep track of goals

- Use *Goal Stimulators* to identify goal possibilities

- Don't bog down trying to find a "best" goal

- Prioritize your goals using an A–B–C approach

- Break big and long-term goals into bite-sized goals with shorter-term horizons

- Create *laser-clear* goal statements

- Make intangible goals tangible and generalized goals specific

- Identify the resources and sacrifices required

- Create an emotional linkage and a personal commitment

- Establish buy-in

- *Imprint* goals using "reach and repeat" techniques

Begin from where you are

Assume you are at your office waiting for me and the telephone rings. You answer, "Hello?"

"Hi," I say. "I'm in my car trying to get to your place. How do I get there?"

What do you do? You ask me a question, right? And this is what you say: "Where are you now?"

You wouldn't begin by describing the street outside your building. You'd ask me to describe the surroundings *where I am*. Only after you knew where I am could you tell me how to get to where you are.

This is a fundamental strategy that operates in all aspects of our lives.

When formulating new goals or updating existing goals, you should start with an analysis of where you are now. A salesperson should analyze past sales results before establishing new sales goals. A business owner should evaluate existing customer satisfaction levels before establishing new customer service goals.

The more specific and complete your "where am I now" analyses are, the better your foundations will be for establishing new goals.

Several years ago Dwight Schar, then the CEO of NVHomes, asked me to help him restructure his company's indebtedness to reduce interest costs and alleviate certain loan restrictions. I first asked the company to summarize home sales by type and price ranges. We then compared these data to published data for the markets served. This revealed that the company dominated certain geographic markets for several price-point categories of homes and town houses.

This information, properly summarized and focused on, pushed over the first domino in a series that resulted in the company's going public and restructuring its debt. Then the company acquired Ryan Homes. Now the company is NVR, and

Dwight is Chairman, CEO, and President of a combined and much bigger organization. Going public and acquiring Ryan Homes became alternative goals to pursue only after the analyses had been made so that Dwight and his investment bankers could assess the company's market positioning and future opportunities.

Knowing where you are, *exactly*, and knowing what you have accomplished and how you accomplished it are more important than most people imagine.

An individual who was applying GOAL-DRIVEN MANAGEMENT for the first time in his financial services business balked when he had to prepare an analysis of his prior sales. But he went along with the recommended approach and prepared the analysis showing the age, sex, and other demographic information for each of his customers, along with information about how he obtained each account.

When the analysis was completed, it was instantly obvious that he had been focusing on the wrong market segments. He was getting only marginal returns in comparison to the results he could achieve if he would shift to a different market niche. It was also obvious that he had not leveraged his productivity. After reviewing his analysis, he identified a couple of techniques to do this. In a short time, his personal sales performance nearly tripled—as a result of his analysis and the new action plan he adopted.

The concept of knowing where you are also applies at the personal level. When I teach at college I have my students keep a time log for two weeks. This provides them a factual basis for planning their study schedules so they can achieve their goals for the semester. The students moan and groan, but the exercise is always worth the effort. One student burst into the classroom after logging her time for a week. "I don't have a life!" she shouted. She had learned how poorly she was spending her time watching television and socializing. This *awareness* made a big difference to her. She immediately adopted new habits and began spending her time effectively.

When it comes to establishing goals, once you know where you are, exactly, you can never again ignore this knowledge. It will affect your future choices and actions.

Don't assume that you or others have knowledge of where you are now simply because information is gathered and made available. Nothing could be further from the truth. To get to the level of "knowledge," four things must happen. First, you have to gather the right information. Second, you have to sort, organize, and arrange that information into the proper context. Third, you have to focus on the information and absorb it. Fourth, you need to apply the information by taking action. *Gather* information, put it into *context*, make yourself *aware* of it, and *act*. *Then* you have knowledge.

A side benefit of analyzing where you are is that the analysis points out past accomplishments. This has a positive and bolstering effect for businesses and individuals. There is nothing like reviewing past successes to encourage pursuit of future goals.

Answer the question: *why?*

The question Why? gives you the opportunity to evaluate the DNA alignment your goals have with your purposes, objectives, and values. *Why* do you want to achieve the goals you have selected? How will achieving your goals make your business or your career better? What will achieving your goals enable you to do or have that you cannot do or have now? How do the goals for your business align with the mission and vision?

Individuals or businesses often pursue goals without focusing on the reasons to do so. This limits the power of their goals.

Companies sometimes adopt goals such as improving customer service or expanding into new markets without taking time to answer the question, Why are these goals important and how do they fit with the mission, vision, and philosophies of the company? If employees understand how the goals they are pursuing and the actions they are taking align with the DNA fabric of the company and support the company's objectives and purposes, they will feel stronger about their goals and their contributions.

Salespeople adopt sales goals. The answers to their "whys" typically are to make more money, win certain prizes, or get bigger territories. These may be good motivators, but they are not always the best motivators. We need to go beyond the superficial reward and identify stronger underlying factors at the DNA level. Will achieving certain sales goals strengthen the competitive position of the company? Salespeople need to know this because then they will understand how their results contribute to the company's development in the bigger scheme of things. In other words, they can integrate the company's goal into their goals and actions on a DNA basis—*DNA Leadership.*

A successful salesman asked me why he should go for bigger sales goals than he had the year before—when he was already making a six-figure salary. "Because you can, and that is what everybody in the company is counting on you to do," is what I told him. Sometimes the best "why" is that we have untapped potential and we have the ability to contribute more.

Establish goals beyond those you are pursuing

A number of years ago I helped an individual become admitted to the partnership at Arthur Andersen by coaching him to go *beyond* the goal of partner even though making partner was his goal.

I told the individual to think of going *past* partner to taking over my job, which was partner in charge of the office at the time. In private conversations I referred to him as "P-I-C," which stood for partner in charge. Immediately he began acting differently— he stepped up to this new level of expectancy. Soon he was bringing in more new clients than any other manager in the office. He seemed to take off and he made partner right on schedule. Now he *is* the partner in charge of an office. He was successful because he never lost his momentum.

There is a danger that we can lose momentum just before we are about to achieve a goal. See *Chapter 12* for additional discussion on momentum, and beginning and ending tasks.

Future goals provide us with continuous energy. This extra power is often needed to achieve an existing goal. This is similar to swinging through the ball in baseball. It is the power of "follow-through" that smacks the ball out of the park.

At the start of a huge systems project, the project manager announced the date of the party we were going to have to celebrate completion of the system. He assigned people to plan the party and described what a grand affair it would be. Then he began discussing what we needed to do to design and build the system we were going to celebrate installing.

Looking back, the project manager's act of establishing a goal, the party, beyond the goal of installing the system, was brilliant. Everyone continually focused on the party, and we pulled together in a Herculean manner to finish on time so we could celebrate. I don't think the completion of the system installation would have created a sufficient *drive* for us to have finished it *on time*—because we could not relate to the completed system emotionally. But we all could relate emotionally to the party, and that created *goal power!*

The way to maintain momentum is to always know what you are going to do next. One of the worst things that can happen to a business or an individual is to run out of goals to pursue and be stuck with no thought of what to do next. This erodes self-esteem and debilitates morale.

So, always have more goals to pursue than you can possibly achieve in your lifetime. This is the advice Ted Turner's father gave him and it worked well.

Think about the goals you are pursuing now. Will the goals for your business continue the momentum of the business? Are there more big goals beyond the horizon that everyone can see? And what about your own goals? Do they bring you to a cliff, with no place to go next? If so, give some thought to the goals beyond your present goals, and start to integrate those into your goal-setting process.

Use a *Goals Journal* to record and keep track of goals

A *Goals Journal* is the heart of the GOAL-DRIVEN MANAGEMENT goal-setting and goal-achieving process. A *Goals Journal* is not a personal organizer, calendar, or other similar time management and productivity aid. It is used solely to record goals and results.

A *Goals Journal* is used to record and keep track of goals we are pursuing currently, goals we may want to pursue at a later date, and goals we have achieved.

Keeping a *Goals Journal* makes sense when you think about it. We each are pursuing many goals, have many more we are considering, and have hundreds of details to manage daily. In many ways we have too much to remember. We need a tool to keep us focused on the important goals we intend to achieve.

I have kept a personal *Goals Journal* for more than twenty years. Mine is a high quality notebook with separate sections for the types of goals I have, such as personal, family, and financial. There is nothing in my *Goals Journal* except information about my goals. My *Goals Journal* contains complete goal statements for goals I am pursuing currently and thumbnail sketches or notations about goals I may pursue later on. My *Goals Journal* is a private, personal, and important record. It is a valuable reference for reviewing and evaluating my progress and for selecting goals to pursue in the future.

By having an ongoing and ready reference of my current and potential goals, it takes little time to update my major goal selections when I sit down near year end and plan the following year.

A side benefit is that keeping my *Goals Journal* has helped me acquire other good habits in my goal-setting and pursuing process.

One benefit of my *Goals Journal* is that I can see what I have been thinking. Last November when I was planning this year I reviewed my *Goals Journal* and realized I had been putting off an important business goal for several years. The dated entries in my journal provided the wake-up call I needed to begin pursuing that particular goal; and, now I have accomplished it.

Another benefit of a *Goals Journal* is that writing our goals creates the catalytic step necessary for achieving them. We operate in a continuous thought→action→thought cycle. Writing your goals is an action step. When you take the step, you reinforce your commitment and initiate your movement towards your goals.

Goals Journals for businesses

The need for some form of *Goals Journal* is pronounced in business. In businesses, there are many complex goals to be achieved and there is a multitude of interdependent relationships among sub-goals and related goals. Most importantly, the goals throughout an organization must contribute to the realization of the organization's overall goals and the furtherance of its underlying mission and purposes. That is, in a *DNA Leadership* environment the goals throughout must be bonded together through the same DNA fabric.

One of the most revealing exercises the president of a company can perform is to wander around and ask associates what top three goals *they* are pursuing. In many instances, individuals will not be able to identify even one, let alone three, important goals they are deliberately pursuing.

Employees are usually able to tell you what they are working on, but often they are not able to relate their activities to the accomplishment of a *specific* goal. Most employees are activity oriented versus goal oriented. This lack of goal awareness represents a gap in the performance measurement, management, and coaching processes—if individuals don't know what they are trying to achieve, they and their managers don't have a basis to evaluate or improve their performance.

Another interesting exercise is to ask employees what goals *the company* is pursuing. I frequently ask this question of the people I meet when I'm visiting another company or traveling. Rarely can employees tell me what their company's goals are. I had a pleasant surprise at a hotel recently when the assistant manager in the restaurant came back with this answer instantaneously: "To have 2,000 hotels by the year 2000."

I was impressed. Someone at that company understands how important it is for employees to know what their company intends to accomplish. The assistant manager said just knowing this goal meant a lot to him— because it assured him that he could advance and grow within the organization. "My goal is to become a full-fledged manager at an international hotel," he said. "With 2,000 hotels there ought to be plenty of opportunities for me."

I asked the manager what actions he was taking to achieve his goal and when he intended to achieve it. He offered general comments like "continue to do a good job" and "keep our customers happy." Those were nice remarks, but that was as far as they went. This young man did not have a specific plan he was following, and he had no target date for when he wanted to achieve his goal. Here was a bright, ambitious, and loyal employee—without the tools he needs to manage himself toward his goals!

What if everyone in your company was required to establish and maintain a *Goals Journal* which always reflects a summary of the goals they and the company are pursuing? Everyone would then know their most important goals and the most important goals of the company. There is power when everyone knows what they are supposed to be focused on so they can make their contribution toward the achievement of the company's goals.

But, what if executives and associates don't have or use a *Goals Journal?* Where do they record their goals? Without a formal record of the specific goals being pursued by an organization and the people in it, how can management hope to know whether individuals are doing the work they should be doing?

Top management can establish and maintain a *Corporate Goals Journal* for recording and monitoring progress toward the achievement of all major corporate goals. Preparation of this journal would be an integral part of the business planning process, and the journal itself would be an integral part of the company's business plan documentation. If you had such a record you would be able to renew the transforming catalysts throughout your organization. This would be like putting your company's DNA under a microscope to evaluate what the cells are going to produce.

A *Corporate Goals Journal* would be part of your *DNA Leadership* control panel. It could be set up with sections for each function or unit such as Sales and Marketing, Customer Service, Administration, Finance, Personnel Development, and Training.

An *Associates* version of the *Corporate Goals Journal* aids individuals in focusing their personal efforts, coordinating and fostering teamwork, and guiding and encouraging their personal performance. These tools are valuable in managing the "work" of an organization and in improving communication and strategic, business, and operational planning.

Use *Goal Stimulators* to identify goal possibilities

Have you ever met an individual who changed his or her priorities at whim—based on the last person talked to, or the last information read or heard? Many of these individuals never really accomplish much. Their problem is a lack of focus.

One reason people skip from goal to goal is they haven't taken the time to consider all significant goal possibilities, to select a few to pursue, and then to commit to achieving them. Their thinking is never finished.

Goals should be identified and selected in a methodical and

deliberate manner. Selecting and prioritizing major goals should not be an afterthought or rushed activity.

To identify and select major goal catagories, you can create and use a *Goal Stimulator* that summarizes the categories and subcategories of goals you may have. These catagories would represent the spokes on your *MOSAIC* graphical displays as described in *Chapter 4*. A *Goal Stimulator* is a quick visual reference that starts your mental juices flowing for identifying goal possibilities.

Illustrated on pages 136 and 137 are two *Goal Stimulators*. These are not all inclusive; they are provided to illustrate the concept of having a reference sheet to stimulate goal ideas. One of the stimulators depicts components of a business with illustrative goal possibilities for each component. The other portrays types of individual goals with goal possibilities for each type.

It may be desirable to develop separate *Goal Stimulators* for particular situations. For example, if you are on the "customer service improvements" team, you may want to have a separate *Goal Stimulator* sheet for your team. Do what makes sense.

A benefit of using *Goal Stimulators* is they force you to *consider* the possibility of having major goals in all areas because they make you consider whether you should have additional spokes in your *MOSAIC* analysis. Businesses can become lopsided with too much emphasis on one area and not enough on others. This can be detrimental since the success formula in business is to do everything required, not just do a few things well. We face a similar challenge in balancing our lives. Balance is an issue addressed in the mission statement and vision statement processes, but using *Goal Stimulators* to drive the identification, prioritization, and selection of goal categories encourages a balanced approach.

Considering all goal possibilities at the outset helps us avoid second-guessing ourselves when we become aware of possibilities and alternatives we did not consider. Second-guessing can be avoided by using a thorough approach.

Goal Stimulator—business goals

Customers and customer relationships

- ❑ Relationships with customers
- ❑ Usefulness to customers
- ❑ Benefits provided to customers
- ❑ Communication with customers
- ❑ Response time
- ❑ Customer appreciation
- ❑ Friendliness of service
- ❑ Customer satisfaction
- ❑ Customer information systems

Sales

- ❑ Sales volume
- ❑ Product and service pricing
- ❑ Sales margin and profitability
- ❑ Sales productivity
- ❑ Product and service mix
- ❑ Customer mix
- ❑ Market and geographic penetration

Selling systems and procedures

- ❑ Prospecting and sales systems
- ❑ Order entry systems and procedures
- ❑ Sales support materials

Marketing and public relations

- ❑ Market positioning
- ❑ Marketing programs
- ❑ Advertising programs
- ❑ Newsletters
- ❑ Public relations programs
- ❑ Affinity marketing programs
- ❑ Name recognition and awareness
- ❑ Corporate image and reputation
- ❑ Product and service positioning
- ❑ Marketing effectiveness
- ❑ Marketing research and information

Products and services

- ❑ New products and services
- ❑ Product and service enhancements
- ❑ Product and service bundling
- ❑ Product and service packaging
- ❑ Suppliers and sourcing channels
- ❑ Supplier relations

Operations

- ❑ Quality
- ❑ Productivity and performance
- ❑ Systems and procedures
- ❑ Speed of operations, simplification
- ❑ Response time
- ❑ Innovations and changes
- ❑ Outsourcing

Management and personnel

- ❑ Planning and decision-making processes
- ❑ Managerial infrastructure
- ❑ Management team strength
- ❑ Executive and managerial education
- ❑ Operating team strength, teamwork
- ❑ Management information systems
- ❑ Training and skills development
- ❑ Performance review and coaching
- ❑ Recognition and reward programs
- ❑ Benefits and related programs
- ❑ Communication

Financial performance

- ❑ Market value and earnings
- ❑ Sales
- ❑ Profitability
- ❑ Liquidity and indebtedness
- ❑ Long-term financial strength

Other pervasive considerations

- ❑ Growth opportunities
- ❑ Global penetration
- ❑ Global infrastructure
- ❑ Channels of distribution
- ❑ Knowledge and brainpower
- ❑ Know-how and ability
- ❑ Safety
- ❑ Corporate citizenship
- ❑ Research and development
- ❑ Proprietary products and services
- ❑ Proprietary information
- ❑ Use of technology
- ❑ Innovations and changes
- ❑ Corporate infrastructure
- ❑ Internal communication

Goal Stimulator—individual goals

Family
- ❏ Family time
- ❏ Family relationships
- ❏ Vacations and travel
- ❏ Communication
- ❏ Responsibilities to family members
- ❏ Family projects
- ❏ Family fun

Friends
- ❏ Selection of friends
- ❏ Time with friends
- ❏ Relationships with friends
- ❏ Responsibilities to friends
- ❏ Projects or trips with friends

Civic and citizenship
- ❏ Civic activities
- ❏ Charitable activities
- ❏ Volunteer activities
- ❏ Citizenship
- ❏ Political involvement

Professional and work related responsibilities
- ❏ Employer
- ❏ Work environment
- ❏ Opportunities and challenges
- ❏ Advancement and achievements
- ❏ Personal growth
- ❏ Compensation and benefits
- ❏ Skills development
- ❏ Professional development
- ❏ Professional relationships
- ❏ Professional organizations

Physical health
- ❏ Indoor and outdoor exercise
- ❏ Exercise facilities and equipment
- ❏ Diet and nutrition
- ❏ Sports participation
- ❏ Personal achievements
- ❏ Physical skills
- ❏ Personal trainer
- ❏ Statistics (weight, cholesterol, etc.)
- ❏ Personal habits
- ❏ Annual physical and other tests

Mental development and growth
- ❏ Goal-setting and self-management
- ❏ Continuing education programs
- ❏ Books, tapes, and videos
- ❏ Lectures and seminars
- ❏ Personal achievements and recognition
- ❏ Skills development
- ❏ Mind-stretching exposures
- ❏ Positive environment
- ❏ Magazines, newsletters
- ❏ Computer skills
- ❏ Internet and World Wide Web
- ❏ Personal time management
- ❏ Personal organization
- ❏ Travel
- ❏ Mentor, coach, personal advisors

Financial
- ❏ Wages and other income
- ❏ Investments and savings
- ❏ Indebtedness and liquidity
- ❏ Budgetary control
- ❏ Spending and saving habits
- ❏ Net worth
- ❏ Financial independence
- ❏ Financial advisors
- ❏ Legal advisors
- ❏ Estate and tax planning

Personal assets
- ❏ Home
- ❏ Home furnishings and decorations
- ❏ Automobiles and boats
- ❏ Technology toys
- ❏ Clothing and personal items
- ❏ Vacation properties

Spiritual
- ❏ Spiritual education and study
- ❏ Worship
- ❏ Ministry and missionary work

Don't bog down trying to find a "best" goal

If businesses or individuals are going to have difficulties in the goal-selection process, it often will be in deciding the exact, right goal to pursue. Sometimes people have difficulty because they try to select a "best" goal among similar alternatives.

I know a management team that spent nearly two days trying to develop the "best" customer service goals. The effort frustrated everyone and nearly brought the endeavor to a halt. Instead of trying to define a perfect goal, an alternative is to establish a stretch goal of *relative* improvement.

An example is "on-time performance" which is measured in many industries. On-time performance means: Did the airplane land on schedule? Did the shipment arrive when it was supposed to? Or, was your car finished at the garage when it was promised? Some companies establish an optimum on-time factor such as having airplanes land within a few minutes of their scheduled arrival 98% of the time, or having 99 out of 100 next-day shipments delivered by ten in the morning. This is a good approach, but sometimes the optimum performance level is not known and sometimes there are no reliable third-party data to compare to. In these cases, a good approach is to seek *continual relative improvement.*

Continual relative improvement is implemented by measuring current performance and setting stretch goals at levels above current performance. Rather than debating whether it should take ten or fifteen minutes to serve customers, a business owner could just determine how long it is taking now and seek relative improvements each month. If this approach is used continually, results will always be improving and approaching optimum levels.

A relative improvement approach works in personal matters as well. Rather than debating which is the best exercise program and never beginning one, just pursue exercise goals that produce relative improvement. An initial goal could be ten minutes of exercise every day for thirty days. The following month your relative improvement goal could be to include an hour walk on Saturdays. Each month as you increase your goals, you are improving.

Prioritize your goals using an A–B–C approach

A stumbling block for many companies and individuals is that they have so many possible goals to consider they don't know how to decide which ones to pick and pursue. In these cases, an A–B–C prioritization approach works wonders.

First, review your *Goals Journal* and prepare a worksheet summarizing all *major* goals you would possibly like to pursue in the next twelve months, or whatever period you are planning. Next, rate each goal as to importance, using your own criteria for A, B, and C designations. Re-list your A goals and prioritize this list on an A–B–C basis. Repeat this process until you end up with two to four A goals to pursue.

Regardless of your approach, the objective is to end up with a short list of major goals to pursue.

Do not underestimate the importance of adopting a formal process for your prioritization of goals. If you select the right goal, you stand a good chance of achieving the right results. If you don't, you won't.

Break big and long-term goals into bite-sized goals with shorter-term horizons

Big and long-term goals should be broken into bite-sized portions so they can be approached on a modular basis. Break long-term goals into monthly, weekly, and daily components, and break major goals into functional components or phases.

Breaking big goals into a series of smaller goals minimizes procrastination. Sometimes the total task is seen as so overwhelming it is hard to get started. Smaller steps make it easier to begin.

A goal of achieving $100,000,000 in annual revenues five years from now should be broken into annual goals; the annual goals for the next year should be broken into quarterly goals; and the quarterly goals should be broken into monthly goals—so progress can be pursued, measured, and monitored in segments small enough for people to relate to.

I was at a meeting when the CEO announced the company's goal of achieving a billion dollars in sales in two years. In his concluding remarks he commented, "Most of you probably *can't* relate to a billion dollar sales goal, but let me assure you it's a big goal we can all be proud to achieve." The problem was right there in the CEO's own remarks. The people he was talking to could *not* relate to the goal. So how were they supposed to pursue a goal they couldn't relate to? What was needed was to put a billion dollars in perspective for the subsidiary company presidents and the division managers.

Bite-sizing goals is important in everything we do. Suppose you are the chairperson of a charity drive and the goal is to raise $10,000 in six months. You could break this into 26 weekly goals of $400 per week. Or, you could set up categories of donors with goals for each category. You might establish a goal of collecting $2,000 from professional services firms, $2,000 from banks, $2,000 from insurance companies, and so on. These smaller bites are easier to act on.

Create *laser-clear* goal statements

Goal statements are *laser clear* when you specify the *exact* goals you want *in no uncertain terms.* There is no room for any doubts.

Your mind cannot work on generalities or vagueness. You must have specifics to focus your attention and guide your actions. You can't accomplish anything until you are able to specify what you want, so your brain sees it.

Try getting into a taxicab and refusing to tell the driver

where you want to go. You won't get very far, will you? The driver can't start until you specify a destination. After you have been in the air for half an hour on your next flight ask yourself this: Does the pilot know our destination? I'll bet he or she knows precisely. Let's hope so.

The lack of precision and specification in setting goals is a limiting factor preventing intended goals from being achieved.

A friend in the public relations business related how he pressed his client to clarify her goals for her public relations campaign. After probing, his client finally said her goal was to have an article in the *Wall Street Journal.* Within 120 days she had it—because everyone had an exact target to aim at.

Some individuals resist establishing *laser-clear* goals because they are not used to being held accountable to achieve specific results. Professionals in sales, research, customer service, and certain other operating areas frequently resist establishing *laser-clear* goals when they begin the *GOAL DRIVEN MANAGEMENT* process because the task is difficult and because they don't want to be held accountable for specific results by specific dates. Regardless of the effort required, *laser-clear* goals are called for if the objective is to optimize performance and results.

The importance of being exact and precise in setting goals cannot be overemphasized. Details and precision are paramount—not only so you aim for the right target, but so you get moving in the first place. You can't plant pumpkin seeds and expect to make apple pie—for apple pie you need apple seeds. Each goal has to be specified as a unique target, with a unique set of circumstances, requiring the efforts of a unique set of people. The primary questions to be answered in selecting goals are *what* and *when.*

What *exactly* do you want to accomplish?

Tony, a manager attending one of our seminars, decided one of his goals was to hire a delivery supervisor. He initially expressed his goal simply as "hire a delivery supervisor." I began to discuss this goal with him, and our conversation went back and forth, something like this:

Jim: Do you have a target date when you want this individual hired?

Tony: Yes, by the end of the year, December 31.

Jim: Okay, we have a deadline, December 31. Do you have any specific qualifications in mind for this supervisor?

Tony: Yes, he must have knowledge of trucks.

Jim: Knowledge of trucks. What does that mean? Does that mean he can recognize trucks if he sees them?
       Tony laughs.

Tony: I want him to have had three years experience driving trucks.

Jim: Anything else?

Tony: I want him to have a good safety record.

Jim: What's that mean?

Tony: A certifiable accident-free record—for the last three years.

Jim: Anything else?

Tony: I want him to have demonstrated some work stability.

Jim: What's that mean?

Tony: To have held a prior job for two or more years. With references I can check.

Jim: Anything else?

Tony: No drugs. Clean appearance. A team player. A self-starter.

Jim: Okay, let me summarize this. Your goal is to "hire a delivery supervisor by December 31 who has a certifiable accident-free safety record for the last three years; has been employed two or more years in a steady capacity; can provide references that you can check; and who does not use drugs, has a clean appearance, is a team player, and a self-starter." Is that it?

Tony: Yes.

Jim: Did you have a salary in mind?
       Tony laughs and tells me the salary range.
Jim: Now, when I add the targeted salary range to what I
       just said, *that* is a *laser-clear* goal statement.

Frequently it helps to use an *iterative* process for clarifying our goals. This happened with Tony. He began with an initial statement, vague and rough, and got it tighter and more precise by adding concrete facts as he answered my questions. This is not unusual and it is the way most goals are refined.

The table on page 144 illustrates goal statements that range in quality from weak to better to better yet as their specificity and precision increases. See what a difference the more precise statements make in terms of providing information that can be acted on immediately. The "better yet" statements have more power than the others because they are specific enough to mobilize actions. The weaker statements mobilize nothing.

Note: it sometimes is not possible to establish a *laser-clear* goal until you write the plan to achieve it. That's okay. Often the writing of the plan provides the *laser clarity* needed.

Make intangible goals tangible and generalized goals specific

"Our goal is to exceed our customers' expectations." "My goal is to get back in shape." "We intend to increase the retention of our new hires to an average of three years."

The problem with intangible and non-specific goals like these is that our brains don't know what the goals mean. What does "exceed customer expectations" mean? What does it mean to "get back in shape?" When do we want to have "increased retention of our new hires?"

Without a specific target, we don't know what to aim at. So rather than guess, we do nothing.

Writing exact and precise goal statements

Weak	Better	Better yet
Improve customer service.	Reduce the number of units that fail when delivered in the field.	Reduce the failure rate of units to 1/10 of 1% by the end of the quarter.
Write the article for our news-letter soon.	Start on my article this weekend.	Start on my article first thing Saturday morning and have it finished by noon.
Our number one goal is to improve sales.	Our number one goal is to increase sales for the year by 10% over last year.	Our number one goal is to increase sales by 10% over last year's sales—by adding six new accounts averaging $50,000 per quarter during each quarter.

A little trick to achieving goals is to make intangible goals tangible and to make generalized goals specific.

Instead of selecting "exceeding our customers' expectations," select a series of tangible goals that will cause customer expectations to be exceeded. For example, select goals like these:

- Telephone answered by the second ring

- Same-day response on all problems

- Same-day shipping on all orders

- Surprise free gift with every order

- Follow-up telephone call after every delivery

By being specific, we have established which expectations we will exceed and those are items we can work on.

Instead of a goal of "getting back in shape," select a series of goals like these:

- Lose ten pounds by Thanksgiving

- Adopt a thirty-minute daily exercise program

- Reduce the fat in my diet by 5%

"When" is the easiest of all criteria to specify, yet it is often left out of goal statements. If your goal is to increase employee retention so you retain new hires for an average of three years, *when* do you want to achieve this goal? If it's the end of this year, that is an entirely different proposition than if it is at the end of three years. What *exactly* do you have in mind?

Identify the resources and sacrifices required

Before you officially adopt any major goal and commit to its achievement, it is good to think through the sacrifices you will have to endure and the resources and time you will have to expend before the goal is realized. If you don't, you can get half-way to the goal and run out of steam, resources, or time, or perhaps even decide the goal just isn't worth the effort.

Do as much as you can to envision the resources, effort, and sacrifices you will have to make so you can prepare yourself mentally to sustain your actions to completion. What will you have to forego to achieve your goal? How long will it take? How much will it cost? How much time will you have to devote to the effort?

Reflecting on and estimating the time, sacrifices, and resources required to achieve business goals is an essential part of the professional management process. It is frequently, but not always, built into a company's budgetary and planning systems. No major goal should be pursued in business without a budget, a plan, a summary of resource requirements, and a timetable for monitoring and managing the effort.

Projecting time and effort is important for personal goals, too. One goal I'll always remember is a family goal when I was twelve of refinishing a mahogany speedboat my dad picked up just for the cost of removing it from a man's yard. We began with enthusiasm, but we had vastly underestimated the task. After two years of sanding, grinding, and fixing in every spare hour we had, we finally had to face the reality that our dreamboat had the best of us. The repairs and refinishing required were just too great, plus the repair materials were costing far more than my dad had imagined. It was a sad day when we hauled that old boat off to the dump. I wish we had done a little homework to learn just what we were getting ourselves into.

The reality of sacrifices

A hurdle many individuals encounter is the gap between the efforts, time, and sacrifices they would like to believe are required for goal achievement and the actual efforts, time, and sacrifices required. There is no easy way to success in goal achievement. Hard work and sustained efforts are required. I know that some individuals say they can be successful in their careers or businesses by working 40 or fewer hours per week, but I remain a skeptic. I do not believe this is actually true for anyone who did not have an extraordinary and unusual advantage of some kind.

In a financial services firm I know, the new professionals joining the company are told, in writing, that they will have to put in 55 to 60 hours per week in their first few years to be successful. They are also told that some time on the weekends will absolutely be required. When I was at Arthur Andersen there was no such thing as a 40-hour week, and working 50–60 hours per week during peak times of the year was common. The successful entrepreneurs I have known put in much more than 55 or 60 hours per week on their businesses; I know I do. The time and effort required to own and grow a business are significant.

Create an emotional linkage and a personal commitment

Two factors that increase your success in achieving your goals are your emotional association with them and your personal commitment to their realization. When these factors are strong, you have strengthened your personal *DNA Leadership* by improving the DNA fabric that aligns and binds you to your goals.

To establish an emotional linkage and a personal commitment to your goals you must grasp them through your senses and feelings. One technique is to visualize accomplishing your goals. You can use your imagination to conjure up images, sounds, smells, tastes, and touches to paint a picture of your goals being realized.

When you think, "I'm hungry," you don't begin to act toward a specific goal until an image of something like a pizza comes to mind through the sensory power of your imagination.

Let's say you have a goal of releasing a new software program by May 1. You could visualize the press releases, trade shows, and internal sales rallies. You could imagine the software in use at user sites. You could almost hear users comment on how well the software works. All of this could be done in your mind to increase your visual linkage to the goal. This same linkage could be created in the minds of others by discussing with and describing to them what it will be like when the software is released.

The power of visualization is increased when you use sensory association. It is not necessary that your senses line up exactly with a goal; the concept is sensory *association*. If you associate smell and sound with a sales goal by imagining the garlic aroma and boisterous conversation in the French restaurant where you will celebrate when you hit a sales quota, that is association. The fact that it is a minor association for a nanosecond does not diminish its effect. Sensory association doesn't necessarily directly cause an action to achieve the goal; it just makes realization of the goal vivid and memorable, and therefore more likely to be pursued.

Emotional association is another tool for increasing the power of your inner drive to achieve your goals. If you perceive your goals as boring or dull, they aren't going to inspire you to act. You need to be excited about your goals.

When a company president wants to achieve a major goal, for *DNA Leadership* she must make sure an emotional appeal and personal commitment exists at the DNA level in the souls of the associates in her organization or the goal is at risk.

The president must "sell" her goals and visions to the associates who must achieve them. This can be accomplished through memos and meetings, but big goals require showmanship and pizazz. For really big goals, there is nothing like a thrilling rally where everyone is bursting with enthusiasm to charge up commitment.

Also important are the words you use to name or specify your goals. One word can paint a thousand pictures—and those pictures can stimulate your senses. Consider a goal of growth versus a goal of *exploding* growth.

A part of emotional commitment is letting go of where you are now and mentally moving to where you want to be. Often an act or series of actions will reinforce this effort. Perhaps the best known example of this is the "burning of the ships in the harbor" (so soldiers could not retreat), which is attributed to Caesar, Hannibal, and other ancient leaders. Burning one's ships is an extraordinary example of commitment, but it does make the point.

An example of emotional commitment is the sales rally where sales leaders stand and yell out the quota they are committing to achieving for the quarter. They buy in to their goals through multiple senses. Another example is where the presidents of subsidiary companies or divisions come together once a month to report their goals and results to the CEO and to their peers. This is quite a bit different from a sales rally, but emotions run high nonetheless.

Establish buy-in

There is no *goal power* unless the individuals pursuing the goals have bought in to the goals and internalized them as personal wants. Individuals must understand how the realization of a goal will affect their self-preservation and gratification, their love and romance, their financial security, or their peer recognition and self-esteem.

Establishing buy-in to company goals

It is not enough to conceive a company's goals and write them down. Goals must be communicated throughout so individuals understand the goals, integrate them into the DNA of their beings, and take actions contributing to achieving the goals.

One of the most important roles a company president fulfills is communicating the organization's mission, vision, and goals. If a company president has a goal of doubling the size of the company in five years, he should make certain everyone knows this goal and also knows what they individually should be doing to help accomplish it.

To communicate corporate goals *in*effectively limits a leader's leadership power because it diminishes the utilization, coordination, and motivation of the individuals left in the dark. How can people help achieve a goal if they don't know what it is?

This buy-in phenomenon doesn't just pertain to rank and file employees; it pertains to executives as well.

If a company president thinks of her company as a $10 million a year business, it will be nearly impossible for her to lead her company to a stated goal of $20 million a year in sales. To lead her company to $20 million in sales, the president must start thinking and acting like the president of a $20 million a year organization.

A vice president of sales will have difficulty achieving a 25% sales volume increase if he sees the goal as an impossibility and does not buy in to it. To achieve his goal, he *must* buy in to it and believe it is possible.

To effect *DNA Leadership* get people to buy in by getting them involved in the goal-setting process from the get go. The more we participate in formulating and specifying a goal, the more we own it and become DNA aligned with its achievement.

Establishing buy-in to your personal goals

The most you can achieve is what you truly want to achieve. If you have not bought in to a goal, it is because you want to maintain the status quo. If maintaining the status quo is what you want, that is what you will get.

Consider the man who has a goal of quitting smoking because there is no place at work for him to smoke. He doesn't want to quit smoking; he is being tormented into it. If at the subconscious level this man thinks of himself as a smoker, he is going to continue to be a smoker regardless of how difficult it is to locate a place to smoke. He will find a way. For this individual to quit smoking he must acquire a reason to want to quit smoking that is stronger than his desire to continue. The moment this occurs he has begun to make progress toward his stated goal, but until it does occur he is nowhere.

It is similar for the woman who says she wants to lose ten pounds. If we can determine where she is mentally, we can pretty much predict whether she will lose the weight and keep it off or not. The question is: "Is she mentally more at the weight she is, or is she mentally ten pounds lighter?"

You will always move to where you are the strongest mentally, at the subconscious level. You can alter your subconscious thinking and establish buy-in using the visualization techniques discussed earlier in this chapter and the imprinting techniques described below.

Imprint goals using "reach and repeat" techniques

One of the primary objectives of GOAL-DRIVEN MANAGEMENT is to put yourself and others on autopilot toward your goals. Autopilot guidance is a powerful force that enhances results and minimizes the need for micro-management.

Think back to when you bought your last car and drove it home from the dealership. You were driving down the road, and suddenly what did you see coming down the highway towards you? A car like you just bought, right? Same color, too.

Now that you own your car, it is impossible *not* to notice another one on the highway within eyesight.

This does not occur by accident. There has been a definite and specific physiological change in your brain. The image of your car has become permanently "imprinted" into your conscious and your subconscious minds. It's in your DNA. Now you are so clearly aware of your car you can't miss seeing one like it on the road if you try. You, in a sense, are on autopilot looking for your make and model of car.

To realize your goals you must similarly imprint them, and your plans to achieve them, deeply into the DNA of your subconscious mind so you can't forget them if you try. This accomplished, if you receive information from any source at any time that pertains to your goals, you will be immediately consciously aware of it and therefore able to seize opportunities or avoid obstacles.

Use visual reminders to drive goals into your subconscious mind

In addition to using visualization techniques to imprint your goals, you need to make your goals visible in physical terms. One way is to create a model or illustration of the completed goal. Builders create replicas of the structures they are building. People in the movie industry create storyboards. Those in the computer world develop breadboards or simulation models. For books I am writing, I develop cover designs, layouts, indexes, and prototypes that remind me of my goal of the completed book.

There are many ways to make your goals visible. You can use charts to show your sales, production, or on-time delivery goals. I know a CEO who kept a picture of the corporate office building of his biggest competitor in a frame on the corner of his desk facing him—to remind himself that his job was to beat that company in the marketplace.

You can even use the real thing to make goals visible. Once when we were giving away a stereo system as a bonus, we installed the system in the lobby and left it on so people could see and hear it as they entered and left the building. This worked well.

In addition to these techniques use a *Pocket Reminder*—a short list of your goals written on a small card you carry in your wallet or purse. This is something you can take out and read often. It is an inexpensive and valuable tool. Some people may dismiss a technique like this as trivial or inconsequential. I don't. This technique has worked well for me. I have my *Pocket Reminder* in my wallet right now.

In a corporate environment put corporate goals on screen savers and pop-up reminders on personal computers, or imprint them on mouse pads—anywhere they can silently work to stimulate subconsciously. Motorola, for example, has produced laminated cards the size of credit cards that state the company's fundamental objective, *Total Customer Satisfaction*, on one side and list the company's *Key Beliefs*, *Key Goals*, and *Key Initiatives* on the other side. It's small and effective.

Use "reach and repeat" techniques
to create an autopilot effect

"Repetition is the mother of all learning." I don't know who said that first, but it was a wise individual.

Repetition is required in learning and integrating our goals into our subconscious minds so we can pursue them on autopilot. Six ways to repeat an *end-result* or *cause*-goal message into our subconscious minds are to:

1. State the goal aloud
2. Read the goal
3. Rewrite the goal statement
4. Imagine the realization of the goal
5. Listen to the goal being stated
6. See a model or demonstration of the goal

As the expression goes, "we become what we think about all day long." Get into the habit of stating, reading, writing, and visualizing each of your major goals daily. I have heard that it's desirable to do this three times a day: on rising, at mid-day, and just before going to bed. I think about my goals off and on literally all day long.

Reminding yourself of your goals three or more times a day sounds easy. It only takes a few minutes. The reality is that many individuals start off with great intentions but never get into the *habit* of repeating and visualizing their goals daily. One of the reasons they don't get into the habit is their goals aren't *laser clear* in the first place. It is impossible to drive a fuzzy goal into your subconscious mind. So first make sure your goals are *laser clear*.

Repetitious reminders of goals are important in business as well. I know many businesses that hold weekly meetings to emphasize and reaffirm sales, customer service, or other goals to employees. I had a client years ago who flipped open his journal and read his goal statements on coming into the office, when leaving for the day, and throughout the day. He was very successful, and he said his habit of repeating his goals daily kept him on track.

I, too, read my goals quite often—not all of them, but the one or two I am working on currently. For substantial goals requiring substantial effort and innovation to achieve, I rewrite my goal statements many times—hundreds of times in some cases when the goals extend over several months.

Keep in mind that stating and writing your goals repetitiously is not enough to motivate you to act. You must have a personal desire and commitment to achieve your goal. For any of these strategies to work, there must be a what's-in-it-for-me factor (the "WIIFM" factor) that combines with the repetition to move you from where you are to where you want to be.

9

Ten elements
every goal should have

One of the most important aspects of achieving goals is fixing them in your mind in no uncertain terms—so they are *laser-clear*. Then the goals can and will be acted on. One of the key responsibilities of a leader using *DNA Leadership* is to help those you are leading select and fix specific goals in their minds as well. Goals get fixed in our minds and acted on best when they possess all ten elements below.

Some of these elements were covered in *Chapters 7 and 8.* Those elements are only capsulized here so all elements are presented together in summary fashion. Goals should be:

1. Written and clearly communicated
2. Visual and visible
3. Prioritized
4. Specific and measurable
5. Deadlined
6. Committed to and rewarded
7. Firm
8. Demanding and challenging, yet achievable
9. Personal, yet participative
10. Backed up by an action plan being implemented

1. Written and clearly communicated

Goals are the catalytic and transforming agents in *DNA Leadership*. To maximize this power, they must be written out in detail and clearly communicated to everyone involved.

Many people have achieved goals without ever writing them down. However, individuals and organizations achieve greater and more consistent results when they take the time and make the effort to write their goals down than when they don't. Writing goals on paper is a positive first step toward achieving those goals. It sets in motion the overall process by allowing us and others to literally see our goals so we can evaluate them and develop plans to achieve them.

Goals kept only in your thoughts have a way of remaining figments of your imagination. They may never get acted upon. Writing forces you to think. When you write a goal down, you see what you are thinking. You have a target to aim for. By writing your goals you are also taking action. This is important. Your first action step leads to your second action step, which leads to your third action step, and on and on.

As the Chinese proverb says: "The journey of a thousand miles begins with a single step." The flip side is true, too. A journey of a thousand miles will never be accomplished without that first step. In setting goals the first step is the thought of the goal. The first *tangible* step should be writing that thought down.

2. Visual and visible

To have focusing power, goals must be *visual* so you can picture them in your mind and "see" them. To have magnetic pulling power, goals must be *visible* so you are reminded of them.

To make a goal visual, write a *laser-clear* statement of the goal describing all aspects in detail. To make a goal visible, create models of your goals, use reminder cards, wall charts, and other devices that you see often. See the topics *Create laser-clear goal statements* and *Create an emotional linkage and a personal commitment* in *Chapter 8* for more on making goals visual and visible.

3. Prioritized

Goals must be prioritized so it is clear which of your goals should receive your attention. There should be no shadow of doubt; no confusion.

You can have many goals, including big goals, but it may not be wise to pursue them all at once. If you pursue too many goals, you may end up achieving none of them.

How many major goals you can effectively pursue in your *business* depends on the nature of your goals, your abilities, the resources at your disposal, and other activities in process. *Individuals* should use a short list approach with no more than one or two major goals being pursued at any one time. See the topic, *Prioritize your goals using an A-B-C approach,* in *Chapter 8* for more on prioritizing goals.

4. Specific and measurable

The more specific and measurable you can make your goals, the better your chances of realizing them.

This applies to business and personal goals. The better job business executives do of defining goals in specific and measurable terms, the better the chances the goals will be achieved.

Our minds have a great capacity to think through facts and circumstances to find ways to achieve our goals, but we are handicapped if our goals are not measurable. To say "I want to improve the profits for my company," or "I want to get in better shape," is non-specific and non-measurable.

What does "improve profits" mean, exactly? Is a $50,000 improvement in profits okay, or is a $2,000,000 improvement the objective? Does "get in better shape" mean lose five pounds, go for a walk once in a while, or get in shape so you can run a marathon? There are differences in these goals, and substantially different levels of effort and different actions are required.

Our minds execute only when we provide exact instructions. An executive who talks about "improving customer service" without specifying what *that* means is going to be waiting a long time for her company's service to customers to improve.

To make goals specific and measurable, quantify and clarify the results desired and answer the questions: What? How much or how many? Where? When? And how?

See the topic *Create laser-clear goal statements* in *Chapter 8* for more on defining goals in specific and measurable terms.

5. Deadlined

We all respond to the call of a deadline. It never ceases to amaze me how much more I get done as deadlines approach, even if I'm the one who created the deadline. Most people are the same. We pace ourselves and put off tasks until we have to do them. There is nothing wrong with this approach so long as it is not just a form of procrastination. It makes sense in many instances to delay actions on some items so other priorities can be focused on. But goals must have deadlines to drive their completion.

A goal without a deadline will never get done "on time" because there never will be a time for it to be done.

If you are serious about achieving your business and personal goals, establish exact day and date deadlines for their completion such as "I want our business plan updated by November 15," or "I want to read one non-fiction book a month."

6. Committed to and rewarded

To have sufficient power to bring you to action, your goals must be committed to and rewarded. We have all established goals that we were not committed to. The chances are good those goals never materialized.

Power from your goals results when you make a commitment to them and when you understand how you are going to benefit when they are achieved. Making a commitment means pledging yourself to take the actions necessary to realize the goal. Making a commitment is more than affirming "I'm going to learn Spanish." It means understanding the effort and sacrifices to learn Spanish. This doesn't mean you can't set goals unless you understand everything required to achieve them. It does mean you should acknowledge the magnitude of the effort and your willingness to undertake it. See the topic, *You must reward the behavior you want to have happen, or it won't happen,* in *Chapter 11* for more on establishing rewards for goal achievement.

7. Firm

Goals are not goals until they are established on a definitive, firm basis. When you commit to a goal, you should do so with conviction and determination. Establishing goals firmly means you recognize that obstacles will be encountered and you intend to overcome them.

Keep in mind that GOAL-DRIVEN MANAGEMENT is a process and a major part of the process is to ingrain habits and patterns. If you get into the habit of setting goals and moving their deadlines as you approach them, moving deadlines is the habit you will acquire and reinforce.

If your goal is to raise $5,000 for a charity by month's end and on the 25th you have only $2,500 in contributions, then don't alter the goal by concluding that $2,500 is good enough. Don't do it—because you will cheat the charity *and* you will cheat yourself out of learning how to use the GOAL-DRIVEN MANAGEMENT process for growth.

Instead of altering the goal, alter your plans and your actions. Figure out whatever you must do to achieve your goal by the deadline date and do it. Be firm in keeping your goals and persistent in your efforts to achieve them. The longer-term payoff from this is enormous.

8. Demanding and challenging, yet achievable

If a goal is not demanding and challenging, there is no power in it for you to grow or for your business to grow. You only grow when you stretch for more than you already have achieved.

If a company has been growing at five percent a year for the last five years and management adopts a goal of growing five percent again next year, I would be skeptical whether that goal is going to cause the company to achieve its potential. A lot depends on the size of the company and other circumstances, but unless the people in the company see the goal as challenging, they will not be enthusiastic in pursuing it, and they and the business will not grow in the process.

This applies at the individual level as well.

If an agent has been selling three insurance policies a week for the last year, a goal of selling three policies a week for next year will not cause growth. There is no challenge. She can already do it. She has already done it. A more demanding goal, say of five policies per week, will require that she change and grow to achieve it, and by the process of changing and growing she will become more valuable.

However, goals don't create power unless you have a reasonable chance of achieving them using the efforts, resources, and time you have available. They must be achievable.

It is important to set *and achieve* goals on an ongoing basis. The more you get into the habit of achieving daily, weekly, and monthly goals, the stronger you become at the overall process.

So, set goals you and others can achieve, goals that are demanding yet achievable. See the topic, *Big goals produce big power,* in *Chapter* 7 for more on establishing demanding goals.

9. Personal, yet participative

Goals must be personal so you will persist until you achieve them, and yet they must be participative so that those who can help you achieve them are involved in a substantive manner.

The "personal" part of this is that each individual recognizes and accepts the responsibility to pursue personal goals to the best of his or her abilities. The individual visualizes them, commits to them, and pursues them.

The "participative" part of this for business or team goals is that all individuals involved have "bought into the goal." They accept it and agree to participate in it and pursue it as a team.

It would be foolish for the president of a company to have a goal of doubling the size of the company in five years and then fail to get everyone involved. The other side of this is that if all the workers in the company wanted to double the size of the company, but it was not of importance to the president, it would be hard to imagine accomplishing such a goal. There would be no basis for DNA bonding.

10. Backed up by an action plan being implemented

Goals must be backed up by a specific plan spelling out the actions to be taken that will result in their achievement; and, the plan must be implemented.

A goal without a plan is like the pressure of water against a dam—it is only potential energy. To get kinetic energy, the water must flow.

It is the same with goals. A goal with no plan has only potential. The plan shows the way to release the potential and implementation of the plan releases it. Action plans are discussed more in *Chapters 11, 12, 13*, and *14*.

10

GET a goal—
Implementation action
steps

GET *a goal* is the first of the five keys in *GOAL-DRIVEN MAN-AGEMENT*. The objective is to select and commit to pursuing goals that are *purpose-driven.*

This involves determining your past accomplishments, identifying goal possibilities and making goal selections, breaking bigger goals into smaller goals, writing *laser-clear* statements for each of the goals you intend to pursue, and then imprinting goals to be pursued so they are locked into your subconscious at the DNA level.

These activities are summarized into the four major action steps to *GET a goal*, which are listed below and illustrated in the flowchart on the next page.

1. Summarize where you are now.

2. Identify goal possibilities, record them in your *Goals Journal*, and prioritize and select major goals to pursue.

3. Break big and long-term goals into smaller goals and write a *laser-clear* goal statement for each goal.

4. Communicate goals to everyone appropriate and imprint goals on an ongoing basis.

GET a goal
Implementation action steps

Step 1:
Summarize where you are now

Early on you should summarize and evaluate the efforts you have made and the results you have achieved for each goal category. For example, if you are establishing goals in the customer service area, then summarize past programs, the nature and quality of services being provided presently, and other relevant information. If you are contemplating goals pertaining to your health, then summarize the state of your health and your past goals, actions, and results.

This is an important step. An assessment of where you are is as important as determining where you want to be. You have to begin from where you are to build a bridge of actions to your new destination.

So, first summarize your past results and create a word picture of where you are. This should be accomplished by completing your *MOSAIC Performance Grid* and your *Current MOSAIC* graphical display as described in *Chapter 4*. The grid and the graphical display provide kindling for the mental fire you must create in establishing future goals.

Step 2:
Identify goal possibilities, record them in your *Goals Journal,* and prioritize and select the major goals to pursue

Begin this step by brainstorming the possible goals or goal categories you want to consider. Write them down. Don't try to evaluate the goals at this point; just compile a big list.

Next, enter your goal possibilities in your *Goals Journal* using a separate sheet or section for each goal type. These entries are for memo purposes; they do not have to be complete goal statements at this juncture. Some examples might be:

Sales and sales-related goals:

- Add a large number of new, small accounts

- Create a sales compensation plan

- Develop a training program for new hires

Product goals:

- Remake existing product offerings, freshen up the packaging

- Add two new products that compliment the present line

Personal training and career:

- Take a course on Internet marketing

- Complete the current year's 40-hour continuing education requirement

After you have compiled a list of goal possibilities, rank them in importance on an A–B–C basis. From these lists select a short list of major goals you *actually intend to pursue.*

After you have selected your goal categories and goals to pursue, prepare a *Goal MOSAIC* graphical display as described in *Chapter 4.* If your graphical display is consistent with what you intended, move to Step 3. However, if your selected goals do not provide the balance and growth you seek, then reevaluate and revise your goal selections.

Step 3:
Break big and long-term goals into smaller goals and write a *laser-clear* statement for each goal

First, break your goals into small, manageable segments. Techniques for this are discussed in *Chapter 8.*

Then write a *laser-clear* statement for each of your goals and sub-goals. Write these goal statements as completely as possible, and then set them aside. After a few days, read them to make sure they are complete in all respects, make sense, and are in line with your other goals and objectives. This passage of time provides a better perspective. The aging process reveals fresh insights. You usually can sharpen your goals considerably if you take this step.

An acid test question to ask for each major goal is: Is this goal compelling? Goals are weak tools for growth unless they arouse a call to action. In many ways the success of a goal can be measured by the actions it inspires.

Step 4:
Communicate goals to everyone appropriate and imprint goals on an ongoing basis

Communicating and imprinting goals are two vital steps often overlooked or not given the attention they require. Goals cannot and will not be pursued unless we know exactly what they are, continuously.

This step is the marketing and sales campaign for your goals. Develop a program to sell your personal goals to yourself and to sell your business goals to yourself and others who must achieve them.

Communication and imprinting activities must continue until goals are achieved. See *Imprint goals using "reach and repeat" techniques,* in *Chapter 8* for more on this.

11

OUTLINE a plan—
Fundamental principles

The second key in *GOAL-DRIVEN MANAGEMENT* is O. O stands for *OUTLINE a plan*. The fundamental principles pertaining to developing and outlining an action plan are discussed in this chapter under the following headings:

- Planning is the most important part of the process
- Benefits of planning
- Why people and businesses don't plan
- Plans are the "dreams" people buy into
- Planning is an Olympics in thinking
- Thought fragments do not constitute a plan
- The objective is to outline the *best* plan possible
- Plans must drive actions
- All actions in a plan must be aimed at the right goals
- The order in which you act will affect your results
- Plans improve with a *mastermind* approach
- You must reward the behavior you want to have happen, or it *won't* happen

Planning is the most important part of the process

A man sent me this letter. It expresses one of the keys to success that many individuals overlook.

> Dear Jim:
>
> In reflecting back over the years, I am constantly reminded of the inscription in Jackson Arch at VMI (Virginia Military Institute): "You may be whatever you resolve to be."— Stonewall Jackson. These same words are found on my class ring. For four years I walked through that arch and saw those words but really never thought much about them. In a way though they have guided much of my life. So the lesson they were meant to teach somehow got through. Yet, it was not until I heard you speak and read your book that I could fully understand what was missing from the lesson the words teach.
>
> I cannot remember anyone at VMI ever teaching us, as cadets, "*how*" to be what we resolved to be. What you offer, that was missing from the VMI experience, is the *"how."* The concept of written goals backed up by a measurable, deadlined, and concrete *plan* is the missing key.

Although all aspects of setting and achieving goals are important, developing an action plan you intend to implement is the most important part of the process. The development of a plan forces you to clarify your goals and makes you figure out *how* your goals can be achieved. Without the how, you have nothing. You can have a good goal without a good plan, but you can't achieve the good goal without a good plan. Plans drive actions and the creation and development of systems.

The principle of "cause and effect," was discussed in *Chapter 5*. For every "effect" you want, you must have a corresponding *cause* to drive it. Plans are composed of action steps. These action steps represent *cause* goals that drive the achievement of the *end-result* goals you want.

When John F. Welch, Jr., CEO of General Electric Company, spoke at the company's annual meeting, his remarks focused on the company's goal of achieving Six Sigma, virtually error-free quality, by the year 2000. Mr. Welch concluded his remarks by saying: "Six Sigma—GE Quality 2000—is a dream, but a dream with a *plan* [emphasis added] behind it."

Many businesses expend tremendous resources without achieving the goals management intended. Similarly, many individuals work hard without achieving the personal goals they desire. Three reasons businesses and people fall short of their goals are they don't have a plan, the plan they have is not good enough, or they don't work the plan they have.

Once you have established a goal, you must turn your attention to your plan of action. Follow-through on the plan of action is one of the great secrets for success. If you take care of the *cause* goals in your action plans, the *end-result* goals will take care of themselves. In other words, the action plan is more important than the goal itself.

Benefits of planning

Sometimes individuals question the need to prepare a *written* plan of action. "I plan in my head. Is it really necessary to write all the steps down on paper?"

For major goals—yes, if you want to have the best possible chance of realizing your goals.

Written plans are an essential management tool. They require more effort than head planning, but there are many reasons to make the effort. Some of the reasons are in the next box.

Here is an example of how the process of creating a plan helped a company achieve its goals. Jeff, the vice president of sales, said that his goal was to increase next year's sales by 20%. The president of the company asked Jeff if he had goals for the sub-components of the 20% increase. "Do you have a goal for sales

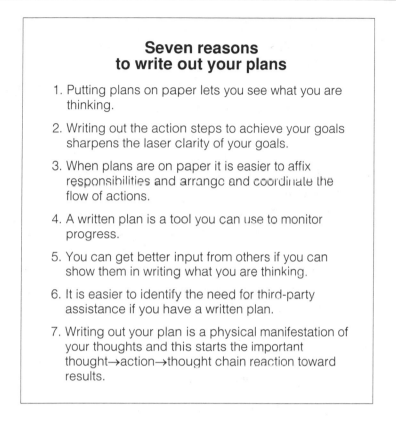

**Seven reasons
to write out your plans**

1. Putting plans on paper lets you see what you are thinking.

2. Writing out the action steps to achieve your goals sharpens the laser clarity of your goals.

3. When plans are on paper it is easier to affix responsibilities and arrange and coordinate the flow of actions.

4. A written plan is a tool you can use to monitor progress.

5. You can get better input from others if you can show them in writing what you are thinking.

6. It is easier to identify the need for third-party assistance if you have a written plan.

7. Writing out your plan is a physical manifestation of your thoughts and this starts the important thought→action→thought chain reaction toward results.

from new customers? A goal for sales increases from existing customers? A goal for sales increases from pricing increases?" the president asked. Jeff did not have a written action plan, and he didn't have a ready answer to the questions.

So, the three of us sat down to develop a plan. As we discussed past results and future opportunities, it became clear that the company had no programs to expand penetration into existing clients. To address this gap we brainstormed several approaches. When we finished, Jeff created an action plan that included two special programs directed to existing accounts.

As a side benefit to thinking through his plan, Jeff reevaluated his goal and increased it to a 25% increase in sales, with specific subgoals for each component of the increase.

I was at a restaurant where a fellow at the next table had one of those loud voices that penetrates. This was great for me, though, because I overheard this relevant conversation. He had just hired a new associate and was telling her how he likes to operate. This is an approximation of what he said:

> "I want to agree with you on our objectives and the plan to achieve them. Then I have a basis to hold you accountable and manage what we're doing together, and you'll have a basis to work on your own.
>
> "I want you to take the ball and run with it—do whatever you need to do—get whatever help you need—just so long as you're working on the objectives we agree on and following the plan.
>
> "What's nice about this is that you don't have to keep checking with me. As long as you follow the plan, you'll know with 100% confidence that I'm behind you every step of the way. If the plan's not working, call me. I'm there to help. We're in this together. I want you to be successful. Do you see what I mean?"

The fellow doing the talking had the right idea. He knew that by planning he and his associate would be able to work together better and accomplish more.

Why people and businesses don't plan

A friend who had just become the president of an association asked my advice on how she should go about leading the organization. During the discussion I questioned her about the specific programs she intended to develop to achieve her goals. "Oh, Jim," she said, "please don't tell me I have to prepare a business plan."

"No," I said, "there is no need to prepare a plan—if you are going to be satisfied when you don't achieve the results you desire. But, if you do intend to achieve your goals, then you need a plan."

In *Association Management*, the magazine of the American Society of Association Executives (ASAE), an article describing ASAE's peer review program identified these results for thirty reviewed associations: 75% did *not* have a strategic plan, and 60% did *not* have an annual action plan on which to base their budgeting for the next year.

I have no way of knowing how many businesses have good, comprehensive plans they are following to achieve their goals. But I know many businesses operate similarly to those peer-reviewed associations. From my experiences with hundreds of companies over the years and from reviewing several thousand business plans in my venture capital business, I know that most business planning efforts are superficial and are focused on number crunching, not strategy and action planning.

I asked a small business owner who was completing the action plans for his business, using the *GOAL-DRIVEN MANAGE-MENT* approach for the first time, How is it going? "It's a lot of work," he said.

Over a four-week period he had spent approximately eight hours identifying and refining his goals and another twelve hours thinking through strategies and action plans. I asked if he thought his twenty-hour investment was worth it. "Without doubt," he said, "this stuff is really cool. I have been flying by the seat of my pants for too long. Now I know where I want to go, and I feel pretty confident I'm going to get there."

Clearly, written action plans deliver multiple benefits. Therefore, why doesn't everyone have a written action plan for each major goal being pursued? There are a number of reasons for this, but four stand out.

1. They don't appreciate the benefits: I read a little story once about the dilemma of a man who had to explain the taste of apple juice to a little boy who had never tasted apple juice before.

The only way the man could solve his problem was to give the little boy a taste. Gaining an appreciation of the value of planning is the same. The benefits of planning may be stated over and over, but you can't appreciate them until you give planning a try.

2. They sense it will take a tremendous amount of time and feel they will get more done by taking action: This is an innocent, but incorrect conclusion. In my dozen years in the venture capital business, the entrepreneurs who took time to plan *well* realized better and more consistent results than those who didn't. The notion that planning doesn't pay is a myth. Planning is an *in*expensive investment and the rewards are great.

Planning does not have to be the long, laborious, and tedious effort many people imagine it to be—particularly if you use the time-saving techniques described in this and the next two chapters. Planning results in substantial time savings over the long term.

3. They don't know *how*: Most individuals don't know how to prepare action plans to achieve their goals. That's no surprise. When were they supposed to have been taught this? Where were they supposed to have gained experience and practice in preparing plans so they could get good at it? What method and techniques are they supposed to be using to guide the process? This and the next two chapters will show you *how to* do it.

4. They don't make planning a priority: This is understandable. If people don't know how to do something and they have no experience doing it, they won't value the effort.

Once individuals and firms understand and realize the benefits of planning by going through the process, then the obstacles above are easily overcome. Learning to plan properly is like learning to use a software package. It takes effort and persistence to get beyond the initial learning curve, but once individuals learn how to plan efficiently and effectively, planning becomes a motivating and even inspiring process. People enjoy creating, and planning is a creative process.

Four reasons people don't plan

1. They don't appreciate the benefits of having a written plan.

2. They sense it will take a tremendous amount of time to prepare a plan and feel they will get more done by taking action.

3. They don't know *how*.

4. They don't make planning a priority, and they keep putting it off as something they are going to get to.

Plans are the "dreams" people buy into

The dream people buy into is more often the *building of the dream* than the dream itself.

The vision leaders must create to inspire their followers is not a vision of their dream, but a vision of their plan to achieve it. For it is through the revelation of the plan that individuals can find and see their role in fulfilling the dream.

When individuals understand the contribution they can make and want to make it, you have regenerated the DNA within the company and that is *DNA Leadership*.

In *Think and Grow Rich*, Napoleon Hill related that many men approached John Pierpont Morgan with the dream of creating the largest steel company in the world but that Morgan was unmoved by their overtures.

It was only after Charles M. Schwab gave an after-dinner speech that Morgan became interested and bought into the idea—passionately. During his speech, Schwab described the world-wide opportunities for steel and his ideas for reorganizing the industry through specialization, consolidation, and capturing foreign markets. *And* he alluded to beginning this grand enterprise through the acquisition of Andrew Carnegie's vast empire.

What fascinated Morgan was not the dream Schwab foretold, but his own role as financier in creating it by acquiring Carnegie's holdings. No one had ever suggested this possibility. Thus, Morgan raised the financing, the United States Steel Corporation was formed, and Schwab went on to head it.

"What's in it for me" is the driving force behind the realization of all entrepreneurial dreams. It is not your dream you can sell me on, for your dream is of little interest to me. It is my role in bringing your dream about that piques my enthusiasm. That is where the excitement is and where my attention lies. That is where I can find my challenge.

Unfortunately, as we know, the plans for our goals do not get the limelight. Plans are relegated to the back office in terms of their importance and prominence in goal achievement.

Therein lies the fault that has cost many men and women their dreams. It is not just your dreams and your goals that you must sell to others and get them to buy into and adopt as their own—you must also get them to buy into your *plans* to achieve those dreams and goals.

When Dan and I founded our venture capital firm, our goal was to raise millions of dollars from investors. To accomplish this, we had to create a vision *and* be able to describe how we would fulfill it. We were successful, not because we discussed our *vision* with prospective investors, but because we showed them a *grand plan*. Our plan provided opportunities for wealthy and influential business leaders to participate in the growth and development of our firm and the companies we would invest in. The individuals and firms who invested with us were interested in more than a passive investment—they were interested in helping us pursue our *quest*. It was our quest and the actionable ideas we described in our plans that our founding investors bought into—and took as their own—not our "vision."

This is the way it has been in every business I have helped start, finance, launch, and grow—and I have been involved in many of them. The honey that attracts investors and management team members to a new company is not a vision for the company—it is the *plan* to achieve the vision. The plan makes the vision plausible. But a plan invokes enthusiasm only if it is sufficiently detailed so individuals can see their role in the endeavor.

DNA Leadership requires that business leaders give people something to sink their teeth into. They must refine their plans: to take them from the general to the specific, and from the intangible to the tangible. The blueprint of what they want to create must be visible to all who have to build it. Instead of keeping their plans behind closed doors, leaders should bring them into the light so their employees and associates can see their plans and find their roles in fulfilling them.

Planning is an Olympics in thinking

Good action plans are important. Even more important is the process you have to go through to create them. Action plans are valuable because they cause you to think, evaluate, and make decisions. They summon your brain power.

There is a difference between planning and writing the plan. Planning is thinking; writing is writing. Once the thinking is complete, the writing is easy. But if the thinking is incomplete, the writing is impossible.

As you go through the planning process you are building a mental blueprint for a bridge that goes step-by-step from where you are to where you want to be. Once this blueprint is in your mind, you can re-create it in real life and fulfill your goals.

In this sense, planning for accomplishment of a major goal is like an Olympics in thinking. And the only way to see how you're doing in a thinking Olympics is to write your thoughts on paper and evaluate them.

Sometimes thinking through the required actions is an obvious and straightforward effort. This happens when you are pursuing goals you understand, or goals that others have achieved and you can analyze.

In many instances, however, you have to conceive the steps to achieve your goals because you have no previous experience or examples to follow. Here the thinking required may pose a greater challenge. In some cases your thinking may have to be extraordinary. The positive side of this is that breakthrough thinking of this type provides extraordinary rewards.

Thought fragments do not constitute a plan

Many individuals have "some idea" of what they are going to do to achieve their goals. They may even have several specific action steps in mind. But their thoughts are loose fragments that haven't been gathered into a specific, cohesive plan that stands a chance of being implemented successfully.

The vice president of a large company told me that one of her company's major goals for the upcoming year was to improve the leadership abilities of the individuals at the management level. When I asked her to clarify the goal she said: "You know, get people to take initiative, act more entrepreneurial. We want our managers to own their areas of responsibility."

These thought fragments did not constitute a *laser-clear* goal by any stretch of the imagination, but I moved on to ask about the company's action plans to achieve their goal. "What programs or actions are you taking to achieve your goal?" I asked.

"Nothing in particular," she said. "We are bringing in an outside speaker to our management retreat, but that's about it."

The lack of specific plans is one of the weaknesses in many businesses today. Bringing in an "apostle" of leadership to speak is not even a good fix, as Raymond W. Smith, CEO of Bell Atlantic pointed out in one of his speeches: "The trouble with [the Apostle] approach is *fairy dust* gets sprinkled on the surface of the organization, but it never gets into the ground to help grow anything.

Managers make speeches, exhort the troops, and get people riled up, but they never develop a specific plan for implementing the quality process, or put forward a systematic, organized approach to accomplishing their goals."

Here's a comparison of an action-driven approach and a talk-driven approach: Two restaurateurs each had goals of opening a second location. One established the goal firmly. He assembled his management team and advisors and developed a three-page plan to establish the second location. The other talked about his goal, but never developed a plan. The first individual now has two locations and is thinking about a third; the second still has only one and is still talking about expanding. Surprised? I wasn't either.

In addition to having no plan at all, many individuals also don't plan as *well* as they should. Gary's goal was to find a new job in another city. He wrote his goal on a sheet of paper, taped it to his front door, and read his goal aloud when he left for work each morning. He had some ideas about what he would do to achieve his goal. He thought he might call several friends in the city he wanted to move to and see if they had any leads. He intended to call a few executive search firms and subscribe to a special service that posted job openings in the area. But after about a year, when "nothing turned up," Gary abandoned his goal and decided to remain in his present position.

Contrast Gary's story with Danielle's. Danielle, who lived in the East, wanted to get a job in Texas with one of the big accounting firms. She created a one-page action plan that outlined a series of steps to approach each targeted firm. Part of her plan was to obtain recommendation letters in advance. She did this. Another step was to research each firm to learn more about its practice specialties. She did this, too. A big step was to schedule a two-week trip to Texas to meet with prospective employers—she scheduled this trip even before she had interviews set up because she wanted to be able to say when she would be available for an interview. The result? She's in Texas working with a big accounting firm. She knew what she wanted, developed a concrete plan to get it, and she got it.

The objective is to outline the *best* plan possible

Don't start taking actions toward your goals too precipitously. First, consider the alternative actions available. A get-started-right-away approach can work for minor goals, but it can burn up time, energy, and resources if used for major goals.

There are always a variety of approaches to achieve given goals. For example, there are several alternatives my firm can choose from to get present and prospective clients to come to a demonstration of our new programs. We could send out formal invitations, place an announcement in our newsletter, have our salespeople invite clients and prospects personally, send an e-mail announcement, place an advertisement in the newspaper, send out press releases, purchase radio or television spots, create a special promotion, and so on.

Any combination of these strategies might work. The question is: Which ones will produce the exact results we want? If our goal is that our top twenty-five clients and prospects attend the event, we might adopt one approach, but if our goal is to have 300 people show up, then a different approach is needed.

Before you prepare a written plan, give some thought to the alternative strategies and actions available. Weigh the advantages and disadvantages of each alternative, and select a combination of the best of each of them.

A useful exercise is to ask questions such as: How can I do this better? Who else has done this? How did they do it? Who would know how to improve upon what I am doing? Where can I see something like this in operation? How can I research this?

Plans must drive actions

The purpose of a plan is to drive actions. While I had dinner with my friend Rob one evening, we discussed the steps he would have to take to reorganize his business and restructure his loans at the bank. He wrote the five items we agreed to on a napkin and put it in his pocket. The next morning we met with his banker, who asked Rob what his plan was. Rob pulled out the napkin, took out his pen, and read off the items on the list. Then he checked off the first two items. "That's done, and that's done too," he said. It was only mid-morning, and Rob had already implemented two of the items in his plan! The banker was pleased; he extended Rob's loans.

Someone has to accept responsibility for each action in the plan and then do it. The importance of acting on our plans is discussed further in *Chapters 14, 15,* and *16.*

As Ray Bradbury puts it, "Want to be a writer? Start by writing to a schedule something like this: One thousand to two thousand words every day for the next twenty years."

All actions in a plan must be aimed at the right goals

There are four corollaries to the principle of cause and effect that must be considered when evaluating action plans and action steps being taken to achieve specified goals: (1) goal achievement is based on actions aimed at the goals to be achieved; (2) for every goal realized there has been a corresponding series of actions that caused it; (3) for every goal *not* realized there has been an absence of actions to cause it; and (4) for every action that didn't cause a goal desired, there was a waste of time and energy.

Your actions must directly cause your goals to be realized. There is no point in expending energy if it is not directed toward a goal you want to achieve.

Also, make sure your plans provide for *all* the action steps

> ## The corollaries to the principle of cause and effect as it pertains to actions and goal achievement
>
> *Corollary # 1:*
>
> Goal achievement is based on actions aimed at the goals to be achieved.
>
> *Corollary # 2:*
>
> For every goal realized there has been a corresponding series of actions that caused it.
>
> *Corollary # 3:*
>
> For every goal *not* realized there has been an absence of actions to cause it.
>
> *Corollary # 4:*
>
> For every action that didn't cause a goal desired, there was a waste of time and energy.

required and make sure you aren't wasting energy taking actions that aren't in your plans.

One of the problems many businesses have is maintaining a focus on essential tasks while eliminating energies expended on unnecessary actions. New entrepreneurs often will do so well in a few areas that they become consumed by their efforts in those areas while neglecting other components of the business.

A company I know spent more than a year designing a product without ever talking to potential customers about what their needs and preferences were. The product was an engineer's dream, but it had far more bells, whistles, and features than anyone was willing to pay for. It was a marketing and financial disaster.

Big oversights like this should have been addressed in the action planning process. Where was the action step that said, "Visit with prospective customers and ask them what they think?"

Or the step that said, "Tell customers the price we are thinking of charging for this and watch whether they laugh."

The order in which you act will affect your results

Once you know what must be done, the next step is to organize the required tasks into groups and create a sequential flow. This is like lining up dominos so they fall in a precision race across the table with the final domino collapsing into the prize.

Arranging your actions in a logical order is not a difficult step, but you should give some thought to it.

I'll never forget the advice I received from a friend when we were planning our first public seminar. "The first thing you do is get people into the room," he said, "then worry about what you're going to say."

What my friend meant was that if no one shows up, it won't matter how great our program preparation was; it was for naught. Obvious perhaps, but at the time we were focused more on the program content than marketing it. His advice was a wake-up call. We immediately altered our actions to concentrate on the marketing side. After our marketing plans were in process, we went back and concentrated on the program. By reordering our approach we ended up with a successful result instead of disappointment.

Plans improve with a *mastermind* approach

There has never been a plan of action that could not be improved. Knowing this, I have formed the habit of seeking input and advice from a network of people with varied backgrounds and experiences. This factor has been a significant contributing element to the successes I have enjoyed.

My approach is simple. I tell people my goal and hand them a list of the steps I'm thinking about taking to achieve it. Then I ask them: What steps can I add, eliminate, or alter to improve my odds for success? By seeing *my* thoughts, they have something specific to focus their attention and stimulate *their* thoughts.

In larger businesses there are many opportunities to create teams or groups to work on problems together. But sometimes small business owners and managers do not have anyone to talk to to test ideas or get input on plans. For this reason I recommend that all businesses, regardless of their size, create an advisory board. This is a small group of individuals with complementary and diverse backgrounds that comes together several times a year to provide input on operations, goals, and plans. I also recommend that individuals create their own personal advisory board. A personal advisory board could be two to five people who meet with you a few times a year to provide input on your goals and plans. These are trusted individuals you can call on for advice and counsel as you select and pursue your goals. (See *Select an advisory board or goals coach* in *Chapter 19.*)

You must reward the behavior you want to have happen, or it *won't* happen

Rewards, incentives, and recognition programs are powerful motivators. An integral part of the process of developing action plans is to think through the methods you will use to motivate yourself and others to take the actions you want taken.

You must believe your efforts will be worthwhile based on what you will get in return for them. As mentioned earlier, this key motivating influence is often called the WIIFM factor— What's In It For Me?

Rewards and recognition work well to motivate people to action and they serve as an enabling catalyst for the regeneration of corporate DNA. The nature and extent of the reward and recognition can vary, but it must exist, or sooner or later the desired behavior will cease. People need to know they are appreciated.

When I was working with a company in the health care field, members of the executive team expressed interest in having associates experiment and innovate to create cost-savings and operational efficiencies. I asked the executives what rewards and incentives they had established to motivate their people to identify such changes. They looked at me with an expression so blank you would have thought I asked them the circumference of Mars. They had never even considered providing rewards to encourage the behavior they desired.

After some discussion, these executives came up with a number of ideas to motivate their employees. These included a special section in the company's newsletter recognizing innovations, an idea-of-the-month program, a suggestion box through the company's e-mail system, cash prizes awarded for ideas that were implemented, and spot recognition programs for great suggestions during management meetings. These techniques were not novel approaches, but they were new to the company, so they got everyone excited and focused on encouraging participation.

One aspect of the management process I have never seen overdone is recognizing people for doing a good job and rewarding them for their efforts. How many people do you know who have been thanked too much for a job well done?

Managers should go out of their way to praise their people and tell and show them they are appreciated. A simple "thank you" or "nice job on that report" goes a long way.

A small business owner I know swears by the free donuts he brings on Fridays when weekly production quotas are met. He claims it is the best $50 investment he makes every chance he gets.

The power of hoopla works well, too. Big celebrations should be considered for large groups with big goals. Companies like Mary Kay Cosmetics and Amway are famous for their rewards and celebrations. Nowadays even traditionally staid companies are getting into the act with big, exuberant programs.

Big recognition programs are important, but don't forget

personal recognition and appreciation programs—these are actually the more important programs in most cases. We all need to know our work is appreciated.

While personal appreciation and recognition cannot be overdone, they can be and many times are underutilized. Some studies show that fewer than half of the employees in most companies feel they are appreciated by the people or the company they work for.

This is wrong. When people come to work for us, it is our responsibility to recognize them and appreciate them for the contribution they are making. A company should be more than just a place to work and make money—it should be a place where employees can grow, develop, and feel good about their contributions. We spend a lot of time at work—much of our lives. There is no reason we shouldn't truly love our work and be appreciated for doing it.

When I ran an office at Arthur Andersen, I created special thank you notes called *Ballgrams*, and I had a cabinet full of on-the-spot tokens of appreciation that I provided for going beyond the call of duty. These items cost peanuts. In fact, one of the spot gifts was a jar of peanuts. But the impact of the little gifts was unbelievable. The size of the gift was not the issue, it was that I took the time to say thank you.

The reward and celebration concept applies to our personal and family goals, too. Years ago I promised myself a trip to the Santa Barbara Writers Conference as a reward for quitting smoking. I loved the conference. I love that I no longer smoke even more. Recently, I offered one of my daughter's friends dinner for six if she quit smoking for a year. Last I heard she's planning her free dinner party. I'm counting on her winning the prize.

Remember, you must reward the behavior you want to have happen, or it *won't* happen. At least it won't happen consistently.

12

OUTLINE a plan—
Success strategies, tools,
and techniques

The success strategies, tools, and techniques for outlining a plan of action are discussed in this chapter under the following headings:

- Use *backwards planning* to drive your thinking

- Do your homework before you plan

- Establish *driving* strategies to focus efforts

- Develop strategies to overcome major obstacles

- Identify all "must do" actions

- Break big steps into bite-sized segments

- Affix responsibility for each primary action step

- Establish solid linkage among interdependent plans

- Allow for changes and flexibility

- Plan for tangible results fast

- Use your plan to establish and maintain momentum

- Begin with a creative brainstorming session

- Write out major assumptions

- Flowchart actions so you can see them

- Focus extra attention on beginning and ending

- Ask for help and get assistance

- Establish rewards when plans are adopted

Use *backwards planning* to drive your thinking

To assist the companies my venture capital business invested in, I wrote *The Entrepreneur's Tool Kit,* a guide for thinking through business plans.

The primary approach I advocate is what I call *backwards business planning*, and the guide includes 270 questions to be asked and answered during business planning efforts. If these questions are answered, it is easy to write a business plan. If they are not, it is impossible to cover all the bases thoroughly.

Backwards planning is still the approach I use in planning efforts—whether planning an entire business or developing an action plan to achieve a specific goal.

To use *backwards planning,* begin with a vision of your completed goal in mind and work backwards to identify the milestones and interim actions that you will have to have taken for the goal to be realized.

In our venture capital business we would write out a description of what we wanted the company to look like when we took it public or sold our investment. We described the desired revenues, products, markets, management team, facilities, systems, and as many other details as we could imagine. Then we would determine the actions required to achieve such results and write them down as our plan. I'm simplifying here, but this was the basic process we used over and over.

To create action plans using this *backwards-planning* approach, ask and answer questions. It is important to ask and answer the *right* questions of the *right* people, but asking questions is the key concept.

Say you have a goal of completing a brochure for your firm's services. In the box below are some questions you might ask.

Goal: Design a new brochure

Questions to ask

- Who is the intended audience for this brochure?
- What are the primary purposes of this brochure?
- What are we using now that we want to replace?
- What actions should the brochure evoke?
- How can we evoke those actions?
- How long do we want the brochure to be?
- How many will we print?
- How can we demonstrate the benefits of our services?
- What can we do to get people to open the brochure and look it over?
- What's the main theme of the brochure?
- Who should have input on this?
- Will we include client testimonials? Whose?
- What's our budget?
- And so on . . .

By going through the process of posing and answering questions such as those in the box, we begin to identify the major obstacles and action steps in the overall task. As an action step, we might hold a brainstorming session to flesh out answers to the questions. Another step might be to interview clients and ask them what they like about our services. Maybe we would add a step to ask if we could quote them in the brochure.

The questions stimulate our thoughts in identifying the actions necessary to achieve desired results. Questions uncover obstacles and reveal possible approaches to overcoming them. Questions expand our thinking and help us reaffirm our intended goals. Questions are a central element of the planning-thinking process. We should use them liberally.

As Rudyard Kipling wrote, "I had six honest serving men— they taught me all I knew: Their names were Where and What and When—and Why and How and Who."

When creating an action plan to achieve your goals, start by preparing a list of questions about what you want to accomplish and the approaches you might employ. Then answer the questions. In the box on the next page are ten questions to consider when developing an action plan. These are not the only questions you might ask and answer, and they may not all be appropriate for your project. They are provided only as food for thought.

Do your homework before you plan

Doing home repairs is not my favorite pastime. But what I really hate is being up on the ladder to fix the floodlights under the eaves only to realize I need the half-inch wrench on my workbench in the garage. Sometimes I try to get by using the tools I have with me. Sometimes I yell for someone to see if they will get me the wrench. And sometimes I come down off the ladder to get it myself. In each case I lose time and energy.

This same phenomenon occurs when individuals develop action plans. They encounter missing facts or realize they cannot develop a strategy without more information. So, they stop the process and get what they need. Or they press forward without having the right tools.

This happened to a friend of mine in the network installation

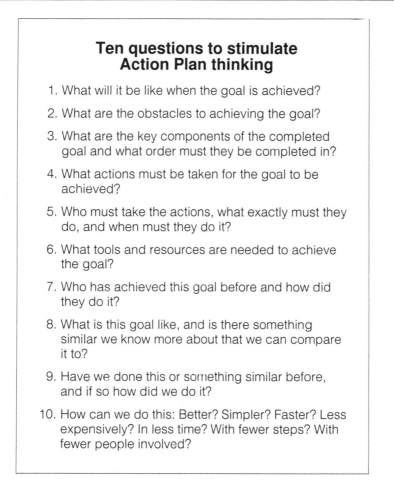

Ten questions to stimulate Action Plan thinking

1. What will it be like when the goal is achieved?

2. What are the obstacles to achieving the goal?

3. What are the key components of the completed goal and what order must they be completed in?

4. What actions must be taken for the goal to be achieved?

5. Who must take the actions, what exactly must they do, and when must they do it?

6. What tools and resources are needed to achieve the goal?

7. Who has achieved this goal before and how did they do it?

8. What is this goal like, and is there something similar we know more about that we can compare it to?

9. Have we done this or something similar before, and if so how did we do it?

10. How can we do this: Better? Simpler? Faster? Less expensively? In less time? With fewer steps? With fewer people involved?

business. A client called and asked if his firm could develop a specialized network for architects who work together in workgroups. My friend's firm was perfect for the task, so he said he would like to be considered for the work and he committed to providing a proposal by the end of the week. That was his goal.

The only problem was, when the project team got together to develop their ideas, they realized that no one had asked enough questions. They had not determined the exact requirements of the individuals who would be using the system, and they had only a vague idea of the kinds of data to be shared among workgroups.

They had other questions as well, and they needed answers before they could plan their approach and develop the proposal. Fortunately, they had jumped on the project immediately and had the time to make calls and get the required facts.

Before any meeting to discuss goals and plans, I like to create a list of information needed prior to the meeting. I also prepare a list of attendees to make certain essential players are present.

The basic question is this: What facts, figures, analyses, and reference information do you want available when you sit down and develop your tactics and plans to achieve your goals?

Establish *driving* strategies to focus efforts

Actions alone are not sufficient to achieve major goals. You must also have strategies and primary tactics to guide your efforts. The *driving* strategy for a plan is the autopilot control center that keeps you on course no matter what obstacles or conditions you encounter on the way.

When it comes to strategies and tactics, deciding what *not* to do is just as important as deciding what to do. A pivotal success factor in business is the ability of management to maintain the focus of the organization. Strategies are a tool of focus.

Advanced Solutions International, Inc. is a young company that has become successful because the founders of the company decided up front what they would *not* do. Robert Alves, CEO, was quoted in *The Washington Post* as saying, "Recognizing what not to do has been a key element in the growth of the company." The company decided *not* to approach more than one major market at the outset, *not* to write too many variations of its software programs, *not* to get into retail sales, and *not* to create an internal sales force.

Instead, the company targeted only the association market, wrote only a limited number of versions of its programs, built interfaces into programs of others as an alternative to multiple ver-

OUTLINE a plan—
Success strategies, tools, and techniques
191

sions, and utilized a distributor network to sell its products. These clean, crisp strategies have worked well and the company has been successful.

We took a similar singular-focused approach with a company I helped start, Automation Partners, Inc. Our primary focus strategy was creating and servicing turnkey systems for law firms, nothing but law firms. Our chief tactics were to provide a state-of-the-art demonstration facility in several key cities and get entre into targeted law firms by offering a preliminary evaluation at a modest base fee. These strategies and tactics worked well and the company went from zero to more than ten million dollars in revenue in about four years.

The beauty of this focused approach is that every time we were about to stray off course and pursue some tangential market, the strategies held us in place. I remember more than one board meeting where we all reminded each other we had agreed to follow certain strategies and we needed to stick to them.

Core strategies and tactics are needed on a smaller scale as well. For example, we have communication goals and communications strategies in our firm. One of the tactics we use to keep clients aware of our work is a monthly brief for executives. This is not a revolutionary technique, but it works well. It is something we deliberately decided to do in a goal and action-planning session. Before we adopted this simple strategy, our effort to stay in touch with our clients was herky-jerky. Now, once a month we focus on the task at hand and knock out the newsletter. We are more effective and so is our communication.

Strategies and tactics to focus efforts should also be used for personal goals. One tactic I use for spending time with my family is to take periodic weekend trips. Another is to schedule one-on-one time with each of my daughters.

A recurring shortcoming businesses and individuals have in developing action plans is that they don't take time to think in terms of strategies and tactics. Often, instead, the most obvious approach is used. Frequently people do things the "way they have been done in the past." Another common approach is to look around and see what others are doing and duplicate their methods. And then there is the approach where you brainstorm a little, identify a few tasks that will get the job done, and adopt those.

All of these approaches are better than having no strategies at all, but they do not necessarily produce the best possible results.

As with other aspects of *Goal-Driven Management*, the approach to narrowing strategies is to A–B–C a list of possibilities and boil it down to a small number of core elements. These are the ones that get summarized into annual business plans and executive summaries of such plans. These are the ones we should focus on to create systems and habits so the intended actions become internalized at the DNA level and performed throughout the organization on autopilot.

Develop strategies to overcome major obstacles

The creation of an action plan is largely an exercise in problem-solving. That is, you identify obstacles and figure out ways to get over, under, around, or through them.

Bob Grafton, Chairman, Board of Partners, Andersen Worldwide, was one of the first persons I met there and he was a mentor to me through much of my career. Some of the best advice he gave me, repeatedly, was to identify all problems or obstacles immediately. "The only real problems or obstacles we have are the ones we don't get out on the table so we can solve them," is a comment he often makes. It's pretty good advice.

In one situation, the product research and development group of a company my venture capital firm had invested in was consistently behind schedule in new product releases and enhancements. We gathered a group of research and development people to brainstorm the problems they thought were obstacles to getting product innovations and new products out more quickly.

We came up with a long list. The marketing people were not providing enough information about customer needs and preferences. The salespeople were not creating any demand for innovations that had been manufactured, so there was no basis to obtain user feedback. There were too many requests for small change orders with no consequential impact. The approval and testing procedures were laborious and had too many steps.

What is interesting is that none of the problems was believed to be significant by itself. It was the collective effect of all of these that caused bottlenecks and slowdowns to occur. So, once the obstacles were out in the open, the project team one-by-one established action plans to remove or alleviate each and every one. The results they achieved were pretty substantial.

Don't think of obstacles in the aggregate such as "we need to raise capital," "I need to do a better job of managing my time," or "we have got to stay in touch with our customers." This provides a blurred picture that is difficult to focus on.

The more clearly you can see the obstacle, the easier it is to penetrate it. Break big problems into components like the company did in the above situation.

An obstacle I faced in writing this book is that I didn't have the time. The true obstacle, however, was not that I didn't have the time, but that my time was committed to other projects. My task became one of eliminating or deferring each of those other projects (the obstacles) one-by-one to create windows of time when I could concentrate on my thinking and writing.

The only real resource in life is time. Therefore, to accomplish more and to utilize our resource of life to its fullest, we must do whatever we can to shorten the time it takes to identify and overcome obstacles. It is better to read the sign that says the bridge is out before we go down the road. If you speed heedlessly toward the gaping hole, you can do little more than swerve off to the side or crash into the ditch at the last minute.

Ask questions like these:

- What can possibly go wrong?

- Where are we likely to encounter our greatest difficulties?

- Who is going to stand in our way?

- What events or circumstances will we have to overcome?

- What tools and resources will we need?

You need an answer for every significant obstacle you might encounter.

A word of caution—don't talk yourself out of goals because of imaginary obstacles. Don't try to resolve every obstacle in your mind before beginning. That is not the intent. If you try to identify and figure out a solution to every single obstacle before you start, you will never begin. The objective is to be proactive with a plan for overcoming major obstacles, rather than to be reactive with no plan.

Identify all "must do" actions

"Must do" actions are the hammer hits that drive the nails into the wood. They are the essential actions that you must take to achieve results. If they are not taken, the results cannot be achieved.

It is easy to get sidetracked by nonessential activities when developing an action plan. Many ideas will be generated during the process. This is good because one objective is to identify alternative strategies and tactics. But when this is done, we must select those actions that are essential. To make the selection, put everything aside and identify the actions you must take for your goals to be achieved. Look at it this way: What actions are there that failing to take them will jeopardize achieving your goals?

You cannot escape the law of cause and effect. Keep it in

Examples of "must do" actions

- A salesperson *must* make sales calls to get sales results.

- An author *must* put words on paper to get her book written.

- An oil company *must* drill holes in the ground to find oil.

- A student *must* study the course material to achieve an A on the test.

- A man *must* exercise to get in shape.

---

mind. No pain, no gain. No ticket, no admission. No action, no goal achievement.

The biggest reason salespersons underperform is they do not make enough sales calls. If a salesperson does not make sales calls, he or she will not get sales. So, a salesperson's action plans should have sufficient steps that *drive* the making of sales calls.

Similarly, the author must have action plans that *drive* her writing of words; the oil company must have action plans that *drive* the drilling of holes; the student must have action plans that *drive* the studying of material; and the man who wants to get in shape must have action plans that *drive* his exercise.

Ask yourself: What are your "must do" actions? Then write them down on paper and build them into your action plan.

Break big steps into bite-sized segments

Break major action steps into subcomponents. Break subcomponents into time-sequenced parcels that serve as milestones for monitoring and managing progress. One of the keys for success is to force yourself to think through the actual actions that are to be taken by groups, individuals, or yourself on a weekly and then a daily basis.

Once individuals get used to this detailed thinking for developing their action plans, the process is easy and takes little time. But most people are not used to planning completely, so this is not going to be easy at first. There is a learning curve. It takes discipline and practice to get the hang of it.

When I work with individuals in developing action plans, invariably, most of them resist thinking through their plans at the nitty-gritty level. Yet this level of thinking produces the big payoffs. When it comes to identifying better ways of doing things and enhancing performance, detailed thinking saves time and provides for quantum leaps.

Carl, a financial services executive, and Skip, an associate, were developing Skip's *Personal Performance Plan* for the upcoming year. Skip identified one of his goals: to pass two securities exams so he could sell certain equity products. Skip adopted this goal and wrote a step in his action plan: "Obtain required securities licenses."

When Carl reviewed Skip's plan, he probed Skip as to what Skip needed to do, specifically, to get his licenses. During the discussion, Skip identified a number of "must do" steps such as:

- File his applications by a certain date
- Sign up for a course by a certain date
- Request advance study materials from the home office
- Establish a specific studying schedule
- Practice taking the exams

This process caused Skip to realize there was more time and effort required than he had contemplated. Plus, he learned he needed to get in gear and get his applications completed soon because he was on the verge of missing the deadline dates. As a result of thinking through the steps and writing them down,

Skip's understanding and awareness of the requirements increased. Because he moved this data deeper into his mind, down to the DNA level, Skip developed a better plan and he was in a better position to be successful.

Skip realized tremendous benefits from this additional level of planning—and all it took was a five-minute conversation with Carl. There was no big ordeal, no humongous effort required, just a few minutes to stop, think, and write it down.

This is not a unique or isolated case; it is the norm when people take the time to pause and think. The few minutes this takes always saves time and effort in the long run. When bigger goals and actions are considered, this process will take more than a few minutes, but the same proportional payoff will exist. A relatively small effort at the front-end will save substantial time and effort at the back end. More to the point, it increases the odds for success.

An action step spanning a long period of time should be broken into small, manageable segments. At a minimum, break action plans into monthly segments and then break monthly plans into weekly segments. Weekly plans should be broken into daily plans for critical items.

For example, an action step to contact 3,000 new prospects during the year should be restated to "contact 60 new prospects each week." The weekly action should then be broken into "contact 12 prospects per day," or whatever plan is desired.

Besides saving time in the long run and identifying better approaches, a big advantage of detailed action plans is there is no question what must be done Monday morning to make progress toward a goal. Management of others and of yourself is easier when you know in advance what needs to be accomplished.

Affix responsibility for each primary action step

DNA Leadership requires that you identify resource needs and affix responsibilities during the planning phase. This involves people and helps them buy in to the plan at the DNA level. If one of your goals is to solicit the help of other department heads, you could have an action item that states: "Solicit participation on the project at next month's management meeting."

When establishing responsibilities, be certain that one person is responsible for each action item. When two or more people are responsible for a task, no one is responsible.

I don't believe in co-chaired efforts or jointly shared endeavors *unless* the responsibilities are divided and defined so one person is *clearly* responsible for each task and result. For example, GEICO has two presidents: Tony Nicely is the President and Chief Executive Officer of Insurance Operations, and Lou Simpson is the President and Chief Executive Officer of Capital Operations. They share CEO titles and responsibilities, but the division of their areas of management is clear as their titles indicate.

An example of affixing responsibility on a smaller scale is the development of an action plan for installing a contact management software package. One individual might be given the responsibility to identify the packages on the market, and another individual might be assigned the responsibility to train users.

Don't assume people know what is expected of them and will do what is required just because their names appear beside an action step in a plan. Go the extra mile. Discuss the plan with them. Get them to ask questions. Ask them to describe how they will approach tasks they are responsible for. Help them create an *Action Plan Recap* for their tasks. See *Chapter 13* for a discussion of *Action Plan Recaps*.

Establish solid linkage
among interdependent plans

Like the cells in our bodies, all actions in business are interrelated and interdependent to one degree or another.

Consider the effect the introduction of a new or revised product or service has throughout an organization. When Mobil Oil launched its *Friendly Serve* service, there was much more involved than just having the marketing department develop an action plan to produce slogans and television advertising spots. Field operating people had to develop a plan to explain the program to station owners and operators and provide the signs and other resources needed. *Friendly Serve* attendants who would greet customers at the pumps had to be hired and trained. In other words, a coordinated *DNA Leadership* effort was required.

The only way to be certain the actions in one plan are coordinated with the actions of another plan is to inform the persons responsible for each of the plans of the actions in other related plans. This can be accomplished by providing copies of plans to each other and by holding meetings where individuals tell each other what their plans and timetables are. An obstacle in this process is establishing clear and common conventions of communication at a sufficiently detailed level so each interrelated party knows what he or she needs to know about what the other party is doing. *Action Plan Recaps,* discussed in *Chapter 13,* address this issue.

Allow for changes and flexibility

"The best laid plans of mice and men often go astray" is a truism. No plan goes exactly as planned. There will always be new information, obstacles, and events that require consideration as action steps are implemented. This does not mean you should change your plans and actions as each new fact or circumstance is encountered. You should not. Once you have developed a plan, you should doggedly stick to it or you will never get results. That said, in reality you can't know everything you need to know when you develop your plans. Additionally, there is always room to improve. Therefore, you must be firm in pursuing your plans, but open-minded to the possibility of changes and enhancements.

Very few plans are implemented 100% the way they were initially established. This should be provided for in the implementation phase. For example, in the middle of one program for executives, it became clear to the individual running the program that the executives were having difficulty grasping a certain concept. The plan did not include stopping the program for an hour to work on this situation, but that is what the instructor did because that was the right thing to do under the circumstances.

An example on a bigger scale was a company's publication of an updated products brochure that the sales team needed to be effective. The brochure was to be published in March. However, a new product line that had been planned for release in February was behind schedule because a key person in product development had had a personal tragedy in his family. I am for keeping deadlines and sticking to plans, but that was not appropriate here. The company released an inexpensive interim update to meet the immediate needs of the salespeople, and then produced the full-scale brochure six weeks later. This was a reasonable and practical solution.

There is a fine line between allowing for important changes and delays when they are essential and necessary, and becoming lax in adhering to deadlines and plans. On the one hand, you must develop the habit of establishing plans and deadlines and hitting them. Don't be easy on yourself, and don't be quick to move deadlines and change plans on a whim. On the other hand, you must use good common sense. When a change or alteration in plans is necessary, you should make it.

Plan for tangible results fast

The purpose of a plan is to move people to action toward a targeted goal and keep them moving. To be effective, plans must provide for tangible results fast—within several days or a week.

It is difficult to keep people motivated unless they sense progress. When early results are recognized, everyone gets the idea that the pace is brisk and the train has left the station. If they aren't already on it, they had better jump on fast.

When I took over the office I ran at Arthur Andersen, I accelerated a revitalization plan right out of the gate so people *clearly* would get the idea we were going to move fast. My first day we held an operational meeting. The partners and managers participated in discussing past results and thoughts on goals and strategies we should pursue. That first week offices were rearranged. Three new people transferred in. The second week the building's front doors were replaced with Andersen's traditional wooden doors, and new furniture was moved into the conference areas. The third week we had our first client and prospective client seminar followed by a social gathering where we could network and renew relationships. The only way anyone could have misunderstood our pace would be if they were dead or heavily sedated.

Our fast beginning created the critical mass and momentum we needed to give us lift-off and get everyone's DNA transformed into the lean and hungry fabric we needed to have to be successful. During the third week one individual told me he had been skeptical that we were going to remake the office as I had announced during that first-day meeting. "Now, I'm a believer," he said. His DNA had been spliced with mine.

Don't underestimate the power of rapid, tangible progress out of the gate. Early results that people can see establish in their minds the DNA pattern for how things are going to be. CEOs and other leaders, including the President of the United States, often make changes and implement new programs immediately after coming into office. They understand how essential it is to establish a DNA precedent and sense of expectancy.

Making sure of a big, bold beginning with tangible results applies in our personal lives, too. Taking off the first five pounds is an effective way to develop the right attitude and build momentum for staying on a diet and exercise program.

Beginnings are fragile. We must take care to make sure they come off right. Action plans for new endeavors should provide for extra effort and energy at the outset. Make sure people can achieve visible milestones fast. Get individuals used to success early—so they know what it is like and will want to continue.

In addition to *early* successes, structure your plans to provide for *frequent* successes. During the formative stages of a new bank, the CEO gave champagne celebrations every time another million dollars was deposited. Soon the bank was so successful he had to alter his approach to prevent everyone from walking around intoxicated. But early on this was an excellent approach.

Use your plan to establish and maintain momentum

Keep two laws of physics in mind when developing action plans: the principles of critical mass and momentum. Critical mass is the fissionable material needed to establish and sustain a nuclear chain reaction. Momentum is the mass of a body times its velocity.

These laws imply three strategies for action plans. First, to get your plans moving forward on a solid and sustainable basis, you must create and provide the initial critical mass necessary in terms of people and resources. Second, to keep things moving you must continue to provide critical mass. Third, to accelerate progress, you must increase the size of the critical mass.

This is like lighting a fire. Three elements are required: fuel, oxygen, and heat. Without fuel, there is nothing to light. Without oxygen, there is no catalytic aid to the burning process. And if we

The principles of critical mass and momentum

Critical mass is the mass of fissionable material required to establish and sustain a chain reaction in a nuclear reactor.

Momentum is the mass of a body times its velocity.

To get your action plans moving and keep them moving, you must create *critical mass* and maintain *momentum* by providing all the resources needed and by always knowing what to do next.

can't create enough heat (the energy resulting from colliding particles) there won't be sufficient catalytic activity for the fuel to ignite. So, to light a fire we put wood in the fireplace, open the damper to allow oxygen to circulate, and strike a match.

These same concepts apply to action plans, but many people ignore these concepts and fail to achieve their goals as a result. In businesses, for example, critical mass is required before a business can operate effectively. At Arthur Andersen we would not open a full-service office unless we projected it could reach a certain size within three years. We believed we needed a critical mass complement of certain types of personnel to serve clients effectively.

I had plenty of painful experiences learning and appreciating these principles in the venture capital business. The critical mass you need in a new venture comprises product, market, and people. You need the right product, demand for the product in the market, and people who create systems to deliver the product and communicate it to the market. We frequently faced obstacles where products weren't ready when the market demanded them. We had other situations where both the products and the market demand were in place, but our marketing communication programs were not. In these instances we did not meet our goals.

I learned this lesson the hard way: Don't let any one aspect of your business get too far ahead of other components. Don't introduce a product or service until you are ready, willing, and able to tell the market about it and deliver it. Don't announce a program to improve customer service until you can deliver it. Don't acquire contact management software for the salespeople in your company unless you are going to train them on using it.

These principles apply in our personal lives as well. If you want to write a novel, you have to create critical mass. You've got to have the desire, time, ability, and discipline all at the same time. If you want to buy a new home of a certain size, you need to earn a certain level of income and have a certain size down payment.

To apply these principles to action plans, ask yourself this: What are the critical elements required to get things moving and keep them moving?

Always know what to do next and always make sure everyone else knows what to do next. When you don't, you have to stop and start again. Stopping wipes out momentum you have built up. Having to start over takes more energy and effort than keeping things moving. It requires more power for a plane to take off than it does to keep going in the air. It is the same with our pursuit of goals—it's harder to begin again than it is to keep going.

To maintain momentum, take time to outline your action plans step-by-step. This way there is an action step to be looking forward to. Plus, there is an action step just completed that makes you feel good about your progress and propels you.

Begin with a creative brainstorming session

To outline an action plan, begin with a creative brainstorming session. Collaborative brainstorming accomplishes three results: It lets everyone involved see what they and others are thinking; it produces new ideas; and it begins building mental critical mass.

Perhaps brainstorming is not practical in your situation

because you are working on a personal project or don't have anyone to brainstorm with. In that case, try starting with some quiet reflective time, a clear desk, and several sheets of plain white paper. It is amazing how thoughts will flow once you start writing on a blank sheet.

How to brainstorm

Brainstorming can be done anywhere. It works best in a big airy room or outdoors if this is practical. There is something about the interrelationships between space and our thinking processes. Most individuals are more creative and prolific when they have expansive visual and physical surroundings with plenty of cubic thinking space.

Gather a group of people, give them the goal being pursued, and then ask them to provide an oral data dump of thoughts and suggestions for achieving the goal. Record comments as fast as possible on flip charts. Keep the pace brisk and the energy moving. Don't judge ideas or comment on them during the process. That inhibits contributions and stops the flow. Just record ideas as they come. Use the flip charts to summarize ideas into action step alternatives, obstacles, and questions to be addressed.

It is useful to use multiple flip charts or to tape paper to the walls so many ideas can be seen at once. We think at the speed of light. This process is enhanced when we can think and see our thoughts at the same time.

Done correctly, brainstorming is a powerful process. It can produce a large quantity of quality ideas fast. Brainstorming sessions are always worth many times the effort.

Brainstorming is one of the instances in life where one plus one equals more than two. One mind plus one mind makes at least three minds: the mind of the first part; the mind of the second part; and the combined mind of each of the parts.

What to brainstorm

Brainstorm the actions, tasks, and strategies necessary to achieve your goals. Remember, the objective is to create the *best* plan. Don't just look for ideas; press hard for great ideas. Ask questions like these:

How have we done this before?

How can we improve what we did?

Who else has done this?

How did they do it?

How is their approach better than ours?

What is this like?

What can we compare it to?

The 100-Idea approach

One of my favorite techniques is to challenge a brainstorming group to come up with 100 ways of solving a problem or achieving a goal. If we are asked for one or two ideas, this is easy. You don't have to call on your big brain power to generate two ideas. But to produce 100 ideas, you can no longer think the way you had been thinking. You must shift paradigms. When this occurs, the logjam breaks and ideas flow.

A derivation of this is to prepare a list showing various formulas that could produce hypothetical results.

Let's say we want to create a $1,000,000 revenue stream and we are trying to decide what to sell to produce this level of revenues. We could prepare a list showing a range of sales scenarios to generate the revenues. An example is on the next page.

We could then look at the list and ask which of the alternatives we like best. Would we rather try and get one customer for $1,000,000; 1,000 customers for $1,000 each; or something in between? How would our business differ on each level? Which option would be the most difficult? The most lucrative?

How you do your brainstorming and creative thinking is not as important as whether you do it. Make time to brainstorm and

---

100-Idea approach

Sell 1 item for	$1,000,000 each
Sell 2 items for	500,000 each
Sell 4 items for	250,000 each
Sell 5 items for	200,000 each
Sell 8 items for	125,000 each
Sell 10 items for . . . , ...	100,000 each
Sell 25 items for	40,000 each
Sell 40 items for	25,000 each
Sell 50 items for	20,000 each
Sell 100 items for	10,000 each
Sell 1,000 items for	1,000 each

---

think creatively. You will end up with better plans and results than those who don't.

The beginning, middle, and end approach

Sometimes we need to jump start our minds. A useful approach is to define action steps at the beginning, middle, and end. For example, at a session for executives in a professional services business, the group decided that one of its goals was to improve its recruiting and retention results. After they wrote several *laser-clear* goals they were ready to brainstorm the action plans they would pursue. But for some reason the group was not responsive to the facilitator—the brainstorming electricity wasn't plugged in.

So, the facilitator changed things around. He put three flip charts in the front of the room instead of one, and he wrote beginning, middle, and end on the charts. He asked for three participants, one to be the scribe for each chart. Then he asked everyone

to stand while he explained that he wanted them to remain standing and begin shouting out ideas for action steps as fast as possible
for any of the three charts. There was an instant uproar of noise
and commotion as the ideas came firing out.

Write out major assumptions

In developing action plans, it is beneficial to prepare a written
summary of the assumptions, logic, and rationale behind the strategies and actions you have adopted. This narrative provides a tool
for seeing what you are thinking so you can evaluate your logic
and get input from others.

This document-what-you-are-truly-thinking approach is
something I have used for many years in planning businesses and
in helping executives and individuals develop their action plans.
As a venture capitalist reviewing business plans for new ventures,
I was more interested in the underlying assumptions and rationale
than in the projected end results because I could evaluate the
assumptions and reach my own conclusions as to whether they
and the strategies and projected results were realistic.

It is difficult to maintain objectivity when you are developing action plans because you get quickly into the middle of the
forest, so to speak. By stepping back and reviewing your written
assumptions, you can regain a big picture perspective and evaluate
if your assumptions make sense and are consistent.

One of the problems we face is underestimating the time and
resources required to accomplish tasks. We tend to overestimate
how much we or others can actually accomplish. By writing out
your assumptions you can spot flaws in your logic and plans.

I can't begin to guess how many business plans I have seen
where the assumptions were faulty. For example, entrepreneurs
will estimate a 10% or greater response rate on direct mail programs when 1% or less would have been appropriate.

Faulty logic crops up in individual action plans as well. A

young man in the insurance business told me he planned to sell a policy a day, or five policies a week, through one-on-one personal presentations. I asked him what his underlying assumptions were. This is what he had used:

Number of prequalified persons contacted per week . 80
Number of persons who agree to meet 20
Number of persons who buy insurance 5

He explained where he intended to get his 80 prequalified leads per week, the bases for his 1 in 4 success ratio in obtaining a meeting, and the 1 in 4 success ratio in closing. These ratios were based on the results he had been achieving. Without commenting on whether those ratios were realistic or desirable, let me just say they were acceptable assumptions to start off with.

The big fly in the ointment was not the assumptions he listed, but the one he had omitted. Historically he was having "no shows" for 1 out of 4 people who had agreed to meet with him. In other words, if nothing else changed, his math was not going to work. Based on his prior performance and beginning with 80 contacts per week, he was only going to end up with 15 meetings and 3.75 sales on average. He needed to alter his plan to take actions to improve his "kept meeting" ratio, increase the number of contacts he started off with each week, or some combination approach.

Flowchart actions so you can see them

My favorite tool for organizing and displaying tasks is a flowchart that shows each step in sequence in relation to all other steps over time. The flowcharts near the beginnings of *Chapters 10, 14, 17, 20,* and *23* are examples of this technique.

You don't need experience to prepare flowcharts. Just use boxes, circles, lines, and arrows on flip charts or blank sheets of paper to provide a visual overview of your plan.

I was working with the salespeople of a company we had co-founded to determine why we were not achieving our sales goals. During an interactive session in a conference room I asked the salespeople to describe each step in the selling process. As they described their steps, I taped flip chart pages together and prepared a flowchart going halfway around the room.

When I finished the flowchart I stepped back and looked at it. In the middle of the sales process was a box labeled "VAR agreement." I asked Fred, the person who told me to put the box on the chart, what it was. Fred explained that new sales orders required a value added reseller (VAR) agreement to be signed before the sale could be made. He explained that new customers resisted signing the agreements and many refused. Those that finally did sign the agreements took weeks to process them.

I couldn't believe it. Right there on the flowchart was a visual, literal, and obvious bottleneck to our sales. No one had focused on it previously.

Now aware of the problem, we eliminated the VAR agreement requirement *entirely*. Sales orders immediately flowed. I doubt that we would have seen the bottleneck significance of the VAR agreement if we had not prepared the flowchart, yet it had been choking the company to death.

Similar to flowcharting, "storyboarding" is commonly used in the entertainment business for developing movie concepts and in the advertising industry for developing advertising concepts. Pictures depicting action vignettes or scenes are developed and placed on boards so they can easily be moved around to present various scenarios of the movie or advertisement. One of my hobbies is to write screenplays. I work with a storyboard composed of big and small Post-it® notes for the major scenes and sequences within scenes.

Regardless of your preferred approach, visually display your planned actions so you can see your plan and evaluate it.

OUTLINE *a plan*—
Success strategies, tools, and techniques
211

Focus extra attention on beginning and ending

Earlier I mentioned the importance of developing action plans that produce tangible results fast. In addition, the beginning of any effort should be planned carefully to make sure you get started in the right direction. There is a correlation between how you start off and how you will end up. The good starts I have observed have yielded relatively more successes than the weak ones. A good or weak start will result depending on how quickly concrete steps are taken, how fast critical mass is assembled, and how fast tangible results are achieved.

My own preference is to go overboard at the outset, to leave no room for slippage, lack of critical mass, or loss of momentum once lift-off of an action plan has commenced.

One client was implementing GOAL-DRIVEN MANAGE-MENT for the first time. Because this approach was new, a DNA cultural change in the way things were accomplished was necessary. At the outset the implementation team decided to leave nothing to chance when emphasizing the importance of the program. Several steps were taken, including creation and distribution of a corporate video announcing and reinforcing the program; establishment of core leaders to serve in a double-teaming capacity in the field to help managers implement the methodology; and creation of customized study guides and quick reference checklists. They really emphasized a good beginning.

Another time to turn up the burners is when action plans are coming to an end. For some reason we often lose our momentum, drive, and enthusiasm near the end of big projects. This was a problem on many of the financial and consulting projects I have participated in over the years—people on the project had a hard time buttoning up the loose ends. The main effort might be completed, but then it would take 20% more effort to wrap-up the last 5% of the project, thus resulting in an unnecessary 15% overrun. I'm simplifying and generalizing here, but the point is real. Many people can't finish. This may be because they don't have anything on the horizon they are looking forward to; thus they feel they must keep their current project alive. Regardless of the reason, plan on strong finishes when action plans are developed. Make sure the ending steps, deadlines, and milestones are spelled out.

Ask for help and get assistance

Don't overlook the step to stop and think: Who can help me achieve what I want to achieve? Identifying where you can use some help and asking for it is smart. Time is the opponent and results are the goal.

When you ask for help, don't be shy. Think big and ask big. It is best to know in advance what you intend to give in return for what you are asking, but don't let this keep you from asking. Sometimes the persons you are asking for help will come up with their own rewards and motivations for helping you.

In business it has been common to build territorial walls and have a "not invented here" approach with respect to the outside world. Worse than this are the interdepartmental factions with the same approach within some companies. In both situations individuals are reluctant to seek and accept advice or share ideas with others because of "turf" issues or pride of authorship or creativity. If you've got a bone of this mentality in your body, surgically remove it fast.

Except for learning experiences, there should be no pride in having done a job by yourself if you could have done it better, faster, or more economically with assistance or input from others.

Don't wait for help to show up by itself. Ask. People are too busy with their own lives to take time to see what they can do to help you and me with ours. This does not mean people don't care and won't help. They do care and will help. But they are preoccupied. We must break through their present preoccupation, get their attention, and ask.

Establish rewards when plans are adopted

The importance of rewards and incentives was discussed in *Chapter 11*. The best time to establish rewards is when goals are being established and action plans are being developed. It is premature to announce incentives before action plans are finalized because individuals won't know what they are being rewarded for. Individuals must understand the effort expected of them.

Benny was the president of a construction company that was involved in a dispute with a customer. As a result of this dispute, Benny's company was filing a claim to collect additional compensation under its contract. Millions of dollars were at stake.

To get everyone focused on the claim, Benny wrote "Two Cardinal Rules" with a black marker on flip chart paper. He hung the big sheet in the center of the wall behind his desk. His rules were that he was not settling for less than three million dollars, and that he was not waiving the company's rights to any future claims. Here is what his sheet looked like:

Two Cardinal Rules

1. We are not settling for less than $3,000,000.
2. We are not waiving our rights to any future claims.

In addition to writing out his cardinal rules, which were his goals for settling the claim, Benny made it clear that when the claim was settled successfully, he intended to throw a bash so big no one would ever forget it, *and* he was going to sweeten the bonus pool by 10% of the settlement amount.

As negotiations continued in the ensuing weeks, Benny frequently stopped mid-sentence, turned to his cardinal rules on the wall, and said, "What's that say? Rule number one: We are not settling for less than $3,000,000. Rule number two: We are not waiving our rights to any future claims." Then he would turn back to everyone and add, "And when we settle this sucker we're going to have a party you'll never forget, and the Easter Bunny is going to put some golden eggs into your baskets."

It became a ritual, so much so that the people in his office began reciting his cardinal rules with him every time Benny turned around and started to read them.

It worked. Benny achieved both goals, had the party, and provided additional cash bonuses. A key to Benny's success was that he established the rewards when he outlined his plan to win the claim. This was true *DNA Leadership* because Benny emotionally locked the goal, the plan, and the incentives together. The strong DNA bond among these factors proved a winner.

Over the longer term most people are not motivated by tangible rewards or by being pushed. We are all pretty much self-motivated. Leaders must create the DNA within associates, teammates, and employees to achieve a vision through implementing an agreed-upon plan. The real reward is the achievement and recognition for setting out to do something and doing it.

13

Use *Action Plan Recaps* to simplify planning and share know-how

Developing action plans can be one of the most exciting and interesting aspects of goal achievement. This is where you determine how to overcome obstacles and cause results. After selection of a goal, the creation of a plan is where individuals have the greatest opportunity to provide creative input.

One reason individuals don't have action plans is they see the effort of preparing them as a bigger job than it is.

An *Action Plan Recap* is a simple to use, yet powerful management tool for creating and documenting action plans to achieve goals. *Action Plan Recaps* can be used by businesses, teams, and individuals for big, small, short-term, long-term, business, and personal goals.

Action Plan Recaps can also be used for sharing *best practices* and company *know-how* and for facilitating *just-in-time* training.

Techniques for creating and using *Action Plan Recaps* to their full advantage are discussed in this chapter under these headings:

- Benefits of *Action Plan Recaps*

- *Action Plan Recaps*—basic form and content

- Use command language to simplify preparation of *Action Plan Recaps*

- Tips for using *Action Plan Recaps* when pursuing group goals

- How to align action plans and cascade them throughout an organization

- Should *Action Plan Recaps* be used when pursuing individual goals?

- Use an *Action Plan Workbook* to keep track of action plans

- Use *Action Plan Recaps* to create and employ the best practices and methods throughout your company

- Use *Action Plan Recaps* to establish a reference library of company know-how

- Annotate action plans after-the-fact to increase their effectiveness

- Use *Action Plan Recaps* for "just-in-time" training

Benefits of *Action Plan Recaps*

Action Plan Recaps provide several benefits:

1. *Action Plan Recaps* focus your attention and document your plans for specific goals. The recap sheet enables individuals and team members to see their thinking in an easy-to-review format so they can evaluate their plans and ensure that their actions will be effective.

2. *Action Plan Recaps* are a catalyst to completing your thinking. You can't prepare a recap sheet unless you have thought through the required action steps. The *Action Plan Recap* is a check and balance on this part of the process.

3. *Action Plan Recaps* clarify responsibilities and provide a basis for sharing information and coordinating activities. The work force of a company must work together in developing and implementing *plans* that will cause the company's goals to be real-

ized. *Action Plan Recaps* make this possible. Once they are developed, all members of a team should receive copies to guide their personal contributions.

4. *Action Plan Recaps* provide a basis to monitor progress and encourage achievement of milestones.

5. *Action Plan Recaps* can be used to solicit input and help from others. Once individuals or teams document their thinking on a recap sheet, other individuals can review the planned approach and suggest ideas for enhancing it.

Action Plan Recaps—basic form and content

On the top of the next page is a blank *Action Plan Recap* sheet. It can be completed manually or on a computer. The first section of the *Action Plan Recap* is used to record a *laser-clear* statement of the goal to be achieved. The second section is for summarizing the "must do" action steps to be taken. Columns are provided to identify the persons responsible for the action steps and the dates they are to be completed. Additional columns are provided for charting the timetable.

An *Action Plan Recap* is prepared in five steps:

1. **Goal:** Summarize the *end-result* goal to be achieved in the top part of the recap as a *laser-clear* goal statement. It is important for your goal to be on the sheet to focus your attention and remove any uncertainty as to the exact goal you are pursuing.

2. **Action Steps:** Enter the "must do" action steps which represent the *cause* goal to achieve the *end-result* goal. Group these by major task and list them in sequential order to the extent practicable.

3. **Person Responsible:** Enter the name of the person who is to implement each action step. This affixes responsibility.

Illustrative *Action Plan Recap*

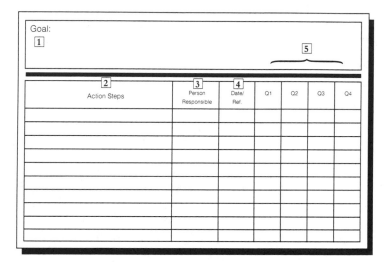

4. **Date/Ref:** Enter the date when the action is to be completed. The "Ref" notation is for "reference." This is used if supporting *Action Plan Recap* sheets provide additional details for the action item.

5. **Q1, Q2, Q3,** and **Q4:** Complete the recap by filling in the cells in these columns or by placing an "X" in them to indicate when the corresponding action item is to be performed. In the illustrative blank form these notations represent the quarters of a year. If an action step is to begin in the second quarter and be completed in the third quarter, the respective cells on the same line as the action step would be filled in or Xed out. These columns can be used in any manner to portray the timeline when tasks will be completed. In some cases it is useful to have twelve columns for the months of the year or five columns for the days of the work week. Do what makes sense for the goal being planned.

Suppose a company has a goal of acquiring and implementing a PC-based contact management software package for tracking customer and prospect data. An action plan for this goal could be developed on an *Action Plan Recap* sheet as shown by the example below.

Illustrative *Action Plan Recap* for acquiring contact management software

Action Steps	Person Responsible	Date/ Ref.	Jan.	Feb.	Mar.	Apr.
Establish system performance criteria	Bob	1/31	■			
Research and evaluate available packages	Bob	1/31	■			
Select a package and install on network	Bob	2/28		■		
Schedule training and train users	Chris	2/28		■		
Load historical data	Bob	3/15			■	
Use for test period and evaluate	Chris	3/31			■	
Document common problems in help files	Chris	3/31			■	

Goal:

Acquire and implement a PC-based contact management system by March 31st.

Use command language to simplify preparation of *Action Plan Recaps*

A technique for simplifying the creation and writing of *Action Plan Recaps* is to use "command language." That is, begin every action step with a command verb that can be executed. Many individuals bog down in writing action steps because they get tangled in their prose. Command language makes it easy.

In the box on the next page are some examples of command language action steps for a goal of establishing a mentoring program for new associates. These steps are not complete and they are provided only to illustrate the command language technique.

Note that each action step begins with an actionable command. It is easy to write in this style. Wordiness and unnecessary

---

**Action steps written
in command language—
Mentoring program for new associates**

(Illustrative steps, not a complete action plan)

Identify mentors

- *Decide* on mentor criteria
- *Schedule* briefing with qualified associates
- *Present* an overview of the program
- *Describe* benefits
- *Ask* for mentor volunteers
- *Screen* and *approve* volunteers

Train mentors and mentees

- *Identify* training objectives
- *Brainstorm* training techniques
- *Outline* the training program
- *Create* case examples and role plays
- *Develop* application aids
- *Draft* training workbooks
- *Review* and *finalize* workbooks
- *Schedule* and *deliver* training

Implement program

- *Receive* mentee applications
- *Match* mentees and mentors

detail are avoided. Give command language a try; I think you'll like it.

Tips for using *Action Plan Recaps* when pursuing group goals

Here are several tips to consider when using *Action Plan Recaps* for pursuing group or team goals:

- Every action step should have the name of the primary person responsible beside it. Tasks can be assigned to subgroups, but to avoid ambiguity and confusion there should be one name only beside each task.

- A firm deadline should be established for every action step. Setting deadlines is important because they drive the flow of tasks. Critical and long-lead items should be moved up on the plan time-wise as far as possible.

- Don't prepare *Action Plan Recaps* and hand them to individuals for implementation. Get people involved in the process of brainstorming and developing the plans—so they buy in to the plan at the DNA level and accept responsibility for *their* action items.

- Don't prepare an *Action Plan Recap* and put it on the shelf. Much of the power and value of an *Action Plan Recap* is realized when it is used during the implementation phase to monitor and drive progress.

How to align action plans and cascade them throughout an organization

The cascading of goals and action plans to create DNA alignment throughout an organization was discussed in *Chapters 1* and *4*. This is a straightforward task using *Action Plan Recap* sheets. Simply establish a coding hierarchy that provides for the indexing and cross-referencing of one *Action Plan Recap* to another.

**Jones Insurance Agency
Cascading Effect**

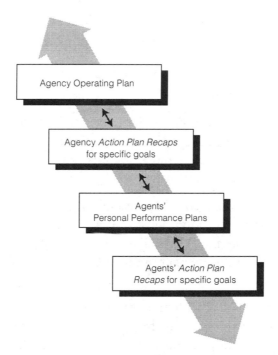

Remember the cascading concept mentioned in *Chapter 4* for the Jones Insurance Agency? The graphic above shows how the cascading would take place. At the top level is the agency operating plan. The agency operating plan is supported by *Action Plan Recaps* for the supporting goal categories in the operating plan. The supporting goal categories are supported by the collective *Personal Performance Plans* of individual agents. And the agents' *Personal Performance Plans* are supported by their *Action Plan Recap* sheets for their supporting goal categories. The agency operating plan and the *Personal Performance Plans* of the individual agents constitute summary *Action Plan Recaps*—there is complete alignment and linkage throughout.

Should *Action Plan Recaps* be used when pursuing individual goals?

Is it necessary to prepare an *Action Plan Recap* when pursuing individual goals? Yes. Anytime you want to achieve a goal, pause, think about the action steps required, and jot them down so you can see your action plan and imprint it into your thinking. Although a special form is not required, I recommend the *Action Plan Recap* sheet format so you acquire good goal-setting habits. Consistency is important.

In *Chapter 11* Danielle and Gary both had a plan for how they were going to get a job. Gary had nothing on paper and he had no timetable to manage his progress. In contrast, Danielle had a written plan with deadlines and a timetable. Gary did not achieve his goal. Danielle did.

The objective of preparing an *Action Plan Recap* sheet is *not* to mechanically complete a form. Many companies and individuals I have worked with like and use the *Action Plan Recap* format. But the precise format is not what is important. What *is* important is application of the concepts. Your goal, your "must do" action steps, and your deadline for each action step should be reduced to writing. This requires you to think things through so you can write down your thoughts. Once acquired as a habit, this thinking-writing process will boost results in achieving goals—whether they are business, career, or personal goals.

Use an *Action Plan Workbook* to keep track of action plans

An *Action Plan Workbook* is an important tool for goal achievement. A *Goals Journal* is the heart of the goal-setting and achieving process, and an *Action Plan Workbook* can be considered the brains or the planning-and-thinking end of the effort. These two tools are core elements of the main control panels in *DNA Leadership through* GOAL-DRIVEN MANAGEMENT.

Many people use a personal planner or appointment calendar to organize themselves and schedule their time. Nearly everyone keeps some form of to-do list—on 3 × 5 cards, memo pads, or Post-It® notes stuck on the wall. These are helpful aids for managing time and keeping appointments. But none of these lay out a step-by-step blueprint to get you from where you are now to where you want to be in terms of your goals.

Even in strategic and business planning efforts of big organizations, there often is a missing link between where those doing the planning want to go and the action steps representing who, what, when, where, and how they are going to get there. There is a break in the DNA chain of communication.

The primary tool for bridging the gap between goals and actions to achieve them is an *Action Plan Workbook*. This workbook is your overall plan. It contains *Action Plan Recap* sheets summarizing in sequential order the key actions you must take to achieve your goals.

Businesses should have an overall *Action Plan Workbook* and each employee should have an associate's portion of the workbook. Individuals should set up a personal *Action Plan Workbook* with separate sections for each type of goal. The workbook for the business is essentially its *Operating Plan*. For individuals it is their *Personal Performance Plan*.

The nature and extent of the workbook will vary depending on the circumstances and preferences of the individuals. The fundamental concept is that every organization and every person in the organization should have a documented series of action plans that are being, or will be, implemented to achieve the goals that have been selected for current pursuit.

Create a new *Action Plan Workbook* each year and update it throughout the year. Organize the workbook with a summary up front followed by sections for functional areas or areas of responsibility.

Use *Action Plan Recaps* to create and employ the best practices and methods throughout your company

Paradoxically, one of the biggest obstacles to business growth is also one of the biggest opportunities in business today: the capturing, transferring, and sharing of corporate know-how—knowledge capital management.

A prerequisite to sustainable long-term growth is to optimize an organization's leverage. This is possible through transferring and sharing critical information, knowledge, and experience with respect to core competencies and operational methods, processes, and techniques. This means more than collecting information and making it available. It means putting information into context, making individuals and workgroups aware of the information, and then showing them, through training, demonstration, and by example, how to use the company's intellectual knowledge and operational *know-how* to enhance their personal contributions toward company goals.

A benefit of using *Action Plan Recaps* as a standard convention throughout an organization is that they provide a readily available library of operating know-how that is easily transferrable from one individual or team to others.

In *Chapter 8* I described how a manager, Tony, was faced with the task of hiring a delivery supervisor for the first time. Tony was an experienced professional, but he had never had to recruit and hire anyone.

Several executives with Tony's company, who had plenty of experience in recruiting and hiring, were in the program that day. They brainstormed with Tony to develop action steps he should take to recruit and hire a delivery supervisor. Tony jotted down their thoughts and ideas for action steps on a flip chart. Then he and the others grouped these ideas into an *Action Plan Recap* that enumerated in chronological order all of the major steps Tony needed to take to hire a delivery supervisor.

The recap specified twenty-two action steps covering everything from writing the newspaper advertisement, to arranging and conducting screening interviews, to performing background checks, to making an offer.

Tony's completed *Action Plan Recap* constituted a documented summary of the company's best available *know-how* on how to recruit and hire a delivery supervisor. Unfortunately, Tony was the only person in the company who had this information documented and available in an easy-to-understand-and-follow format. Tony had no way to share his know-how with others and those who needed the information had no way of knowing where to find it. No one except the people in the room that day even knew the information existed.

What will happen the next time a manager like Tony has to figure out for the first time how to hire a delivery supervisor? They'll do what Tony would have done. They'll create the wheel on their own, or else they'll ask one or two people for a few ideas and then they'll create the wheel on their own. No matter how you look at it, they won't be able to take advantage of Tony's newfound know-how.

Tony's example is a small part of the bigger picture of how an organization works. The greatest asset of a company is the quality of its people. Next is the collective know-how of those people. Know-how is what enables a company to achieve its goals and exploit its competitive advantages. The more a company can share and increase its know-how, the greater the advantage it will have in the market and the greater its growth, profits, and customer satisfaction will be.

Action Plan Recap sheets can become one of the most impor-

tant strategic assets in any organization if they are shared throughout and continually improved.

Use *Action Plan Recaps* to establish a reference library of company know-how

Companies need a reliable system for sharing techniques and
action plans. *Action Plan Recaps* are a simple tool for doing just
that: standardizing, communicating, and sharing helpful information for how to set and pursue similar goals. The collective *Action
Plan Recaps* of an organization can become a dynamic reference
tool to reinforce a company's DNA fabric and to assist employees
in fulfilling their responsibilities. They could be stored and shared
as an electronic library to enhance the know-how within an organization. They would be invaluable to a new person or anyone
else pursuing one of those goals for the first time. In an instant, an
employee could determine the steps others have gone through to
achieve a goal the employee now is faced with—like writing an
advertisement, hiring a new employee, creating an incentive plan,
penetrating a new market, giving a speech, developing a brochure, or releasing a new product.

The beauty of this is that if everyone adopts the same *Action
Plan Recap* format to document plans to pursue goals, then the cost
of establishing and maintaining this valuable library of know-how
will be modest in comparison to the enormity of the benefits.

Suppose your company develops a practice of compiling and
maintaining an "annotated" electronic reference library of *Action
Plan Recaps* used throughout the organization to pursue goals—all
goals in all shapes and sizes. This would be a library of *Action Plan
Recaps* actually used to achieve goals, with annotations to describe
the results and recommended changes to improve performance.

Let's say your manager in San Jose wants to create a marketing campaign to sell services to accountants and attorneys. With
the collective efforts of co-workers this manager does an excellent

job of defining her goals and subgoals. She then develops a step-by-step *Action Plan Recap* to penetrate the targeted market, implements the plan, and it is successful. That's step one.

Now suppose a manager in Boston decides to pursue a similar goal for his market. With access to the goals documentation and the *Action Plan Recap* of the manager in San Jose, the manager in Boston has a tremendous advantage. He doesn't have to re-create the wheel. He begins with a running start. He uses the San Jose manager's *Action Plan Recap* as a foundation and then develops and uses an improved plan in Boston—also with successful results. That is step two.

For the next step, a third manager, from Tampa, decides to go after the same targeted market segments, accountants and attorneys, in Florida. Since this person has both the San Jose and the Boston *Action Plan Recaps* available, she is in an even better position than her colleagues to start developing her plan—because she can select the best strategies and tactics from both plans and still create her own innovations. Rather than re-creating the wheel, the manager from Tampa begins with the "wheels" already created and improves them to develop her own enhanced approach.

This approach can be used for any goal and its related *Action Plan Recap* sheet, regardless of the nature of the goal and the length or complexity of the recap sheets. It could be used for sharing know-how for something as routine as the protocols for sending and receiving e-mail, to something as complex as installing equipment at a customer's site. There is a right and wrong way to do everything and it makes sense to tell people the right way at the outset.

Annotate action plans after-the-fact
to increase their effectiveness

We needed to develop an action plan for a one-day seminar for the local chapter of a professional association I belong to. As chairperson, I gathered a small group and brainstormed the project in a computer lab where individuals typed in anonymous input to questions posed by a facilitator. We used this to create a half dozen action plans for the goals we had, such as ticket sales, product sales, program content, sponsor participation, and take-home materials. Then we implemented the plans and produced a successful event.

After the program several of us met to discuss what worked well and what didn't work so well. We prepared a summary of recommended changes in the action steps for the following year. The next year's chairperson had the benefit of both our plan and our recommended changes. From a national association perspective it would have been advantageous to provide other chapters access to this plan so they could see what we did and use what works best for them. This was several years ago, and cost factors prohibited reproducing the plan and distributing it, but now with the Internet this would be a real possibility.

The most powerful ways to learn anything are by demonstration and actual experience. *Action Plan Recaps* that have been used to achieve results are metaphors that demonstrate actual experiences—they show you *how it is done*. *Action Plan Recaps* portray how knowledge was actually applied to achieve a result. *That* is the critical information individuals need to leverage their capabilities and fulfill their potential.

Imagine what it would be like to electronically post an *Action Plan Recap* sheet throughout an organization and ask for constructive input on it. Or think about the possibilities of developing these on a virtual group basis. The quality of the plans could be enhanced instantly through input from people across the organization.

To the person with the vision to see the opportunities for using *Action Plan Recaps*, the potential is enormous.

Use *Action Plan Recaps* for "just-in-time" training

"Just-in-time" training is a current topic in the training arena. The theory offers a solid conceptual advantage: Rather than train individuals on skills they might forget or never use, provide the training when they need it. Just-in-time training is not always appropriate because at times there are desired direct and indirect benefits to training that go beyond the content being delivered.

But in many situations, particularly when dealing with vast amounts of rapidly changing information, technical material, precise specifications, and other similar situations, just-in-time training offers many advantages. Pop-up computer help files for training on software programs make sense. It also makes sense for professional and technical practitioners to be able to look up information on procedures and processes on a real-time basis. Perhaps a doctor or nurse wants to review the recommended steps for performing a surgical procedure or an accountant wants to know how to file an extension for an estate tax return.

Some of the hurdles to just-in-time training include:

- Capturing the right information from the right people at the right time

- Storing and organizing information and putting it in context so the information becomes knowledge and individuals can find and use it quickly

- Updating information and knowledge on a real-time or other timely basis

- Making information and knowledge easily accessible

A continually updated library of electronically stored *Action Plan Recap* sheets could be used to create a data base for just-in-time training. It could address and overcome each of the above hurdles to the training.

Here is an example. Gina is pursuing a career in retailing and she is being groomed to be the assistant manager of the jewelry store where she works. One of Gina's new responsibilities is to do nightly "closings" where she is responsible for: making the night deposit; alarming the security system; taking the register readings and resetting the registers; and locking the doors. For each of these tasks the manager has told Gina what needs to be done and then done it with her once or twice to make sure she understands. I believe in hands-on training, but wouldn't it be better for Gina also to have a listing of each of the tasks to be completed, so she can refer to the list if she needs to?

If Gina's store manager had access to an *Action Plan Recap* for "closing a store" on the company's intranet, her manager could bring up the *Action Plan Recap,* go over it with Gina, and Gina would then have the advantage of high quality just-in-time training. This is a modern day, easy-to-implement approach to the documentation of policies, procedures, and systems, and to the training of associates in their use.

14

OUTLINE a plan— Implementation action steps

O*UTLINE a plan* is the second of the five keys in *GOAL-DRIVEN MANAGEMENT*. The objective is to develop a plan that is *action-driven*.

This is accomplished by determining the obstacles to be overcome and then identifying, selecting, and organizing a series of action steps into a workable plan that will overcome the obstacles and achieve the desired results.

These activities are summarized into the five major action steps to *OUTLINE a plan* which are listed below and illustrated in the flowchart on the next page.

1. Identify obstacles and possible actions

2. Create a preliminary *Action Plan Recap*

3. Establish rewards and incentives

4. Develop a final *Action Plan Recap*

5. Communicate and imprint the plan

OUTLINE a plan
Implementation action steps

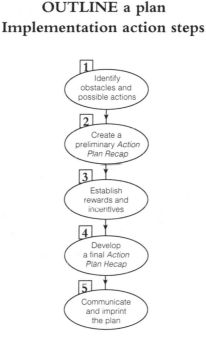

Step 1:
Identify obstacles and possible actions

The two questions that drive the development of action plans are: What are the obstacles to achieving the goal? and What must be done to overcome the obstacles?

To develop an action plan, first identify potential obstacles that may be encountered. Then identify possible action steps to overcome these obstacles. Brainstorming and other techniques to identify obstacles and action steps are discussed in *Chapter 12.*

At this point in the process, the objective is not to select the best possible action steps to achieve your goals; it is to get a data dump of all the possible actions you can think of so you can evaluate, pick, and choose from among them. If you are working on a group goal, brainstorm possible action steps with the group. In addition to action steps, identify strategies that can drive the actions in your plan. Strategies are also discussed in *Chapter 12*. The end result of this step is a flip chart or worksheets listing possible obstacles, actions, and strategies.

Step 2:
Create a preliminary *Action Plan Recap*

An action plan comprises a series of detailed steps and tactics that, taken together, will result in the realization of a goal. *Action Plan Recap* sheets described in *Chapter 13* are summaries of these action steps and tactics.

To prepare a preliminary *Action Plan Recap*, evaluate the action steps and tactics identified in Step 1 and determine which of them are "must do" actions required for achieving your goal. Select the tactics and actions that are the most appropriate and that will best achieve the results desired. Arrange these steps in a logical order and assign preliminary deadlines and preliminary responsibility for each step. Summarize the information on an *Action Plan Recap* sheet.

Step 3:
Establish rewards and incentives

Determine the reward, incentive, recognition, and celebration programs that will be used to motivate yourself and others to implement the overall plan. Rewards and incentives, discussed in *Chapters 9, 11,* and *12*, are important for business and individual goals. Incorporate the reward and incentive programs you select into your preliminary *Action Plan Recap*.

Step 4:
Develop a final *Action Plan Recap*

Develop a final *Action Plan Recap* by obtaining input and evaluating your preliminary *Action Plan Recap* with the individuals who must implement it and others you feel appropriate. Discuss the preliminary action steps and overall timetable. Obtain commitments from individuals to do their part. Affix responsibilities by entering final assignments and final deadlines on the *Action Plan Recap.* When completed, this becomes the final *Action Plan Recap* for managing and monitoring progress.

Action Plan Recap sheets are valuable tools *only* if you use them. Don't file these sheets and forget about them. Keep a copy of your *Action Plan Recaps* for each of your major goals handy on your desk and in eyesight. Review the sheets frequently to reorient yourself. Update the information during periodic reviews. Use the sheets as a basis for decisions with team members.

Step 5:
Communicate and imprint the plan

Communicate and imprint the plan and the related rewards and incentives for implementing it and achieving the goals. Imprinting was discussed in *Chapter 8.*

The adage, "out of sight, out of mind," is alive and well when it comes to maintaining your awareness and focus on action plans you have created. The world is full of distractions, and we are all susceptible to many of them. You must go overboard when communicating and imprinting your plans and timetables, even if you are communicating just with yourself.

To communicate plans so they are imprinted on an autopilot basis, use a variety of techniques centered around the advertising principle reach and repeat. Reach the right people with the right message, and repeat it often so they absorb it.

Don't assume anybody knows or understands anything. When it comes to big goals, leave nothing to chance. Create wall charts. Establish recital rituals and routines. Do whatever you must to drive in the plan and the reward messages permanently.

It is not enough to complete an action plan. The plan should be used and referred to often until the action steps become rote— because they are built into the fabric of a company's DNA. CEOs and other leaders must imprint goals and rewards into the minds

of the people responsible for achieving the goals. Successful leaders make sure that individuals understand that it is in their personal
best interest to achieve a given goal, and not just in the company's
interest. *That* is *DNA Leadership.*

15

ACT on your plan—
Fundamental principles

The third key in *GOAL-DRIVEN MANAGEMENT* is A. A stands for *ACT on your plan*. The fundamental principles pertaining to acting on your plan are discussed in this chapter under the following headings:

- "It is more important to do the right things than it is to do things right"

- The most important progress is *daily* progress

- *Act* and you will receive

- Action powers the *thought→action→thought* engine

- To win you must cross the finish line

- A good plan poorly executed is a poor plan

- Concentration creates the power that produces results

"It is more important to do the right things than it is to do things right"

That's what Peter Drucker said years ago. His advice was solid then and it still is today. If you want to achieve your goals, you must take the *right* actions at the *right* time. The overall strategy for achieving your goals is not just staying busy with "feel good" activities; it is implementing your action plans that spell out the critical steps leading to your success.

During the 1957 World Series, Yogi Berra, the catcher for the New York Yankees, noticed how Hank Aaron grasped the bat. Berra said, "Turn it around, so you can see the trademark." But Aaron, ignoring Berra and keeping his eye on the pitcher's mound, said, "Didn't come up here to read. Came up here to hit." Achieving your goals is the same: You must do what you came to do. You must take the actions that will produce results. You must do the right thing.

My venture capital firm invested in a company that developed a technical product for use on networks. The company's founders were engineers bent on perfecting and enhancing the product even though they already had a good working prototype. The company ran out of money while a competing firm brought to market an easy-to-use, stripped down version of the same product. The company we invested in was sold for cents on the dollar. The right thing to do in this case was to produce a "useable but improvable" product. This is essentially what Netscape did with its Internet browser. Rather than continually tinkering to remove all possible imperfections and make it right, Netscape got its product to market and then continued to improve it. Netscape did the right thing—it staked out a key position in the market.

Pat owns a travel agency. One of his goals is to acquire new accounts in a unique market segment. Pat established this as his top priority, and he developed a written action plan with a series of strategies to penetrate the new market. That was three months ago. Pat knows what he must do: he must implement his plan. Unfortunately, he has been so busy "fighting fires" he just hasn't been able to make progress. "I'm too busy," Pat says. "Maybe next month." Pat is not working on the right thing. He is spending all of his time solving yesterday's problems, so he has made no progress toward building his future. Pat should figure out other ways to deal with the fires. He may be using the fires as an excuse to put off addressing his top goal.

Betsy is a college faculty member whose goal is to be tenured. To be considered for tenure, she must complete her doctoral work. Betsy knows this, and her main goal is to complete her dissertation. But instead of concentrating on completing her degree requirements, she allows herself to get diverted and involved as a faculty adviser in student activities. Betsy feels good about her work with the students because it is important work and she is superb at it. But Betsy is working on the wrong thing. In so doing, she is jeopardizing her career on a long-term basis. The right thing for Betsy to be working on right now is her degree.

The dividing line between individuals and businesses who achieve their goals and those who do not is this: Those who achieve their goals take the actions they must take and those who don't, don't.

It takes discipline to get up every day and implement a plan step-by-step until it is completed. Working the plan isn't always the fun thing to do. But working the plan is the right thing to do, and it is what you must do if you desire success.

Long-term results often demand sacrifices. As Muhammad Ali put it, "I hated every minute of the training, but I said suffer now and live the rest of your life a champion."

The most important progress is *daily* progress

Daily progress is the most important progress you must make towards your goals. One of the great secrets of success is getting down to the day, and then to the hour, when it comes to taking actions toward your goals.

Daily progress drives weekly progress; weekly progress drives monthly progress; monthly progress drives yearly progress; and yearly progress drives lifetime achievement. So all progress depends on *daily* progress. If you are making *daily* progress, you are making progress. If you aren't, you aren't.

What is the most important goal in your life right now? Stop and think for a minute and answer that question in your mind. Now, after you know what your most important goal is right now, let me ask you this: What actions did you take yesterday and today to move closer to your goal? And what actions do you intend to take tomorrow to move closer still?

Within the preceding paragraph is the secret to success many people never seem to get. Here it is: Work toward your important goals every single day.

The extent of your daily efforts and progress is not as important as whether you make the effort. If every day you make an effort toward your goals, you can maintain momentum. But, if you let a day or two go by your momentum disappears and your hot trail of pursuit cools.

Among my major goals are a number of specific writing projects. Although projects change from time to time, I do everything I can to write something every day. I am hard-nosed about this. There are not more than five days in a year when I don't write at least a few hundred words; most days I write considerably more. Day-by-day, step-by-step, I am achieving my goals.

The three critical questions you should always be able to answer are: What did I do yesterday to make progress toward my major goals? What am I going to do today to make progress toward my major goals? and What will I do tomorrow to make progress toward my major goals?

The most important choice you make each day is how you will spend yourself. Tomorrow, will you spend yourself working toward your goals, or will you allow yourself to be spent working only toward someone else's goals? This choice establishes who you are, what you are all about, and what you will become.

Nevertheless, many people wake up and essentially say: "Here I am, day, take me." They enter each new day without a

---

> ## Three critical questions
>
> 1. What did I do yesterday to make progress toward my major goals?
>
> 2. What am I going to do today to make progress toward my major goals?
>
> 3. What will I do tomorrow to make progress toward my major goals?

---

plan or any preconceived notion of how they will spend the next twenty-four hours of themselves. They go to work, come home, eat, watch television, go to bed, and then get up and start the humdrum process all over again. This is a reactive approach to life, and it is debilitating.

Don't leave your days to chance. Get proactive. Be in charge of yourself. Become *goal-driven*. Have a daily action plan to follow in working toward your goals. Don't wake up and say "Here I am, day, take me." Wake up each day and say, "Here I am, day, and this is what I am going to accomplish!"

Act and you will receive

Ask and you will receive is not enough. You must also *act*. We all must sooner or later face the realization that we are responsible for ourselves. I am responsible for me and for achieving my goals. You are responsible for you and for achieving your goals.

This is fundamental. But many people seem to have a blind spot that prevents them from fully facing up to this reality. They act as if someone is going to take care of them and their business or as if something is going to "turn up" in their favor.

This invisible dependency is understandable. We grew up with someone taking care of us. But now we are grown up. As adults we should not remain reliant on others to initiate actions on our behalf. Business owners and business leaders *certainly* shouldn't do so.

Does this mean we shouldn't seek and accept help from friends, family members, and associates? Absolutely not. No one makes it on their own. No business is successful because of one individual. But we each must take responsibility for our actions and for achieving our goals.

Some individuals have interpreted the concept of "ask and you will receive" literally. Ask and you will receive is not a stand-alone maxim. It is overly simplistic to think that asking is all that is required.

When Dr. Norman Vincent Peale wrote *The Power of Positive Thinking,* he did not imply that positive thinking is *all* that is required. Before he passed away, Dr. Peale wrote me about my book, *Soar . . . If You Dare®* and said I was a "benefactor to my readers" not just because I "told them what they could become," but also because I "showed them *how.*" *How* means to act.

In addition to thinking positively and receiving by asking, you must also ACT to receive.

Action powers the
thought→action→thought engine

Taking actions to achieve your goals accomplishes two things.

First, an action, even in the wrong direction, will move you closer to your goals than no action at all. If nothing else, an action produces a data point you can use to evaluate how well you are proceeding. A data point can tell you that you are headed in the wrong direction and provide the information you need to get back on track, or it can confirm that you are on the right path and spur you forward.

Second, actions reinforce your commitment to, and your desire for, your goals. First you think; then you act. When you act, you reinforce what you are thinking. When your actions move you closer to what you want, this revitalizes your energy. As the following diagram illustrates, momentum toward your goals is built on a continuous spiraling circle, where each thought reinforces each action and each action reinforces each thought. Action, itself, creates power and momentum toward your goals.

The Power Cycle
for producing momentum

To win you must cross the finish line

To win the race the horse must cross the finish line. Almost there doesn't count.

That's the way it is with the implementation of action plans and the realization of goals. You must cross the finish line by persisting until the deeds are done and the goal is achieved.

Many individuals simply cannot complete a project or task. They get almost there, but not quite.

A manager who worked for me always delivered the reports the client needed. He was a great guy and everyone liked him. But he couldn't finish. He never took care of billings to the client and other housekeeping items without a great deal of effort on my part to follow-up and make sure the loose ends were tied down. He had what I call "a lot of baggage to carry," and as a result he had limited career opportunities. I was sorry to see him go, but I would have been sorrier to see him stay.

In another business endeavor, a real go-getter salesman generated more quality leads than any other two salespersons. But he could never get around to getting the proposals prepared and submitted to make the sales. He, too, had to go.

The same problem can affect companies. A firm announced its intentions to improve customer service. The announcement described how the firm intended to spend time with customers to determine their needs and how to serve them better. I was one of their customers, and I got the notice. But I never heard anything from them except the announcement telling me their new, great service was coming. I'm still waiting for that new, great service.

To win the race and capture the prize, you must cross the finish line. This means completing all steps in the plan.

A good plan poorly executed is a poor plan

Occasionally Dan and I have looked back over our experiences as venture capitalists and the investments we made in new companies. We have compared the companies that met or exceeded our expectations with those that performed below our expectations, either because they were not successful in the final analysis or because they were less successful than we thought they could have or should have been.

Many factors contribute to the differences in success of the companies, but implementation, or lack of implementation, of the agreed upon action plans is clearly one of the most significant.

It does no good to spend time and money crafting a watertight plan if the management team is not disciplined in implementing it and does not create systems and procedures to drive the daily actions required by the plan. In other words, a good plan poorly executed is not a good plan, it is a poor plan.

Implementing a plan is not easy. You can't just write a plan, hand it to associates, and hope for the best. It takes organization, follow-up, attention to detail, and day-in, day-out persistence. These are the requirements for success. There is no easy way.

Concentration creates the power that produces results

Our power of concentration is released when we gather our physical and mental resources and focus them on a common objective. When a magnifying glass focuses sunlight toward a single spot on paper, the paper ignites. But until this focusing, this concentration of energy, has occurred, nothing happens.

Unfortunately, many businesses are run without ever applying the power of concentration and most people live their lives without benefiting from its power.

The problem is that when we get wrapped up doing a little bit of everything, we tend to do not a lot of anything—and this leads to mediocrity and minimal accomplishments.

The power of concentration can be applied in all aspects of our businesses and our lives. When it comes to implementing your action plans to achieve your goals, the three areas that provide the biggest payoffs are concentration on the goals you are pursuing, your daily activities, and your expenditures of time.

First, you must limit the number of major goals you pursue at any one time. Anyone who tries to pursue too many goals will end up achieving none of them. Second, you must limit your daily actions to those "must do" steps that will actually bring you closer to achieving your goals—while forgoing actions that will not. And third, you must concentrate your time expenditures during the day.

In *Chapter 16* several suggestions are provided to increase daily concentration. Two of these, using *Thunderbolts* and *Chunking your time,* are extremely effective for managing personal time and boosting daily performance, and in turn, long-term results.

16

ACT on your plan— Success strategies, tools, and techniques

The success strategies, tools, and techniques for acting on your plan to achieve your goals are discussed in this chapter under the following headings:

- Begin strong and never, never, never quit
- Build your primary actions into daily habits
- Make hay while the sun shines in the morning
- Get yourself a hideaway
- Help people follow their plans
- Break big action steps into small action steps
- Use *Thunderbolts* to drive daily progress
- *Chunk your time* for increased effectiveness
- Don't move deadlines; change your actions
- Address obstacles head-on
- Use this "secret" technique to overcome obstacles

Begin strong and never, never, never quit

Determination and persistence are prerequisites for success. Winston Churchill summed up this idea best when he said: "Never, never, never quit."

There is a difference between determination and persistence, and both are required. According to *Webster's*, determination is the "act of deciding definitely" or the "power or habit of deciding definitely and firmly."

We become determined when we know exactly what our goal is, when we have placed a high priority on it and know why we want it, and when we make a definite decision to achieve it.

To reinforce your determination you should begin strongly and boldly as though you mean it and are to be taken seriously.

History is full of examples where bold actions were the firepower needed to bolster determination. Perhaps the greatest bolstering act in American history was the signing of the Declaration of Independence. There was no turning back after that document was signed.

When Kathy Clark co-founded Landmark Systems Corporation, one of her early actions was to print an expensive brochure. She then got on a plane to Europe to find prospective distributors for her company's products. Kathy says her company spent far more on the brochure and the trip than was probably prudent at the time, but in hindsight, the expensive brochure bolstered her self-confidence during her meetings, and the trip to Europe was a turning point in the company's growth. She made a bold move and it worked.

Being persistent is different from being bold and deliberate. Checking *Webster's* again, persistence is when you "stand firm" and continue to "go on resolutely or stubbornly in spite of opposition." It is not easy to hang in when the going gets tough and the future looks bleak, but that is what you must do if you want success. You must persist; you must not quit.

At times in my career I have been beaten down to the point of nearly throwing in the towel, but I persisted and I am glad I did. A major setback was when I was nominated for partner at Arthur Andersen but was not admitted that year because there was a "numbers problem." This meant that too many people had been nominated for partner that year. If they were all admitted, it would dilute partners' earnings too much. So, I was one of those cutback. I could have given up and quit, and the thought did cross my mind for a nanosecond. But I had decided to become a partner and I wasn't going to give up on my goal that easily. So I sucked in my pride, put my nose back to the grindstone, made partner the next year, and in two years was running an office.

Unfortunately, some people do quit; often on the verge of success. One reason is they underestimate the size, difficulty, or required duration of their efforts before they begin. This can be mitigated by making a realistic assessment of the action steps, time, and effort required and facing up to the reality that it usually takes longer and costs more than you estimate at the outset. It is not possible to know all you need to know when you begin.

Another reason people quit is that they lose their "invisible support system." That is, their internally generated enthusiasm wanes, and their belief in themselves begins to pale. I've never met anyone who didn't need periodic recharging, stroking, and nourishment of their self-confidence. There are many ways to keep your belief in yourself and your fire of enthusiasm stoked. First, you must avoid negative and limitation-thinking people. Second, you must feed yourself a constant mental diet of positive reinforcement and encouragement through the information you read, hear, and see. Third, you must continually get new exposures to people, events, and places. Fourth, you must find periodically some quiet time to think and reflect. And fifth, you must make time to be with those you love and to live at least a little bit by the Epicurean philosophy of "eat, drink, and be merry, for tomorrow we shall die."

Build your primary actions into daily habits

Judy and Ron were promoted to district manager at the same time. Both had aspirations to be promoted to regional manager. They had similar talents, abilities, and experiences. In three years Judy received a big raise and her desired promotion. Ron was passed over for promotion and left two years later. What difference caused Judy to be successful and Ron to leave?

It was their *daily* habits. From the get-go in her new position Judy got into the daily habit of calling several of the managers in her district to touch base and see if they needed her assistance. She set up a follow-up system to monitor projects her managers had committed to, and she spent a lot of her time in the field with her managers. Judy planned her days and worked her plans.

Ron, in contrast, never established a routine for visiting his units and monitoring the results his managers were achieving. Their results were inconsistent and usually below budget.

The difference between Judy and Ron was their daily habits. Judy acquired good daily habits for staying close to her managers and operating units; Ron did not.

To turn any action into a habit requires discipline and persistence for extended periods. You probably have heard it takes twenty-one days to exchange an old habit for a new one. In my own experience, twenty-one days isn't enough time to acquire the new habit. For me, twenty-one days is just for openers. It has taken me months to permanently internalize some good habits I wanted to acquire.

Instead of relying on a twenty-one day approach, commit to doing whatever it takes for as long as it takes until you create and acquire the daily habits you desire.

A technique that works well in creating new habits is to develop and follow a ritual. I have several rituals for the work I do. When I write, I clear everything off nearby surfaces in my office and I get a fresh cup of coffee before I begin. When I am going to be on the telephone interviewing people or making callbacks, I establish a block of time and make as many calls as I can in a specified time slot. Before I hold a meeting, I develop a checklist of the outcomes I want to have.

Two groups famous for their rituals are athletes and entertainers. Many athletes practice in the same manner in the same clothes every day. Before they compete they go through mini-rituals to psyche themselves. Performers do the same.

Rituals are useful because they usually involve many of your senses and they trigger a series of patterns that allows you to perform on autopilot.

Make hay while the sun shines in the morning

One of the best habits I have developed over the years is to start work a little earlier than most everyone else. I get more done in the two hours before others arrive than I do in four hours when the office is humming away. This is partly because my mind is fresh in the morning and not weighted down with the day's activities; but the bigger reason is the quiet and absence of the hustle and bustle of telephones, conversations in the hallway, and other minor distractions.

Many successful people arrive early. The president of one of the fastest-growing high technology companies in Virginia has a breakfast meeting every morning around seven. I know a few real early birds who arrive at the office around five in the morning. That's too early for me, because I often write late into the evening, but those predawn risers swear by their habit.

Mary Kay Ash, Chairman Emeritus and founder of Mary Kay Cosmetics, Inc., is very time-conscious. She formed the *Five O'Clock Club* in her organization. It's easy to join: Just get up and get going at five o'clock. Ash explains in her book, *Mary Kay,* that she formed the *Five O'Clock Club* after hearing someone remark that three early risings a week make an extra day in the week.

Writes Ash: "If I get up at five o'clock for three mornings, I'll have an eight-day week. That's what I've been looking for!"

If you would like an extra productivity boost several days a week, give Mary Kay's *Five O'Clock Club* a try.

Get yourself a hideaway

We are plugged in everywhere—by telephone, cellular phone, facsimile, e-mail, the Internet, beeper, cable, and now by satellite through direct broadcast television. Like attached tentacles, each of these plug-ins is constantly pulling us outward and draining us of physical and mental energy.

We can't totally unplug ourselves from the world and I am not recommending that we try. But it is important to pause periodically and look inward to our own thoughts. Many individuals are so interconnected and networked that they don't spend a single hour a month, let alone a week, in quiet time thinking about their goals, themselves, and their plans. But they should.

Get yourself a hideaway—someplace you can retreat from your busy world and reflect on what you have been doing, where you are going, and how you are going to get there. Danielle Steel, one of the most prolific authors of our time, claims she is able to be so productive only because she has a place to concentrate that she calls her hideaway. Steel's hideaway happens to be an entire separate residence, but most of us can do with smaller solutions.

The hideaway you use doesn't have to be devoid of human activity, but it should be someplace where you feel truly unplugged. Some individuals go for long walks in the woods. Others spend a weekend at the beach. Sometimes when traveling I will have a cup of coffee in a quiet cafe or off in a corner of a grand hotel lobby. Where and how you hide and get away is not important; doing it is.

Help people follow their plans

One aspect of leadership we sometimes forget is leaders must help people achieve their goals. This means leaders must guide and motivate individuals toward the implementation and completion of their action plans. This can be accomplished in many ways, but it certainly includes giving input into the content of action plans; offering advice, guidance, and encouragement during implementation of action plans; and measuring and monitoring progress as plans are being completed. See the related topics, *Achieving alignment through the creation and management of doer-centered goals,* in *Chapter 1;* and *Create a goal-achievement environment* and *Demand excellence and press individuals to fullfil their potential* in *Chapter 27.*

Break big action steps into small action steps

Failure to begin causes failure to achieve goals. More people fail to achieve their goals because they never begin than for any other reason. Hockey pro Wayne Gretzky puts it this way: "You miss 100% of the shots you never take."

How many goals have you *failed* to achieve after you earnestly pursued them? Most individuals cannot compile a large list.

But how many goals or dreams have you not realized because you never pursued them? The list is longer there. Many of us have discovered a book in the bookstore that is "our book," the one we were going to write, but didn't. And how many new products have you found advertised in the paper that were "your ideas" not acted upon? Software for keeping personal accounting records and telephone calling cards are just two of many ideas I had *years* before someone else made them a reality. And I've got others I know someone is right now acting on, while I am not.

People don't know where to begin to convert their ideas and dreams into goals to be pursued. Or they see the task as overwhelming. Those two reasons prevent a lot of good beginnings.

An important first task when developing an action plan is to analyze major, multi-faceted efforts and break them into small, easily defined *workable* steps. This is essential.

Start by defining a beginning, a middle, and an end, or a phase one, phase two, and phase three. "Beginnings" and "phase ones" then can be further broken into their own beginnings, middles, and ends until you wind up with beginning steps small enough that you can actually accomplish them.

We have to form the critical mass necessary to begin building momentum. This is done one step, one small piece at a time.

In a company I co-founded we established an initial marketing action step of contacting and prequalifying 1,000 targeted firms. This sounded like a formidable task, so we broke it into a palatable undertaking of calling on six companies per day; that's less than one an hour. By the end of the first week we had achieved 3% of our goal. By the end of the first month we were 12% of the way there. In six months we had achieved 78% of our goal. And in less than nine months we were finished and off onto the next goal.

The same concept applies in personal situations. Let's say you have a goal of reading twenty-four books the next year. This could sound overwhelming, and it may be difficult to figure out how to begin. Instead of twenty-four books in a year, let's say your goal is to read twenty pages a day. Does that sound more reasonable? At an average book length of 300 pages, if you read twenty pages a day, in a year's time you will have read twenty-four books. In addition to providing a smaller, less onerous action segment to work on, with an action step expressed as twenty pages a day, you now have a basis for creating a daily ritual or habit.

Use *Thunderbolts* to drive daily progress

I have read many accounts of a story where one man received advice from another man that was so valuable he paid the man $25,000 for it. The first rendition I read related that the man who paid the $25,000 was Andrew Carnegie and the man he paid it to was Charles Schwab, who worked for him. I've also read it was actually Schwab who paid the money to an efficiency expert named Ivy Lee. And, I've read the amount paid was $65,000. I don't know who paid what to whom. But I know this: The advice provided was worth whatever price was paid.

The advice is simple. Every day before you leave the office prepare a list of the five most important items you need to complete the next day. Then come in the next day and work your list. Begin by working on the first item until it is completed as far as possible. Then go on to the second item and complete it as far as possible. Follow this process until you have completed all items on your list as far as they can possibly be completed.

Mary Kay Ash wrote about this technique and the story involving Ivy Lee and Charles Schwab in her book, *Mary Kay*. She wrote that Schwab paid Lee $35,000. Mary Kay adopted the technique and attributes much of her success to it. She writes (paraphrased): "I have continued making that $35,000 list every single day of my life—it became my mechanism for keeping on track."

I have used this technique for more than twenty-five years. Of all the techniques I have tried, used, read about, or heard about for enhancing personal productivity and effectiveness on a daily basis, this is one of the two most important and valuable techniques that exists.

I call this my *Thunderbolt* technique. It's named after a quote from Mark Twain: "Thunder is good, thunder is impressive, but lightning does the work." A thunderbolt is "a single discharge of lightning with an accompanying clap of thunder"—the best of both powerful forces.

Thunderbolts are daily action items toward major goals. An example of a *Thunderbolt* card is shown on the next page. The box on the next page contains four steps for creating your daily *Thunderbolt* list.

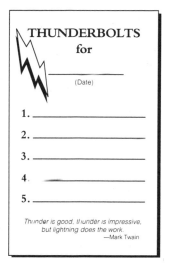

THUNDERBOLTS
for

_____
(Date)

1. _____

2. _____

3. _____

4. _____

5. _____

Thunder is good, thunder is impressive,
but lightning does the work.
—Mark Twain

Instructions for preparing a *Thunderbolt* list

1. Before you go home from work each day or before you retire for the evening, make a list of the five most important "must do" actions you have to complete the next day. These are your *Thunderbolts*. Write your *Thunderbolts* in priority order on a single card or sheet of paper with the most important *Thunderbolt* first. Highlight those items that pertain to your major goals.

2. After writing your *Thunderbolt* list, take a couple of minutes and think through the implementation of each item on the list. Visualize yourself completing each *Thunderbolt*. Excellent times to do this are before leaving the office or before retiring.

3. First thing the next morning, begin immediately to work on your *Thunderbolt* list, in order. Complete the first *Thunderbolt* as far as you can before moving on to the second one. Complete as much of the second *Thunderbolt* as you can before moving on to the third one, and so on. As you complete a *Thunderbolt* cross through it.

4. At the end of the day, take out a new card or sheet of paper and repeat the process.

Thunderbolt tips

Prepare your list the day before: A list of *Thunderbolts* must be prepared before leaving the office or before retiring for the evening. Individuals who use this technique, but prepare their list of *Thunderbolts* in the morning instead of the day before, will not get the same results. Like the missing ingredient in a secret recipe, this aspect of the technique is paramount. People who prepare daily lists in the morning are more susceptible to distractions because until they have a plan, they have nothing to draw their focus. Once you are distracted, it is very hard to get back on track, particularly if you have no plan to get back on track to.

Another advantage of preparing your *Thunderbolt* lists the day before is that your mind will work all night long on the items you identify. You then begin the next day already mentally in gear to take the required actions.

Use a special card: Enter daily *Thunderbolts* on a special card called *Thunderbolts* as illustrated. Having a single, special card emphasizes the importance of the items and concentrates your attention.

Visualize your actions: In thinking through the implementation of your *Thunderbolts* the day before, imagine yourself completing the action steps. Actually visualize what you will be doing and what the surroundings will look like when you do it. This doesn't have to be a major effort, but visualization is an important step and should not be omitted. Visualization clicks on your autopilot switch for the next day. A minute or two of thoughtful reflection and visualization is all that is required. It will work wonders.

Cross off completed items: Crossing through a *Thunderbolt* when it is completed is a trivial act, but it reinforces action from having achieved results and is a mini-reward in and of itself. It is a thrill at times to cross a *Thunderbolt* off your list.

Keep your list visible: Keep your *Thunderbolt* list on your desk or in eyesight during the day so it serves as a constant reminder of your plan for the day. Concentrate as much time as you can on the items on your list without taking time for any interruptions that you can avoid or defer.

Highlight major goal *Thunderbolts*: Each day when you write out your *Thunderbolt* list, highlight those *Thunderbolts* that correlate to the major goals you are pursuing. This little step is rarely taken by most individuals, but it makes all the difference in the world.

By highlighting the items that correlate to your major goals, you are focusing on whether or not you are making daily progress. It is easy to lose sight of the fact that days and weeks are going by without making discernible progress toward major goals. This easy highlighting technique keeps you from fooling yourself by sharpening your awareness. If nothing is highlighted, you aren't moving forward toward your goals, are you?

Adopt a daily *Thunderbolt* **habit:** The *Thunderbolt* technique is simple and easy to use. To get long-term benefit, it must be acquired as a daily habit on a lifelong basis. Saturdays and Sundays excluded, I have prepared a *Thunderbolt* list every day for as long as I can remember; for more than twenty-five years. I don't recall how long it took me to develop this habit, but whatever time it took, it was worth it.

Chunk your time **for increased effectiveness**

The other of the two most valuable techniques responsible for my personal results is to *chunk your time*. I first heard the word "chunk" used in reference to time more than twenty-five years ago in a Peter Drucker training tape on time management. Drucker believed, as I do, that one of the problems we face in maintaining our effectiveness to achieve our goals is our failure to focus on one thing long enough. One of Drucker's recommendations was to spend time in *chunks*, instead of small drabs and dribbles.

This is the most important advice I have ever received for

managing my own personal effectiveness and for achieving my personal and business goals. Let me repeat that because it is so critical: Drucker's advice, to spend time in "chunks," instead of drabs and dribbles, is the most important advice I have ever received for managing my effectiveness and for achieving my goals.

A chunk of time is a *one-hour uninterrupted* segment *at a minimum*. There is something special about a one-hour segment. An hour seems to be the time necessary to form mental critical mass. Your mind takes ten minutes to clear everything you had been thinking so you can give your full attention to a new matter. Then, you concentrate for thirty to forty minutes. When you become aware the hour is soon to be up, you begin to lose your attention span. So within an hour chunk, you actually have only thirty to forty-five minutes of in-depth concentration.

This in-depth concentration is required to produce breakthrough results. You can't make mental or physical progress in drabs and dribbles.

Every great inventor, artisan, entrepreneur, business leader, or other accomplished person I ever met spends substantial portions of their day in chunks of an hour or more. This doesn't mean they go from one one-hour chunk to another throughout the entire day, but much of their day, perhaps half of most days, is spent in uninterrupted chunks.

In many companies I have invested in, some of the greatest breakthroughs were realized when software or other engineers were working alone in the quiet of the night, *chunking their time.*

The chunking-time technique produces the power of concentration because it crowds out unwanted interruptions. When we want to concentrate and really get something done in our office, we use our custom-printed doorknob hangers that say "Please do not disturb, I'm chunking my time." We call these door hangers CTAs or "Chunking Time Activators." It's amazing how much more I get done with a CTA hanging outside my door than without one. It is also amazing how much more others in our office get done when I respect their need to have chunks of time to do their work. People are happiest when they are permitted time to do a good job.

Note that the one-hour chunk of time is intended to be *uninterrupted*. Even the slightest interruption can break your concentration, and you may never regain the thought you were just about to have. Keep meetings with others uninterrupted as well.

Chunking time with managers, team members, and associates is a powerful management technique. If you are going to conduct a performance review with someone you are grooming for promotion, don't try to cram it into a half hour. Spend an hour with the individual and make it an uninterrupted hour. If you have never done this before, you will be pleased with the results.

Time chunking is also effective in personal performance. When my youngest daughter was in high school, I observed her studying for an exam in ten-to-fifteen minute drabs, in between telephone calls, trips to the kitchen for a snack, and other assorted interruptions. Over a week's time, she had gotten nowhere to speak of. Then one Saturday, I insisted she sit down and study in three uninterrupted one and one-half hour chunks, all in the same day—one in the morning, one at midday, and one in the evening. Even she was surprised with the results—when she was done studying in those three chunks, she was done! She took the exam and got a good grade. Why? Because she concentrated.

And by all means *chunk your time* with your family members and friends. A friend recommended I chunk time individually with my two daughters years ago, and I began having one-on-one "dates" with each of them. The first time I did this was with my youngest daughter when she was twelve. She wore a pretty new dress, and we went to a fancy restaurant. I went in with my twelve year old little girl and came out with a friend I had never really known in many ways. It was a great evening in my life and I highly recommend it. I've continued my time chunking with both daughters ever since.

Don't move deadlines; change your actions

Serena, a student in a college class I taught, called at 3:00 P.M. to ask if she could have an extension on her final paper that was due at 7:00 P.M. that evening. She had been caught out of town in the worst winter storm we had had in decades. Serena was distraught because she knew my rule that to get an "A" for the semester, her final had to be turned in on time.

I thought about Serena's request for several minutes and then denied it. I knew this was harsh, but I thought it was the right decision. I reminded Serena that she had known for more than ten weeks when the paper was due and said I was holding every other student in the class to the same standard, no exceptions. I told her I thought she was an "A" person, but if she wanted an "A" in the course, her paper was due at 7:00 P.M.

"Isn't there anything I can do?" Serena pleaded.

"Yes," I said. "Start writing."

At precisely 7:00 P.M. that evening Serena popped into the classroom, on time, with her final paper in hand. I read it that evening, and it was one of the two best papers in the class.

When we had a graduation dinner for the class, Serena came up and gave me a hug. "I'll never forget you, Jim Ball," she said. "I'll never forget how you taught me what I could do under pressure if I would just get started and apply myself."

Instead of moving the deadlines for any goals you may not be achieving, first adjust the actions you are taking. Sadly, the most common approach when goals are not being achieved is to change the goal or move the deadline. Not only does this delay and endanger achievement of your goals, it also establishes a dangerous pattern you may never be able to break.

We often are too easy on ourselves and on others. But to tolerate mediocrity is the worst thing a leader can do. Once goals are established, we should be demanding of ourselves and others, and we should act as aggressively as we can toward achieving our goals. If you aren't getting the results you want, don't change your goals; change your actions.

Address obstacles head-on

No matter how great your plans are, you sometimes will encounter obstacles that will stop you in your tracks. This is to be expected. Obstacles are a part of life. But obstacles should be only temporary hurdles. They should not be permanent deterrents from your goals.

When you encounter obstacles the questions are: What are you going to do about them? Are you going to let them slow you down or block you from achieving your goals? Are you going to bull your way forward and press through until you get breakthrough? Or are you going to pause, reflect on the obstacles and your present plans, and then revise and refine your plans and move forward again from there?

You have heard the phrase, "when the going gets tough, the tough get going." This is good advice for goal achievement. You will never achieve your stretch goals if you lay down your tools and quit at the first sign of trouble or difficulty. To get results, you must persist and persevere.

But sheer force and determination will not always win out over obstacles. Sometimes a better strategy or plan is needed because the one you have adopted isn't going to work.

Individuals often have difficulty seeing the need for a new plan because they have integrated their present plan so completely into their minds that they are mentally blind to new possibilities.

A four-step approach for overcoming obstacles is: (1) quantify and specify in writing the obstacles you are encountering; (2) review your existing plan to determine if your planned actions are being taken; (3) determine why your planned actions aren't working; and (4) get fresh input on the approach you are taking.

1. Quantify and specify the obstacles you are encoun-

Four steps to overcome obstacles

1. Quantify and specify in writing the obstacles you are encountering so that you can "see" them.

2. Review your existing plan to determine if your planned actions are being taken.

3. Determine why your planned actions aren't working.

4. Get fresh input on the approach you are taking.

---

tering: Writing a description of obstacles and then reading it *aloud* goes a long way toward putting obstacles in their proper perspective. We often tend to exaggerate the significance of obstacles and problems. When you define them they become less onerous.

Another advantage of writing out obstacles is that you have a basis to get input and assistance. An entrepreneur I know asks his key people to provide him with a brief weekly report of their major goals and progress toward them. At the end of their reports, they write a thumbnail sketch of any obstacles they are encountering and whether they need help overcoming them. This is a smart technique for developing people and promoting teamwork.

2. Review your existing plan: In many instances, individuals aren't following the action plans they developed. If this is the case, a new plan is *not* needed; what is needed is more discipline in following the agreed upon plan.

Sometimes individuals act too quickly to develop new plans. Constantly changing approaches can be debilitating in organizations. When it occurs, people become resistant to change and innovation. "Another fine approach" is their tongue-in-cheek comment. Follow preconceived plans long enough to give them a chance to work. Suppose a golf pro offers a tip or two to improve your golf swing. You try it two or three times and your drive gets worse, not better. What should you do? Should you abandon the pro's tips and go back to what you had been doing, or should you first check to make sure you are implementing the tips properly?

3. Determine why your planned actions aren't working: Don't be bitten by the *du jour*-approach-to-management bug. Don't be too quick to abandon what you have been doing and adopt the next new idea that comes down the pike.

A six-member sales team was not achieving its sales goals. First, the sales manager tried enforcing the number of calls his people were supposed to be making. When this didn't cause an instant increase in sales, he started tinkering with spot bonus programs for a month. That didn't work, so he tried offering price reductions to customers. He never did look into the quality of the calls the salespeople were making. Who were they calling? What were they saying when they called? How did they follow up? This, it turned out, was the core of the problem—they were not executing the plan very well.

4. Get fresh input for the approach you are taking: This simple step can yield great results. Once your brain locks onto a pattern of thinking, it is hard to break out of that pattern and identify new approaches. You can get fresh input by asking for input from others, or you can get yourself some new exposure—by reading new material, changing your environment, and so on. In addition, you can jolt yourself out of mental ruts by using the special technique discussed in the next section.

Use this "secret" technique to overcome obstacles

I was working with the top salespeople in a large homebuilding company to identify fresh ideas for improving the company's products and sales approach. We decided to brainstorm. I asked Bart, one of the company's best and most experienced salespeople, to give me a couple of ideas to start the process.

Bart was a hulk of a man sitting in the back row. He folded

his arms and leaned back, tipping his front chair legs up a few inches. He didn't say a word, and I sensed that he was annoyed that I had put him on the spot. That was not my intention; in fact, I thought Bart was going to be the biggest participant in the group. Nonetheless, he wasn't a happy camper. Several moments of silence passed and finally I broke it. "Come on, Bart," I said. "Just start us off with one idea."

Bart leaned further back from me and cleared his throat. "Jim, let me explain something," he said. "I'm a commissioned salesman. I make more money if I sell more units. Don't you think if I had a good idea to sell more houses I would already have made it known?"

The room turned stone silent. I turned away from Bart and took several paces toward the front of the room while I pondered the situation. Then I eased around and walked back to Bart. "Bart," I said, "I know you would tell us all your ideas. I'm not questioning that. But what if I gave you a million dollars just to provide us with one or two more ideas to improve our products or our selling techniques? Couldn't you give me just two ideas for a million dollars?"

Bart frowned, indicating he was a little perplexed by my new tactic. "A million dollars for just two ideas," I said again. Then I repeated it once more. "Bart, what if I gave you a million dollars for just two ideas?"

By now, everyone was looking at Bart. Bart shifted in his chair. "A million bucks? For two ideas?" he said.

"A million bucks," I said. "Tax free."

Bart smiled and unfolded his arms. He brought his chair down and leaned forward on the table. Then he began: "Well the first thing I would do is . . . ." Bart went on and gave us a half dozen good ideas to improve the products and increase sales. He had the ideas all along; he was mentally blocked from releasing them.

The technique I used with Bart can be used in any situation

to get "out of the box" you are trapped in mentally. I call the technique *Genie Power* because it can be used in so many situations to grant seemingly impossible wishes—like it did with Bart.

When you or someone you know encounters an obstacle you can't figure your way out of, use *Genie Power.* First, restate and acknowledge the obstacle you are encountering. Next, begin with "what if" or "just suppose" and then *postulate* an incentive. Then press for ideas.

How to create *Genie Power* to think out of the box

First, restate and acknowledge the obstacle you are encountering. This is a critical step because our minds will not begin to move into a new direction if we think the present circumstances are being ignored or overlooked.

Next, begin with "what if" or "just suppose" and then *postulate* an incentive or the introduction of something that does not exist or is not being done.

Then press yourself or others to come up with a number of ideas to answer the question.

With Bart, first I restated where we were by acknowledging that I knew he would have provided any ideas he had. This way he knew I understood where he was. If I had not done this, Bart would not have cooperated because I was not where he was mentally. To use *Genie Power,* you must always begin from where people already are if you want to move them in a new direction.

Postulation, the technique in the second step, is a method where you advance a hypothesis based on an essential new presupposition. This approach is used in mathematics to generate fresh perspectives for problem solving. I postulated when I said to Bart, "What if I gave you a million dollars?"

Postulation is not brainstorming; it is more powerful. In brainstorming, individuals generate all the ideas they can think of, but brainstorming does not require a new presupposition.

In using the *Genie Power* technique, the introduction of a presupposition forces your mind to make a paradigm shift. This provides you with a fresh perspective and gets you on a positive new track. After several repetitions of "What if I gave you a million dollars . . . ," Bart finally bought into the "game." When he did, he made a visible physical change. He relaxed, leaned forward, and began thinking on a whole new path. He was a different person.

There are many ways to introduce this technique. My two favorites are "*What if I gave you a million dollars . . .*" and "*Just Suppose . . .*" Here are some examples of introductory phrases using the *Just Suppose* approach.

- Just suppose you were the president of the company, what would you do then?

- Just suppose you could have all the resources you needed, what would you ask for?

- Just suppose you were able to get an extension of time, how much time would you want and what would you do with the extra time?

Interestingly, the presupposition you insert doesn't have to be real or even realistic. Individuals will go along and start thinking on a new path just by having the mental possibility introduced. The objective of this technique is not to produce an immediate new idea or approach. Rather, the objective is to break the existing pattern of thought—to get you out of the mental rut you are in, so you can develop fresh ideas. Give *Genie Power* a try. It works magic.

17

ACT on your plan—
Implementation action
steps

ACT *on your plan* is the third key in *GOAL-DRIVEN MANAGEMENT*. The objective is to take daily actions toward your goals that are *results-driven.*

To do this, break your overall action plan into weekly and daily action plans. Be persistent. Implement your action plans so that tangible results are realized daily. Monitor the progress of your actions every day and every week.

The four major action steps to *ACT on your plan* are listed below and illustrated in the flowchart on the next page. These steps flow from one to the other continually until goals are achieved.

1. Prepare a weekly *Action Plan Recap* sheet

2. Prepare daily *Thunderbolt* lists

3. Implement daily *Thunderbolts*

4. Review weekly results and adjust plans

ACT on your plan
Implementation action steps

Step 1:
Prepare a weekly *Action Plan Recap* sheet

Don't let a week go by without a plan. Planning doesn't have to take long. With a plan, each week brings you closer to your goals. Without that regular, weekly plan you accomplish less toward your goals than you could.

Each week is a mini-planning opportunity to act, evaluate progress, get back on track if necessary, and recharge. Take some time *before* Monday morning and reflect on where you have been and where you want to go. Pay particular attention to what you want to accomplish for the upcoming week.

Friday is the natural time to plan for matters that pertain to your career or business, but Saturday or Sunday is fine, too—just be sure to be ready *before* Monday. People who do not plan their weeks beforehand get a slow start on Monday mornings. Those who have a plan in hand before Monday get a jump on progress.

Planning a week doesn't take a lot of time and isn't difficult. Fifteen minutes to a half hour is all that is required. This is a small investment, and the return is great.

Do your monthly, weekly, and daily planning in a quiet place where you won't be interrupted. If you are going to use your office, let the telephone go to voice mail and ask co-workers to leave you alone.

To begin the process, break your annual *Action Plan Recaps* into *Action Plan Recaps* for each month.

On Friday, think through the "must do" actions you have to take the upcoming week to make the desired progress toward your goals. Identify obstacles that will sidetrack you and decide how to avoid, defer, or eliminate them. Think about how much you can accomplish in the week and what you could do to accomplish more. Establish goals for the week.

Jot down your major goals and planned activities onto an *Action Plan Recap* sheet for the upcoming week. This should include a *laser-clear* statement of each major goal for the week and a list of all "must do" action steps required to complete these goals. Often I add my other major tasks to my weekly recap so I have only one place to review what I am doing during that week.

The action steps on my *Action Plan Recap* for the past week included these items:

- Finish chapters 16 and 17 of this book
- Get information to trademark attorney
- Complete interviews for upcoming programs
- Meet with Jennifer and Greg to plan upcoming programs
- Finalize software licensing agreements
- Update marketing plan to reflect revised strategy

Only the first two entries on the list above relate to major goals. The other items are important, but I first listed those that related to the major goals I am pursuing currently; that is, finishing this book and securing trademark protection for certain assets in our business.

I had a number of less significant business and personal items on my running "to do" list for the week, but none of them was important enough to be summarized on my basic plan.

To make sure I worked my plan, I cleared the decks and made way for progress. I blocked out 2½ days completely for writing; I scheduled time with Jennifer and Greg; and I put away everything in my office that I would not be working on during the week.

Because planning on a weekly basis is something I learned to do years ago, it comes as naturally to me as walking down the street. But this kind of planning takes some getting used to before it sets in as a habit. Once acquired, though, this habit serves its master for life.

Step 2:
Prepare daily *Thunderbolt* lists

Thunderbolts are the top four or five major actions you intend to accomplish for a given day. At the daily level your actions have become your goals and vice-versa. The concept of *Thunderbolts* is discussed in *Chapter 16*. You should prepare your *Thunderbolt* list the day before the items are to be accomplished. Preparing a list the morning the items are to be accomplished is not as powerful as preparing it the day before. Also, it is important to take a few minutes and visualize completion of the tasks the day before. This focuses your brain on the tasks ahead.

Keep the list short. Include only major items to be accomplished. Write the items in the order you will perform them.

Step 3:
Implement daily *Thunderbolts*

Now is the time to act.

Start the day and work your *Thunderbolt* list—this is your daily plan. Complete the first item on the list as far as you can before moving on to the next item, and so on down the list. *Chunk your time,* and fend off nonessential interruptions and distractions.

Take a mid-morning, lunchtime, and a mid-afternoon check to evaluate how you are doing. If you find yourself off track, pull yourself back on.

The goal is to manage yourself and spend the day as you want to spend it—according to your daily plans—not the way others would have you spend it.

At the conclusion of the day, record activities, progress, obstacles, and significant events in your *Daily Journal*.

Step 4:
Review weekly results and adjust plans

Review the results you are realizing or not realizing daily and then again weekly. Adjust your plans to get back on track as appropriate. It is also important to review progress monthly, quarterly, and annually. These reviews are discussed under the concept of learning from your progress, in *Chapters 18, 19* and *20*.

18

**LEARN from
your progress—
Fundamental principles**

The fourth key in *GOAL-DRIVEN MANAGEMENT* is L. L stands
for *LEARN from your progress*. The fundamental principles pertaining to learning from your progress are discussed in this chapter
under the following headings:

- Learning is how you navigate to your goals

- Learning must be timely

- Continual improvement provides the edge for success

- The best way to improve performance is to involve the
  people doing the work

- Awareness is the key to the lock on learning

- Learning must be fast because changes must be fast

- The first step toward improving performance is
  measuring performance

- You can't learn anything from experiences you're not
  having

- It is better to crawl out of the desert alone than to try to
  drag a dead camel with you

Learning is how you navigate to your goals

Bill Lishman, a reclusive sculptor, adopted a gaggle of geese in Canada, flew with them in an ultralight airplane, and taught them to migrate to Airlie, Virginia, a country town near my home.

In *Father Goose*, Lishman's book about this experience, he relates that birds use many systems to migrate. "Birds are doing much more than simply orienting in the proper direction, for they often do not proceed toward their goal in anything like a straight line," Lishman writes. "Thus, they are actually navigating, keeping track of where they are in relation to where they want to head. And given the extreme fidelity of many birds, like geese, to the same bend of river or nest site year after year, they must be navigating with extreme precision."

Businesses and we, as individuals, are like Lishman's geese when it comes to pursuit of our goals. We, too, often do not proceed toward our goals in anything like a straight line. We, too, must navigate. We, too, must keep track of where we are in relation to where we want to be. We, too, must establish systems to stay on track.

The importance of always beginning from where you are when you establish goals was discussed in *Chapter 8*. There I also described how to specify exactly where you want to be through *laser-clear* goal statements. The final piece of the puzzle to enable your navigation is to know *on an ongoing basis* where you are in relation to where you want to be.

This isn't just knowing physically where you are in relation to where you want to be; it's also knowing how you're doing in the process. You must evaluate whether the actions you are taking are going to produce the results you desire.

Therefore, to navigate successfully toward your goals you must evaluate not only where you are, but also the rate and nature of your progress. Then you can determine whether you should be tweaking your approach or changing courses completely. One of the keys to success is to learn from the progress you have been making. Regardless of the actions you have taken or the results you have achieved, it is always progress if you take the time to learn from it.

Just as DNA is built into every cell in your body and is essential to your existence, in *DNA Leadership* the processes for learning and navigating must be built into your business and into your personal life. This isn't something you should do once a quarter, once a month, or even once a day. Learning and navigating must be continuous because the environment you are in is continuously changing. Like birds that migrate at night using the stars to guide them, you must collect numerous data points and you must identify markers to guide yourself.

Learning must be timely

An obstacle businesses and individuals face is not knowing how they are doing on a real-time basis. Without information in the right form and context so you are aware of it, it is easy to fool yourself into thinking you are making progress when you are not.

Individual sales performance and customer service and satisfaction are two areas where businesses frequently fool themselves because they have not measured results.

The worst question you can ask a salesperson is "How's it going?"—because the canned answer will be "great," "good," "okay," or something similar. Problem is, what does great, good, or okay mean? Instead of asking "How's it going?" ask to see the call list and the order book—those measurements will *tell* you how it's going.

Kevin, an investment advisor, asked what he could do to increase his closing ratio on new accounts. I asked Kevin if he could send me lists of his calls and sales for the past two weeks—analyzed to show the name, age, occupation, sex, income, and other information for each person contacted, and whether they purchased or not. Kevin said it would take him awhile to compile this information because it was not readily available. "Not readily available" means Kevin didn't know the results of his calls or why he was successful in making his sales.

Not knowing your exact prospecting results is like shooting at a target at 100 yards and not checking to see how close your shots are coming to the bull's-eye. The only way to improve performance is to get a snapshot of current performance *and interpret it.* How can Kevin improve his sales performance unless he knows how he's doing and what he's doing? Could a golf pro give you advice without watching your swing?

An executive mentioned that his company had successfully responded to 1,200 calls on its customer service lines in the past month. I asked if anyone had prepared an analysis of the calls to determine their nature and cause and the response. No one had. What's more, no one was even capturing the information. What do you think are the chances of reducing the number of calls on this company's customer service lines? I'd go with your bet if it's close to zero.

In many environments, feedback information must be better than fast; it must be real-time to affect performance. MBNA, the credit card company, has a number of performance factors that are measured and monitored on close to a real-time basis throughout the day. This sharp attention to detail and precision has enabled MBNA to outperform many of its competitors. And yet they are doing nothing more than paying close and careful attention to *where they are* performance-wise, in comparison to *where they and their customers want them to be.*

Lee Gorman, a regional sales manager with Tab products, quoted in *Sales & Marketing Management,* said, "It took years for it to sink in, but I realized that selecting goals is only the first step. A critical ingredient is a consistent method for monitoring progress toward goals, otherwise the goals get lost in the shuffle."

Continual improvement
provides the edge for success

"Learning" is important, but don't stop there. An overall objective should be to act on what you learn and take actions to provide for continual improvement.

The expression, "If you keep on doing the things you have been doing, you are going to keep on getting the results you have been getting," isn't true. In today's changing world if you keep on doing the things you have been doing, more than likely you are going to get poorer and poorer results. You must constantly improve what you are doing or you are going to fall behind.

The same goes for business. Nothing a business is doing today will be adequate tomorrow. Nothing. Customers will continue to demand more and more for less and less. *And* they are going to want it faster and faster. If the store on the corner doesn't respond to these demands, the national chain in the next town will soon move in to do so, and if that national chain doesn't meet customer expectations, another one will.

An article in *Forbes* magazine related how "Friendly's [restaurant chain] is dying, not from terribly sloppy management, but from a far more insidious disease: an inability to adapt to changing tastes and more focused competition."

People and environments are changing. Businesses must respond by continually improving all aspects of customer service—including enhancements to products, services, and delivery methods. Businesses must find ways of doing everything better. They must process transactions faster. They must improve the quality, functionality, and value of their products and services. They must become more effective and productive. They must be more useful to their customers. And they must be more fun to do business with and more pleasant when we call.

Life means living, changing organisms. In *DNA Leadership* this means we should have living, changing processes that are continually improving. It's not that we should change for the sake of change or fall victim to a "What's the latest fad today?" approach. But we should create an environment that cultivates and encourages change and improvement as a way of life in business. A business that is doing today what it did yesterday the way it did it yesterday will not be here tomorrow.

Relative improvement

There are many ways to create an environment for change and innovation. Plenty of books are written on these subjects. Because change and innovation are integral to successful leadership and goal achievement, I recommend programs that drive continual *relative improvement.*

The beauty of a relative-improvement approach is that you don't spend time debating "optimal performance" or "maximizing potential." Instead, you just measure your current performance levels and adopt higher levels of performance as your goals. It's smart to choose a performance level that is a stretch goal, but even this is not as important as *continuous* relative improvement. Compounding improvements over time will do for a business or an individual what compounding interest does for an investment. A small percentage improvement every month compounds into a substantial overall improvement.

A business that answers 95% of its customer calls by the second ring only needs to find ways to increase this to 95.1% next month and then to 95.2% the following month. Before long the business will have a substantial relative improvement thus achieving its goal of improving customer service.

If, in your personal life, you improve a little each month, you will achieve enormous results there, too. So your personal objective should also be to achieve *continuous relative* improvement in each important facet of your life.

The best way to improve performance is to involve the people doing the work

I was in the gourmet cookware section of a department store buying a gift last Christmas, and I laughed out loud when I observed the poor salesclerk trying to enter my purchase into the touch screen register. She laughed, too, because the process she had to go through was ludicrous. "I'd like to get a hold of the little nerd who designed this fiasco and wring his neck," she said. Then she added her poignant insight: "Why didn't they ask me how to set this up? I'm the one who has to work here."

This is not a unique example. From my years of observations from inside companies, I know that the persons actually doing the work are often ignored when systems and processes are changed— and the resulting effect is the touch screen the salesclerk and I had a good laugh over.

If you want to improve performance, get the people doing the work involved. Many companies have extensive programs to get their hands-on workers involved. General Electric has a program called Work-Out sessions where people close to the work gather to identify problems and opportunities and deal with them on the spot. Hewlett-Packard's version is called a Work Innovation Network to facilitate the sharing of knowledge among employees and operating units. Landstar System sends its executives to ride in the trucks to seek ideas for improving operations from the company's truck drivers.

Like many aspects of achieving goals, this goes back to the fundamentals of *DNA Leadership*. That is, the processes for improving how a company achieves its goals must permeate the company and the people actually doing the work, or the operation is not going to work as well as it could. Individuals must know how they are doing. They must be able to evaluate their progress. This requires self-measurement and recordkeeping.

Awareness is the key to the lock on learning

Information is an essential element in the learning process, but information alone is not sufficient to stimulate progress toward goals. *Awareness* is also needed to drive actions. To improve your performance or change your plans, you must become aware of where you are in comparison to where you want to be. Information must be organized and put it into context for your purposes. Then you must become aware of the information and act on it.

If you have a production goal of 100 units per day and become aware that you are producing only 85 units per day, this creates tension in your mind. This tension can stimulate you to take actions to remove it.

Tension in this sense is good. It serves as a positive stimulus to action. No business and no individual should ever become so "comfortable" that they lose their drive for growth and development. Businesses and individuals that are comfortable are usually coasting. As someone said, "Don't ever forget, coasting is always a downhill proposition."

We should create positive, growth-stimulating tension in our businesses and within ourselves as often as we can. To produce this tension, you first must know exactly where you are in comparison to exactly where you want to be.

When you know for certain you are on the wrong road, you take action to get on the right road quickly. But if you are driving along ignoring landmarks and road signs, you may continue on the wrong road for a long time without knowing you are lost.

It is the same in pursuing your goals. First you need information; then you need to pay attention to it.

The information has to be the right information, and it has to be presented so you understand its significance. It does no good to know you are lost on an unknown road. You need a map that illustrates your position, your destination, and the roads in between. This is knowledge with awareness.

After you gain awareness you must ask yourself: What does this mean? and What should I do? You must make decisions and alter your actions based on what you learn. You must read and follow the signs.

In business, the intensity of this kind of positive discontent can be measured by looking at the size of the gaps between the results a business is realizing and the expectations of customers, employees, management, and the owners and other stakeholders in the business. Are the gaps between these expectancies and the realities of the business being measured? Are the right people aware of them? Are they acting on them?

The *LEARN* key in the *GOAL-DRIVEN MANAGEMENT* method is more important than many people realize. *LEARN* determines how well a company is able to anticipate, identify, and respond to market conditions and customer needs. It influences how well a company innovates and improves its business even in the absence of external stimuli to do so. Again, this type of learning and the related drive to improve must be present at the DNA level within a company—it must be built into the people in the company at all levels.

Learning must be fast because changes must be fast

The speed of change is a popular topic. It's not just that business and life are full of changes; it is that the rate of change has increased and continues to increase. If you are to keep up, you must speed up the rate you learn and apply what you learn. Regardless of what has worked in the past, you must experiment to find ways to improve.

Consider the guided missile. It is off course nearly all the time, but as it travels, it is being corrected constantly and placed back on course. Similarly, you should constantly correct your path to your goals as you progress and learn. Or think of the sail boat—

it tacks to zigzag from one shoreline to another. And so must you, to take full advantage of changes of current as they occur.

Many aspects of goal achievement develop in a back-and-forth mode. At the Santa Barbara Writers Conference, every instructor stressed that good writing results from good *re*writing. It is not try, try again. It is polish, modify, revise, and *improve* until you learn what words work best.

Children practice spelling until they learn words correctly. Great chefs experiment to create their recipes. Computer chip manufacturers experiment with materials to perfect silicon chips. And DNA diagnostics firms label one strip of DNA after another, searching for the right combinations to unlock the secrets of genetics and conquer disease. The process of life is learn and grow, learn and grow.

Think about this: The faster you encounter experiences, the faster you learn, and the sooner you can achieve your goals.

We should not be trying to speed up every possible aspect of life. As a wise philosopher once said, "There is more to life than increasing its speed."

But it makes sense to speed up our learning because time is finite. Businesses must speed up their response to customer feedback—whether the feedback is provided through point-of-sale terminals or through calls into the company's 800 number. Businesses compete with other businesses and like it or not, individuals compete with each other in their careers. Those who speed up their learning will have advantages over those who do not.

Speed up and increase your attempts

This doesn't mean you should race in without thinking and without a plan; but it is worthwhile to speed up and increase the number of your attempts, move past your failures, and go on to achieving your goals. In many ways, those who have difficulty or fail early and often have advantages over those who never fail or who have early successes. Sometimes individuals who have had early successes fail later in life. Learning to overcome obstacles makes people and businesses tough and resilient.

We have heard about pioneers spending years performing thousands of experiments to develop today's inventions. Thomas Edison reportedly tried nearly 10,000 experiments before he found the right material and conditions to create the light bulb. A business with Edison's one-after-the-other linear approach probably wouldn't be successful today. Today, you must experiment faster, you must get multiple inputs faster, and you must find out what *won't* work faster—so you can go on to discover what does work faster.

Look at the way software is developed. No firm tries to make a so-called "perfect" software program anymore. In the first place there is no such thing. But, even if perfection were attainable, it would take too long. Markets move at blinding speeds. To compete, software firms get a product into a good, workable state, release it, and then make enhancements as more development is completed and user feedback is obtained.

This approach is appropriate where technology drives the speed of change; it is also applicable in consumer and other markets where personal tastes and preferences are subject to subtle, but rapid change. Many corporate giants have been asleep at the switch. To keep up they must wake up and move.

Look at coffee. A mundane product, right? Starbucks Coffee Company had been in business for awhile before management figured out a successful formula. Then the company's growth exploded. Suddenly Starbucks turned a latte and a scone into a business with more than 20,000 employees and new store openings occurring one a day—and these are company-owned stores— Starbucks had to learn fast to move fast.

We are learning machines. We must learn and apply what we learn if we are to succeed in fulfilling our potential. Business executives have finally figured out that their businesses must be learning machines, too, if they going to fulfill their potential.

The way to increase the power of your learning is to set goals, develop plans, begin implementation, and then monitor your progress closely while improving as you go. When you improve your know-how and skills, you improve your chances of achieving your goals; you speed up your time frame for success; and you expend less energy and resources in the process.

The flip side is also true. If you don't learn from your progress, you reduce your chances for achieving your goals; it will take longer to reach them; and you will use more energy and resources. You apply the *LEARN* key by being specific and timely in capturing and evaluating the results you are realizing.

The first step toward improving performance is measuring performance

The expression, "Things that get measured get managed," is accurate—particularly when managing action plans. Management doesn't mean management in the parochial sense—it means DNA-like management that includes management of others, team management, and self-management.

Measurement means more than taking the measure of an item. It means inspecting results so they can be compared with expectations or with benchmark references.

I visited a clothing manufacturing plant where the production of every employee was monitored and measured. Daily, each person at the sewing, pressing, and assembly functions entered the number of units completed on a card posted at each station. Copies of the cards were compiled into a daily production report that was provided to everyone in the plant—so individuals could see how their production compared to other workers. In addition, there were inspection stations where seam and size tolerances were continuously checked.

All this checking and measuring takes time, but the owner of that clothing business is adamant that he can't maintain his quality standards or control his profitability without these efforts.

Today everyone must do more with fewer resources. But many businesses and individuals don't know how to approach this challenge because they don't have any way to evaluate what they are accomplishing in comparison to what they could be accomplishing. As a result, they have no bases for improving their performance. They have no way of knowing how well they are performing the "must do" actions necessary to achieve their goals.

Measure the right things

It is important to measure and manage the *right* performance indicators—those that provide insights into whether your goals are going to be achieved in the manner desired.

A salesperson might measure and evaluate data such as these on a daily, weekly, and monthly basis:

- Number of calls made
- Number of interviews set
- Number of interviews held
- Number of sales made
- Average dollar per sale

An accountant, attorney, or other professional might measure and evaluate chargeable hours, average billing rate per hour, and chargeable hours supervised.

Speed is a common measurement. A fast-food restaurant may measure how long it takes to fill an order. A telephone company may measure how long it takes to process new service requests.

In addition to *quantitative* factors, it is also important to measure *qualitative* factors. Some people contend their performance or the performance of their companies cannot be measured because the output is qualitative and the measurement would be subjective. It may not be easy to create measurement criteria, but every activity can be measured using objective information. This may be objectively compiled surveys of subjective opinions, such as is the case in taste tests, but a measurement can be made.

This book is not intended to provide examples; it is intended to convey the concept of management by measurement and the reality that self measurement is the best form of measurement. Each of us should determine our own particular actions and results that are appropriate for measuring and monitoring. These will vary widely from person to person.

A company president I know monitors and manages how many days he spends in the field visiting operating divisions. Another president monitors the quantity and dollar value of new proposals in process and the success ratios being achieved.

I asked the president of a direct mail insurance company what he measured and monitored. He took me down to an application processing room and introduced me to Carl, the man stamping applications. Carl's counting stamp advanced to the next number each time he used it.

"What's the number, Carl?" the president asked. Carl looked at the application. "9,766," Carl said. The president stepped to the wall beside Carl's desk and entered 9,766 in the cell designated for that day. He subtracted the number from the previous day, and entered the difference, 366, in the next cell. "That's what I watch," he said. "The number of new applications. As long as that grows or holds steady we're in good shape."

Measurement may be more important in bigger companies. There, a small degree of difference is magnified many times because of volume. For example, American Express reported in its annual report: "For the third year in a row, we measured client satisfaction to determine where we excel and identify gaps between our performance and what customers expect from us." Note the reference to the measurement of the *gaps* between results and expectations.

As mentioned earlier, MBNA is maniacal when it comes to

improving customer services and increasing the speed of processing transactions. A *Fortune* magazine article reported that MBNA
has established fifteen specific performance measures that are
tracked religiously—details like how many rings occur before the
telephone is answered, and how long it takes to respond to customer inquiries.

The measurements at MBNA aren't just captured on a computer report; they are posted real-time on more than fifty score-
boards at MBNA offices throughout the country. "The net effect:
'If you are an MBNA employee and go to a store or restaurant and
hear the phone ring more than twice, it drives you nuts,' says Jan-
ine Marrone, a division head."

You can't learn anything
from experiences you're not having

Mike Vance consults with organizations on thinking out of the
box. I heard Mike speak years ago and he made a remark that he
attributed to Louis L'Amour. I have used Mr. L'Amour's words
myself many times since: "You can't learn anything from experiences you're not having."

These words provide a heap of wisdom. When identifying
new and innovative ways to improve what you are doing, you
increase your odds for success by increasing your experiences.

One of the dangers we face is adapting to a life that Faith
Popcorn, the futurist, refers to as "cocooning." That's where you
go to your cubbyhole with your computer, I go to my cubbyhole
with mine, and we retract inward to the point where our relationship is only a virtual relationship over the Internet.

We were not born to stare at a ten-inch computer screen or
a sixty-inch television screen. This kind of zombied approach to
life will clog your thinking and desensitize your abilities to love
and care for others. You must have real emotions for life and other
human beings—not because you read in a book that it's what you

should do, but because inside you is a little murmur telling you it's why you are here.

To get experiences you must access life through your God-given senses. This requires touching, smelling, tasting, and feeling, in addition to listening and seeing. This is not the movies. This is real life, and you have got to get out and experience it. The goals you want to achieve are not goals you dream about when you see a movie on the big silver screen; they are your real life honest-to-goodness goals. To improve your odds for success you must resist the temptation to kick back and veg out.

Even if you don't think you need to, get out and expand your experiences. Improve your reference points to evaluate your progress and actions. New, fresh experiences will also expand your goal horizons. You may discover ideas for goals you hadn't thought of before. Richard P. Carlton, former CEO of 3M Corporation, commenting that 3M had accidentally "stumbled" onto some of its greatest product discoveries, said, "Our company has, indeed, stumbled onto some new products. But never forget, you can only stumble if you are moving."

It is better to crawl out of the desert alone than to try to drag a dead camel with you

I was on a trip with a friend. As we were discussing goals, he asked what I recommend when you have tried everything and nothing is working. He and his business associates had tried everything they could think of to achieve a certain goal, but nothing worked.

I offered several ideas to overcome the obstacles my friend had encountered. To each suggestion he said, "right," "yes," or "tried that one, too."

When I ran out of ideas, I was convinced that he and his associates had made a go of it. So, I turned to him and said, "You know, it is better to crawl out of the desert alone while you still can than to try to drag a dead camel with you."

My friend had described a situation that had become a debilitating factor in his organization. He needed to abandon the effort, get it behind him, and move on. But everyone was hanging on to the project. They hadn't recognized it, but it was a dead camel. They were exhausted in the desert dragging it, and unless they let go, they were jeopardizing other goals and operational aspects of their business.

Sometimes there is nothing more to measure and manage, and the only thing left to do is abandon ship. When I sense I'm involved in efforts where we can't be successful, I say, "I feel like we're adjusting the deck chairs on the Titanic."

When you've exhausted your search for life boats and you see the front half of the ship underwater, don't try to brainstorm new ideas. Jump.

19

LEARN from your progress—Success strategies, tools, and techniques

The success strategies, tools, and techniques for learning from your progress are discussed in this chapter under the following headings:

- Adopt DNA-based strategies for monitoring progress
- Institute a planned approach for managing progress
- Create an environment for change and improvement
- Learn from what works
- Learn from your mistakes and the mistakes of others
- Don't look at objective information as a report card
- Define "success" and short-term learning intervals
- Establish performance benchmarks in advance
- Review your progress and plans periodically
- Display performance to increase awareness
- Select an advisory board or goals coach
- If nothing works, try these strategies

Adopt DNA-based strategies
for monitoring progress

One of my jobs during college was assembling electrical junction boxes at a steel fabricating plant. We were paid hourly wages plus a "piece-rate" bonus if we assembled more than a standard production quantity of boxes during a shift. My foreman explained this compensation structure on my first day of work. It took about seven seconds to grasp the concept. It wasn't rocket science: Make more junction boxes, make more money.

The moment I sat at my bench I felt the pressure to start producing junction boxes as fast as I could. In two hours I completed half of the minimum daily standard. Things were looking up, until I turned the boxes in for inspection. Every one was rejected, and I had to rebuild them.

It took me two weeks, but I finally got the hang of the system. I remember my mentor at the mill, a huge man named Emil, coming over two hours before the end of each shift to look at my production card. "Big money here!" he would yell to everyone if I had a shot at earning bonus money that day. Every time Emil yelled that, I worked even harder.

This story makes several points. First, and most importantly, I was *self-motivated* to achieve the bonus money. Yes, someone established the bonus structure, but making bonus money was not required; it was my choice to go after it. Second, although the money was important, it wasn't the money that motivated me. It was Emil's encouraging "Big money here!" As the youngest worker in the plant, what I wanted most was the respect of Emil and my co-workers, some of whom were pretty rugged individuals. Third, the little act of turning in a completed junction box, watching it get tested, and seeing my production card punched by the inspectors was a tremendous stimulus to maintain my production throughout the day. During my first few days on the job, I waited until I had completed several pieces before I took them for inspection. It was then that Emil told me to take each box over *as it was completed.* I can see him grinning at me now, saying, "It gives ya a little thrill, plus you don't make too many mistakes, you know what I mean?"

Associates must be able to evaluate their contributions toward the company's goals, and individuals must be able to evaluate their progress toward *their* goals. So we have to create mechanisms to measure and evaluate progress at the DNA level.

A consultant told how he helped a brokerage firm increase performance. He gave the brokers call slips that they wadded up and shot into their personal call baskets, small buckets with basketball hoops attached, as they completed calls during the day. In a playful way each broker was visually aware of his or her personal performance throughout the day in comparison to other brokers nearby. The result was increased performance across the board.

It is important for leaders to tell associates how they are doing, but it is more powerful for associates to know themselves, without being told. A reason individuals move from one employer to another is that they don't know how well they are doing on a frequent and timely basis. Leaders can help individuals establish their own self-appraisal reference points.

Institute a planned approach
for managing progress

The planned approach is the best approach to manage toward goals. This does not require a burden of paperwork, non-productive meetings, or a bureaucratic structure. The simpler the approach, the better.

When I co-founded the Century Club of George Mason University, an organization of businesses that support the university, we established a committee structure presided over by the president of the club. Ten committees were created, each with its own goals, budget, and programs.

Once a month the chairpersons came together around a table to maintain *esprit de corps,* keep each other informed, and discover opportunities and obstacles we should address.

This was a simple infrastructure. I don't think anyone recognized the strength or elegance of it when we created it, but ten years later the same structure is in place and working well.

The illustration below depicts the three-step management formula in operation at the Century Club: (1) establish goals and plans; (2) create an infrastructure; and (3) implement, monitor, and manage. This formula works well for all business and personal situations.

Three-step management formula

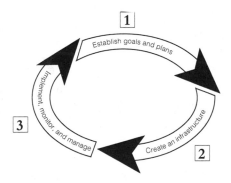

The three steps provide a systematic approach for monitoring and managing progress. Everyone always knows the next step and when the next opportunity will arise to discuss obstacles and seek input. All work groups should have a planned basis to come together, learn from their experiences, and coordinate efforts. Individuals should have a planned approach to evaluate their progress.

LEARN from your progress—
Success strategies, tools, and techniques
293

There are a number of mechanisms that can be used to monitor progress, including:

- Schedules that specify milestones to achieve

- Checklists stating tasks to complete

- Graphs, charts, and tables illustrating quantitative results

- Performance appraisals and reviews

- Surveys, polls, and customer feedback cards

How and when you monitor and measure your performance will vary. The key is to find approaches that work for you and your organization and use them.

Create an environment for change and improvement

In *DNA Leadership* leaders must create opportunities for change. To be successful, businesses must change. They must create better ways of doing what has been done. They must create new approaches, new products, and new services.

The central questions to ask are: What can be done to improve what was being done yesterday? How can it be done faster? Simpler? What steps can be eliminated? How can it be made better—perhaps to last longer, be more durable, taste better, or be easier to use?

Leaders must create environments that encourage constant change and improvement. There should be incentive mechanisms that encourage experimentation and change. There must be specific action steps to find and make enhancements. 3M has a goal of having at least "30 percent of sales from products introduced within the past four years." This goal provides solid encouragement to innovate and improve.

Learn from what works

It is important to perpetuate and amplify those actions that produce the results desired. This is particularly valuable in organizations because the sharing of ideas, techniques, and knowledge enhances the performance of others while reinforcing the corporate DNA fabric.

A vice president asked a group of managers what techniques they were using to motivate and retain night shift supervisors. Several individuals offered ideas that others in the group could use immediately. A sales manager asked his sales team which of their sales openings achieved the best results. The discussion enlightened two individuals who realized they had been overlooking the most important benefit of the service being provided. They learned from shared experience.

A common approach when seeking performance improvement is to ask people to do better or to produce more. These requests often are made when fewer resources are being provided and less time is being allowed for results to be achieved. A better approach is to find islands of superior performance and benchmark against those.

Seek out natural systems developers

One of the biggest opportunities in business is to identify individuals or groups who have a natural ability to create procedures and systems and clone what they create. Some people are much better than others at creating and improving systems. Their unique skills should be utilized.

At our local grocery store, a check-out expert named Steve is a joy to watch. This guy is a machine. Every time we go to this store we get in Steve's line, no matter how long it is. Somehow Steve can carry on a conversation and still zip customers through faster than everyone else. Steve's manager shouldn't try to get the other clerks to do better; instead he should have them study Steve and learn what he is doing that they are not. What is Steve doing differently? That is the question.

If one salesperson is outperforming two others, what is she doing differently? Is she calling on different prospects? Does she stress different benefits? Does she have a special closing approach? Is she doing some commonplace but important action that is helping her results? What is it? Why is she so good?

If one store in a chain is outperforming another, what is it doing differently? If one customer service unit handles more calls than another, what is it doing differently?

Or just try something different every now and then. When hunting, my father used to fire a shot once in awhile "to see if there is anything in the bushes." This approach has merit. Sometimes you should check and see if there is anything in the bushes. To do this, businesses must continually test and experiment—even if there is no apparent pressing need to do so.

Learn from your mistakes and the mistakes of others

Two questions I like to ask groups of executives are: What is the worst mistake you ever made? and What are you doing differently as a result?

Those present always perk up and pay attention. We all want to avoid making the same mistakes.

Making mistakes is an integral part of the learning process. The important aspects are not the mistake, but what you learn from it and how you will act differently the next time.

In my venture capital firm we provided start-up capital for a company in the computer peripherals market. In three years the company grew substantially. Several products were in the market, sales were over two million dollars per year, and the company had two plants and a sales presence in Europe. I remember telling my wife that this company was going to pay off big for us—soon.

Was I ever wrong. The company was eventually placed in bankruptcy and our investment was worthless.

Shortly after its demise, one of our investors and I met for dinner. Over coffee he asked me, "What did we learn from our experience that we're not going to do again?" That was it. He didn't rehash the whole nine yards; he simply wanted to know what we had learned and what we would do differently next time.

When something goes wrong, do you just feel miserable and move on? Or do you take the time to sit down, identify, and learn from the mistakes you have made?

Joe Mancuso, founder and president of the Chief Executive Officers Club, has studied business failures and learned much from mistakes others have made. It is informative to hear Joe provide an autopsy on what he feels went wrong at W.T. Grant and in other instances when big blunders were made. In his own business ventures, Joe says he has learned more from his failures than his successes.

We should also learn from the mistakes and experiences of others. Fred Brinkman was the country-managing partner I reported to at Arthur Andersen. If Fred told me once, he said fifty times, "Put an 'A' player out front if you want to see a great parade. If you put a 'B' or 'C' player in charge, everybody is going to be banging into everybody else and all you'll have is a big mess." Fred's advice was solid and valuable, and it was based on mistakes he had made and learned from earlier in his career. I benefited from his experiences.

Increase your rate of trial and error

"If I only knew then what I know now." It's a cliche, but it's a powerful concept to remember. There are two things worse than making mistakes. One is to make the same mistake twice. The other is to make mistakes over a long period of time without checking to see how you are doing.

A company our venture capital firm invested in created a line

LEARN from your progress—
Success strategies, tools, and techniques
297

of products and produced them in a family of colors that Dan and I thought were too dull for their intended market. Despite our suggestions to try brighter colors, management forged ahead with its color choices. Sales progressed slowly. Four years after the products were first released, the company experimented with new, dazzling colors. Sales took off exponentially. How many sales were lost because the company did not experiment with new colors sooner? How much time was lost? I don't like to think about it.

If you are going to make a mistake, it is better to make it early on. That way you have a chance to learn and correct while you still have the time, resources, and energy to continue.

Consider the person seeking a new position who sends out ten resumes. He or she intends to see what happens and then send out more. What this approach fails to consider is the time lost. Time is our most important asset, and we must accomplish as much as possible in the time we have. To do that, we must avoid linear approaches and adopt multi-faceted strategies. Anyone seeking a job should blitzkrieg the market to find out fast where to focus and where not to waste time.

The objective is to learn as much as you can, as well as you can, as fast as you can. The method is to try as often as you can. Increase the incidents of what you want to get better at, and learn from the experiences. If you want to get better at batting, start swinging your bat more. If you want to get better at speaking, make more speeches. If you want to get better at sales, increase the number of sales calls you are making. What skills do you want to improve? How can you increase your attempts to master those skills?

A friend who aspired to become a published author sent me a letter asking what steps I recommended for him to become a better writer. I returned a one-word response, "Write."

Don't look at objective information as a report card

Objective information is a tool, one you have to get familiar with using. Just as you read a speedometer to see how fast you are going, you should view information about your goal progress as an instrument to help you get where you want to go.

The purpose of measuring performance is to help individuals, teams, and companies improve their performance. This overriding objective must be kept foremost in mind. It is easy to slip into the pattern of using objective information as a basis for criticizing others. This will happen if the information is seen as a report card. For example, I know a manager who always rides the person with the lowest production during his weekly meetings. This approach is not productive, it causes resentment, and should be avoided. Try altering the questions. Instead of asking What happened? What went wrong? or Who screwed up? try How can we do better? What can we improve? and How can I help? These questions set the tone for positive discussion and minimize defensive posturing.

Define "success" and short-term learning intervals

Individuals like to know exactly what is expected of them, as specifically as possible, so they can evaluate how they are doing in comparison to the expectations of others. This is true at all levels.

The CEO of a large company gathered his top executives to explain how he, as CEO, was evaluated by the board of directors. He took a full hour to illustrate the quantitative performance criteria he was judged on. He showed charts depicting how the criteria were broken into categories and monthly components, and he explained the board's performance review process. He wanted his top executives to know his targets so they could help him achieve them. When the CEO finished his presentation, he asked those in the room to develop supporting targets broken into segments so they could be aware of their "successes" or "misses" on a week-to-week basis.

Sometimes it is qualitative success we seek. A regional manager placed a great value on the ability of his district managers to develop the "bench strength" of their teams. The problem was that no one knew what he meant by bench strength. The regional manager told me, "I'll know it when I see it." I told him that this was not a good solution. It is always possible to establish tangible parameters if you work at it, so I pressed him with several questions. In a few minutes he clarified his criteria by defining specific experience levels and skill capacities his district managers should be developing in others. In so doing, he placed quantitative criteria into the process. For example, he thought district managers should have associates who had taken certain courses or worked in certain functional areas. Now he knew what he was looking for *before* he saw it.

Establish performance benchmarks in advance

The time to establish performance benchmarks is when you develop your action plans. That way individuals can evaluate the tasks before them, lock into a mental frame of reference, and pace themselves. They start off knowing the rules of the game and how it must be played to be successful. They are DNA bonded.

The purpose of performance benchmarks is to make yourself and others aware of the gap that may exist between actual and desired levels of performance. It is this gap of discontent that you and others must act on.

Third-party and other empirical data provide benchmarks to boost and motivate performance. If Sam knows that Julie processes two hundred applications daily and he only processes a hundred and fifty, then he has a tangible reference point to motivate him. If the management of one hotel chain knows that another hotel chain checks guests into their rooms within five minutes of arrival, then this may be a good benchmark for the first chain to strive for. But, it doesn't have to be a hotel chain that management benchmarks against; it could benchmark against the time it takes to get oil changed. Here's the logic: How can it take ten minutes for a guest to check into our hotels when they can have their oil changed in five minutes? What are the fast oil-change franchises doing to process transactions so quickly? Do they train their people better? Do they have simpler procedures? Less paperwork? What *do* they do that we aren't doing?

Review your progress and plans periodically

In addition to reviewing daily progress, discussed in *Chapters 16* and *17*, you should evaluate goals, plans to achieve them, and progress on a weekly, monthly, quarterly, and yearly basis.

The weekly review consists of evaluating the past week's progress and planning the next week. Look over your *Action Plan Recaps* and evaluate whether you are following your plans. Are you doing what you set out to do? Did you accomplish what you had planned? If not, why not? What must you do to get on track?

A weekly review for a team or business unit may take one or two hours. A weekly review for personal goals usually requires a half hour or less.

A monthly review is a step up. You perform the same tasks of a weekly review, but more completely. Check each task on your *Action Plan Recaps* and evaluate progress. Modify your plans as required. Summarize results achieved and determine if you are on track for the year. A monthly review for business purposes could be two to four hours or more; for personal progress it may take one to two hours.

A quarterly review is even more complete. We tend to think in calendar quarters when making bigger, more official evaluations. A quarterly review for team or group efforts could be a half to a full day event; for an individual it would probably still take one to two hours.

An annual review is a complete update and reappraisal. While goal planning should be ongoing, annual reassessments are an opportunity to review progress and start fresh.

The time required to update annual goals and plans for a business will vary widely depending on the business.

While you shouldn't try to complete planning for your business in a single weekend retreat, retreats are an integral part of an overall approach. Retreats provide opportunities for fresh minds in relaxed bodies, camaraderie, no distractions, and a new environment. These elements refocus and recharge you, and they stimulate new ideas while strengthening teamwork.

Annual planning for a business or business unit could take four to five days over three to four weeks. This does not include time gathering information; rather it is time thinking, discussing, and deciding among alternative goals and courses of action.

Chunks of two to four hours each, spread over several weeks, work best for us in our business. Ideally, you should do the planning for your business prior to November 30 for the new year, assuming your business is on a calendar basis.

An individual's annual planning efforts could take ten to twenty hours spread over several weeks. For many of us, the ideal planning period is November 15 to December 15 because that's when things are slower. If your personal plans are set by mid-December, you won't have to rush through them during the holiday season or in the first weeks of the new year.

Keep in mind that the purpose of reviewing results is to decide which actions, if any, you should change to improve performance and progress in achieving goals. If you never alter your approach, it is a waste of time to evaluate and monitor results.

Display performance to increase awareness

When I ran an office at Arthur Andersen, I created charts that displayed individual performance data for all professional personnel. The performance factors included personal chargeability, unbilled fees expressed as a percentage of fees generated, aged accounts receivable data, number of new client contacts, and so on. During operational meetings, I would bring out the charts and review them so everyone could see how we were doing as a group and how they were doing personally.

I organized the performance data so the individuals with the best results were at the top of the charts and those with the weakest showing were at the bottom. When I reviewed the data with everyone, I recognized and praised those on top of the charts, and I provided prizes or incentives for outstanding performance.

Though I never commented on the bottom of the charts, individuals rarely stayed there two meetings in a row. While we recognized individual contributions, we were focused on the results of the office as a whole. This created peer pressure to do one's part. Since the charts were so big and visual, weak performers could not avoid seeing their results in comparison to everyone else. There was no need to specifically comment on their underperformance.

Another effective technique is for individuals to "report out" their results at group meetings. A corporation I know calls its subsidiary presidents to a monthly meeting to report to each other on their results. To open the meeting, each president who did not achieve targeted goals stands up and reports why goals were not met and what steps are being taken to make up for the underperformance. At the conclusion of the meeting each president announces goals for the next month. A similar approach could be used for team leaders or team members.

Select an advisory board or goals coach

A *Business Advisory Board* is a group of individuals who periodically come together to provide advice to management on solving problems and managing toward the company's goals. An advisory board is not necessarily the board of directors.

A friend of mine owned twenty clothing stores. He, his wife, and his father were the sole shareholders, officers, and members of the board of directors. The advisory board was separate. It included a consultant in the retailing industry, the owner of a non-competing chain of stores, an attorney, a relative who was in a similar business, and me.

This advisory board met quarterly and provided advice on new locations, product lines, vendors, incentive compensation plans, financial strategies, and other topics. In addition, the advisors introduced the president to business contacts and professional consultants. Members of the group provided second opinions by interviewing key employees to be hired.

When Dan and I co-founded our venture capital firm, we assembled a board of advisors before we raised the capital. In every company we helped start, an early step we took was to assemble an advisory board. We used these advisory boards to provide additional information, experiences, and resources, and to act as sounding boards to check our thinking.

A few of the benefits of advisory boards are in the box at the top of the next page.

Craig A. Ruppert, president of Ruppert Landscaping, says his advisory board was "instrumental in helping us take advantage of opportunities we might not otherwise have recognized, and more importantly, avoid mistakes that were not readily apparent."

Personal advisors

In his book, *Think and Grow Rich*, Napoleon Hill described the benefits of creating a *Master Mind Group* to provide advice on

---

Benefits of Advisory Boards

1. Advisors provide frank and objective information and opinions to help keep you from fooling yourself.

2. Advisors bring dimensions of thought and experience to the table that you cannot possibly have on your own.

3. Advisors expand your universe of resources through the people and organizations they know.

4. Advisors serve as sounding boards to check your thinking.

---

personal growth and goal achievement. A *Personal Advisory Board* is the modern day term for this concept. It consists of trusted individuals who serve as personal advisors, coaches, and mentors.

An alternative to a *Personal Advisory Board* is a personal performance coach or personal goals coach. This is an individual who helps you achieve your goals as a personal trainer might help you implement an exercise program or a tennis coach might help you improve your tennis game.

Consultants are available to offer personal performance coaching services and some companies are experimenting with coaching programs. The concept is sound, but personal performance coaching should not be entered into willy-nilly.

Two aspects should be looked at carefully. First, the individuals doing the coaching must be qualified. Have they done this before? Can they provide references? Why would they be good personal performance coaches? What makes them qualified? Second, coaching of any type is *not* effective unless it is done pursuant to a method that serves as a framework for skills training and for managing the effort. *MOSAIC* and *GOAL-DRIVEN MANAGEMENT* provide such a framework.

If nothing works, try these strategies

Sometimes, after you've tried to work your plan and you are not making any progress, you need a fresh start. There is much to be said about a new broom and how well it can sweep. Fresh starts revitalize, and they help you avoid boredom and complacency in pursuit of your goals. To get a fresh start, go back to the beginning. Start by clarifying and reconfirming your goals. Then build your action plan all over again from the ground up.

Also, ask these questions many times during the year: What did I improve, and what innovations did I create and begin using this past month? What can I improve, and what innovations can I create and begin using next month?

These questions can drive continuous improvement in all you do. That is a major goal you should have.

Finally, in the box below are several questions to consider if nothing seems to work no matter how hard you try.

Questions to ask
when nothing seems to work

- Is the goal I am pursuing really important? Why?

- What is the worst that could happen if I abandoned efforts to pursue this goal?

- Who can I ask for help or guidance?

- Who else has had a similar situation and how did they handle it?

- What could I possibly be overlooking?

20

LEARN from
your progress—
Implementation action
steps

L*EARN from your progress* is the fourth of the five keys in G*OAL-*
D*RIVEN* M*ANAGEMENT*. The objective is to modify the actions
you are taking so you are continually *improvement-driven*.

This is accomplished by measuring and monitoring the
results you are realizing and then adjusting your plans as appropriate to increase those results.

These activities are summarized into the four major action
steps to *LEARN from your progress* which are listed below and illustrated in the flowchart on the next page.

1. Establish a plan to monitor and manage

2. Arrange third-party input

3. Record and evaluate results

4. Modify plans as appropriate

LEARN from your progress
Implementation action steps

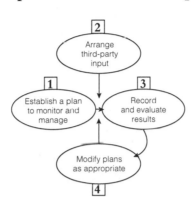

Step 1:
Establish a plan to monitor and manage

Take time to establish a plan to monitor and manage your progress before you begin implementing action plans. Once you begin implementation, it is easy to get wrapped up in activities and forget to check periodically how you are doing and determine what you should be doing differently to make better progress.

What to monitor and manage

What "must do" actions and results should be monitored and managed to ensure optimum progress toward your goals?

The key here is to determine the driving forces or "must do" actions that produce results. Measure and monitor those forces or actions. The more specific, the better.

If a business wants to improve service, should it monitor complaints by tracking the number of calls received? Or is it important to also know the *nature* of the calls, how fast they were responded to, and what was being done to avoid future complaints? If the manager of a jewelry store wants to monitor the sales performance of individuals, is it sufficient to know each salesperson's sales for the day, or is it also important to know what items the individuals are or are not selling, and whether their sales are at list price or negotiated discounts?

In deciding what to measure and monitor, it is essential to take into account your individual circumstances. Find a practical and realistic approach that you will actually use. Keep it simple. Limit the factors being monitored to a few meaningful items.

Measurement and information needs

What measurements or information are needed to monitor and manage actions and results? How are the measurements and information to be obtained? Who is going to obtain them?

Do you need someone to record the number of units produced each day? Should customer service operators code incoming calls so they can be analyzed? Who needs to record the information needed?

Compile a list specifying the information required and the persons responsible for recording the information. Many businesses create a summary of items they call their *Key Factors*. We have a list in our business. One of the key factors we monitor is inquiries. We track requests for program information, and the individuals who answer incoming calls know it is their responsibility to complete a mini-questionnaire for each call.

Monitoring and management processes

Who is going to be involved in the review and evaluation of actions and results? How will they monitor and manage actions and results? What will they do? When will they do it?

The next step is to create systems and procedures for capturing and organizing information so it can and will be used. *Chapters 18* and *19* gave several examples of this process.

Creating and administering a measurement and monitoring system takes time and effort, but they are well spent. Without such a system most efforts to monitor and improve performance are ineffective. This should be a serious effort. Set up routines to review progress weekly, monthly, quarterly, and annually. Learn from your progress as you go. Decide your approach. Establish concrete dates. Let everyone know the schedule, log dates on your calendar, and then follow through. See *Chapters 21, 22,* and *23* regarding the creation of systems.

Step 2:
Arrange third-party input

Third-party input is most beneficial if it is obtained when goals and action plans are conceived and then continued during implementation of the plans. As discussed in *Chapter 19,* it is important to benchmark against internal and external performance factors. An advisory board for businesses and a personal advisory board or a goals coach for individuals can also be helpful.

Step 3:
Record and evaluate results

Record, summarize, and review your results at least weekly. Daily evaluations often are appropriate. Accomplish this by preparing charts or analyses to show specific information depicting results being achieved in comparison to results desired. In group efforts results should be reviewed with all individuals so they can assess their personal contributions. Charts and analyses were discussed in *Chapters 18* and *19.*

Step 4:
Modify plans as appropriate

Modify your plans and revise your actions on an ongoing basis. No plan is ever implemented exactly as written, and no planning effort is ever perfect. Minor corrections and adjustments must be made. Sometimes major changes or complete overhauls are required.

We are thinking machines. We continually gather information, process it, and alter our thoughts and actions based on new information and experiences. This is natural. It is unnatural to attempt to remain the same without changing and growing.

There is nothing worse than trying to hold on to a fixed point of view about what should be done or how to do it. Any CEO or manager who attempts to force fixed-point management will fail. The name of the game is dynamic change and improvement. Businesses are living, breathing entities and we must treat them that way—by providing for their nourishment, revitalization, growth, and development.

You should continually evaluate and modify your plans and goals. Ask yourself how you can improve what you are doing to achieve your goals. How can you achieve your goals faster, more assuredly, or in greater quantity? Who can help? What small modifications could produce a quantitative jump?

21

SYSTEMATIZE
your efforts—
Fundamental principles

The fifth key in *GOAL-DRIVEN MANAGEMENT* is S. S stands for *SYSTEMATIZE your efforts*. The fundamental principles pertaining to systematizing your efforts are discussed in this chapter under the following headings:

- The best kept secret of successful companies and people is that they have a method for everything they do

- An organization will not grow beyond the capabilities of its methods and systems, and individuals will not grow beyond their habits

- *Orchestral Management* is a better approach than *Hockey-Puck Management*

- There are big differences between creating methods and improving them or using them

- New methods will always be met with some resistance

- Methods take time to learn and implement

- You can't break old methods or habits; you can only exchange them for new methods and habits

The best kept secret of successful companies and people is that they have a method for everything they do

Have you ever wondered how they put that little "M" on M&M's® candies? It is pretty interesting.

The candies are processed through devices resembling over-sized metallic rolling pins with rows of inverted dimples the size of M&M's®. The colored delicacies are vibrated into the dimples, and at blurring speeds the rollers bring one row at a time under mechanisms that stamp little Ms on each candy as the rows pass beneath them. Then the candies are packaged in bags, bags are packaged into boxes, boxes are packaged into cartons, and cartons are placed on pallets and moved into trucks. From beginning to end, the candy-making process is all mechanized—beautifully so.

I don't know how long it took the engineers at M&M Mars to figure out the method for stamping Ms on candies, but I'm sure it took considerable time and effort before they perfected it. Now the method works day-in, day-out, 365 days a year, and it proba-bly is taken for granted.

The *method* for stamping M&M's® is *know-how*, and it is just one of many methods the company has developed over the years. Have you ever wondered how Uncle Ben's Rice, another subsid-iary of Mars, Inc., keeps the off-colored grains of rice out of its boxes of white rice? Another fascinating process. Again, the pre-cision of the method represents the company's know-how.

The greatest "secret" of successful businesses and individuals is that they have predefined methods they follow in a disciplined manner for everything they do.

Some businesses and individuals do this consciously and deliberately. Arthur Andersen deliberately created methods for designing information systems (Method I), performing examina-tions of financial statements (Transaction Flow Auditing), and hundreds of other activities.

A successful attorney I know consciously acquired dozens of good habits to control his daily life. He follows the same exercise regimen every morning—twenty minutes on his rowing machine, twenty minutes of aerobic exercise, and twenty minutes on the treadmill. He has a light lunch and goes for a walk in the park every day—rain, snow, or shine. At three in the afternoon he has a snack. At four he takes a fifteen-minute nap on the sofa in his office. In the top left drawer of his desk there is a stack of note pads, and in the bottom right drawer there are two candy bars, a box of tissues, and an extra pair of reading glasses. He is even more methodical about his professional work and how he manages his law practice. He is the successful product of his good methods, which he created and implemented until they became habits.

You may run into some successful businesses or individuals who are not aware of how systemized they have become. Yet if you analyzed how they do what they do, you would realize they faithfully follow a series of methods and habits in their endeavors. There is always a pattern to success.

Many businesses and individuals exert enormous efforts but are not successful. Unfortunately, they do not realize that it is not their efforts that have failed them, but their lack of methods.

What's a method?

A "method" is one or more systematic procedures or processes that *drive* actions on a continuous basis towards obtaining one or more goals. A method can be an individual technique or the aggregate of all procedures working together as a system.

Like the tracks the train runs on, methods guide and drive actions that lead to results. Good methods lead to good results. Better methods lead to better results. The best methods lead to the best results. First it is important to make sure you are using a method, and then it is important to make sure you are using the *best* method possible.

It wasn't until several years ago that I realized how systematically I "chunked my time" and approached the preparation of my daily *Thunderbolt* list (see *Chapter 16*). Every day for more than twenty-five years I have prepared a short list of the major tasks I want to accomplish the next day and scheduled out chunks of time to accomplish them. Preparation of my *Thunderbolt* list and chunking time may seem inconsequential, but they are important to me. My accomplishments would be considerably less without my use of these techniques.

Success is the result of good methods and habits. Athletes use methods to train and develop themselves for competition. Their training routines are collectively their method. When they follow sound training methods, they improve their chances for success.

Business methods are the systems, procedures, policies, strategies, tactics, processes, structures, and other elements that a company employs to do its work. Collectively these establish the know-how of the company and its employees. Companies with the best methods get the best results. In these times of rapid and continuous change, a vital role of management is to continually upgrade and improve the methods of the company.

Our personal methods are our habits. If we have good habits, we get good results. If we have poor habits, we get poor results. To achieve your goals, you first must acquire the habits necessary to drive the required actions. If you want to write a book, you must adopt daily writing habits. If you want to accumulate wealth, you must adopt good saving and investing habits. If you want to stay healthy, you must adopt good exercise and eating habits.

You can take steps to implement what you learn in this book, but your efforts will not help you achieve your goals on a long-term basis unless you apply what you learn by making changes in your habits. Let me repeat that because it is so important: You must apply what you learn by changing your habits.

Put another way, if you want to improve your results and increase your successes, then you must first adopt improved habits.

Unfortunately, the flip side of this is that if you don't change your habits, you won't be able to change your long-term results.

Every successful personal development or improvement program is a collection of techniques knitted together as habits into a series of rituals resulting in a method, and it is these methods that drive results.

Weight Watchers® and Pritikin®, for example, have developed specific procedures to help individuals lose weight and become healthier. The accumulation of all their procedures and systems results in their method; it is their collection of habits.

Methods encourage creativity and innovation

Some individuals may feel that methods create a cookie cutter or cookbook approach and thereby stifle creativity and innovation. Paradoxically, just the opposite is true. Step back and look at the big picture. Methods and standardized systems and procedures do not stifle creativity. Instead, they eliminate the need to spend time and effort re-creating the wheel on routine aspects while providing individuals freedom to think both within the system and outside the box.

For example, ask anyone in Hollywood how long a screenplay for a full-length motion picture is. They will tell you 120 pages plus or minus a page or two. This is because motion pictures run about a minute per screenplay page and industry executives believe the ideal length for most motion pictures is two hours. In addition to their common length, virtually every screenplay has exactly the same conventions as to the placement of dialogue, scene descriptions, and other matters. Thus, the format, or method, for "writing" a screenplay is rigid and standardized. But look at the innovation in the development process. What could be more creative? Screenplays are creative and innovative because the writers and collaborators focus their time not on form, but on the substance of the content.

Other benefits of methods and habits

The understanding, creation, and control of methods and habits are the means to achieving business and individual goals through *DNA Leadership*.

To achieve your goals you must determine the methods and habits you will need to get you there. Then you must acquire those methods and habits. You also must determine which of your present methods or habits are obstacles, and replace them.

Business leaders should not allow individuals to become totally dependent upon other people to make their contribution toward company goals. Rather, leaders should create an environment where individuals can utilize and rely upon processes and methods. While we all must work interdependently with one another, each of us must have our own independence, responsibility, authority, and ability to create a positive result.

Businesses benefit from methods in many ways:

- Methods provide bases for identifying and replicating the best practices dynamically throughout an organization. Best practices can be identified by comparing the results of one method with another.

- Methods enable portability, the transfer of know-how from one individual or group to another. Without methods there are no common bases to communicate with others and train them.

- Methods provide bases for evaluating existing know-how so improvements and enhancements can be made—if you don't know exactly what you are doing, it is difficult to determine how and what to change to improve results.

- Methods ensure know-how is in the hands of companies, not just individuals within companies. A company cannot afford to have an indispensable individual possessing critical know-how. If the individual leaves or is incapacitated, the company loses a vital asset. I have observed situations where "indispensable" individuals made outrageous demands on companies because of their unique know-how that was acquired while employed at the company. These difficulties can be avoided by reducing know-how to documented methods that are known and used by more than one individual.

An organization will not grow beyond the capabilities of its methods and systems, and individuals will not grow beyond their habits

There is a saying, "The pack can't go beyond the lead dog." A company can't go beyond the capabilities of its systems and methods for doing business. An individual can't go beyond his or her habits. This being the case, a substantial portion of our efforts must be directed toward creating, improving, and in business, sharing our methods and habits.

If leaders and managers want their businesses to grow, they first must improve their methods of doing business. Then they must improve the training and development of the individuals who use those methods to do their work. In the box on the next page are examples of how we should work on methods to achieve sales, customer service, productivity, quality, operations, and profitability goals.

The power of methods is demonstrated by franchising. The explosive franchising phenomenon was possible only through the standardization and systemization of operating methods to such a degree that they could be transferred and taught *en masse* to individuals with disparate backgrounds and skills. Every day hundreds of entrepreneurs go into business for themselves by acquiring a franchise, and with it, the *methods for doing business.*

Franchises expand under a "cookie-cutter" strategy. That is, create a prototype unit or two, make sure the prototypes work,

First work on the methods

Sales: If the goal is to increase sales, first work on improving the methods to get sales.

Customer service: If the goal is to enhance services to customers, first enhance the systems and procedures to produce the services.

Productivity: If the goal is to expedite production, first work on improving the design and operation of the manufacturing system.

Quality: If the goal is to improve product or service quality, first work on improving the processes that produce the products or services.

Operational: If the goal is to improve the bench strength of associates, first look at the methods used to recruit, train, reward, and coach associates.

Profitability: If the goal is to improve profits, first look at the methods for creating profits.

then stamp units like crazy into the market as fast as you can using the same recipe. Every franchise—from McDonald's and Mrs. Fields Cookies to Jenny Craig International—was possible only because someone figured out a series of methods that work, and then packaged those methods and sold them to others. There are more than 500 different franchises to choose from, and they are all built upon this same foundational rock: standard and portable methods.

Cookie-cutter expansion is not just for franchised businesses; big businesses use this strategy, too. Look at gas stations, Wal-Marts, automobile dealerships, banks, retail stores in the mall, and Starbucks coffee shops. These all have grown following the same proven approach: Get it right; freeze the design; then expand. Cookie-cutter expansion is one of the strategies venture capitalists try to utilize because it is easier to grow a business based on a set of proven business concepts than it is to keep re-creating the wheel to produce more revenues.

Orchestral Management **is a better approach than** *Hockey-Puck Management*

Compare the rambunctious game of hockey to the disciplined performance of the symphony orchestra to discover some basic truths about management.

Hockey-Puck Management is management by chance. In hockey, the puck is dropped, and furor breaks loose. There are some plays, some teamwork, but in hockey there isn't a predictable approach.

Businesses managed in a hockey-puck manner operate the same. When the doors open, it is every man or woman for themselves and there are few, if any, methods driving the business activities.

Orchestral Management is the opposite. In orchestral performances the conductor works from a score; each musician has a part to play; and on the one hundred and eighty-eighth beat the conductor raises his baton, points it to the tall man in back, and the timpani begin their soft pom, pom, pom—precisely on cue.

Businesses managed in an orchestral fashion operate the same. There are precise methods to be used and exacting procedures to be followed. At precisely 6:00 a.m. you get your wake-up call in your hotel room—because someone created an exacting method to drive the actions required for the telephone to ring.

Below are four levels of management development: best methods; orchestral; emerging methods; and hockey puck. Which of these best describes your business?

Best methods: Orchestral methods are in place, *and* there are constant and continual efforts to find and use the *best possible methods* to achieve the results a company desires.

Orchestral: There is a method for every important facet. These are documented, enforced, and working smoothly, but they are not necessarily the best possible methods available; they can be improved.

Emerging methods: Standard methods, processing policies, conventions, and procedures have been established. But these may be in the formative stages, and they may not be documented fully. Utilization of the methods may be erratic.

Hockey puck: The organization is managed "by the seat of its pants." Little is documented. There are few prescribed policies or procedures. No standardization. It is pretty much every person for himself or herself.

The closer a company moves its operating functions toward the orchestral and best methods categories, the more successful and profitable it can be. Domino's Pizza is what it is today because it adopted an orchestral approach to delivering pizza in thirty minutes or less. FedEx got there by orchestrating overnight delivery. As Domino's and FedEx continue to refine and hone these and other aspects of their businesses toward best methods, they continue to grow stronger and more competitive.

There are big differences between creating methods and improving them or using them

There is a big difference between using or improving methods others have created, and conceiving and implementing those methods in the first place.

Some individuals are good at using and improving methods, but not so good at creating them. In designing methods and procedures, it is essential to involve users in the process, but users often lack the perspective or experience necessary to identify and evaluate the alternatives and best approaches. Because different skills are required, the way to get the best methods is to use a collaborative approach.

In new business endeavors everything must be created anew. The development of initial methods is a major undertaking. It often makes sense to adopt methods others are using successfully rather than create new methods. In a sense, if your competitors don't want to steal your methods, you probably should want to steal theirs—not literally, but in spirit.

Regardless of whether you are developing a method from the get-go, or fine-tuning what is in place, make sure your methods are designed by people who know what they are doing. Get input from someone experienced. Ten rules of thumb to keep in mind are in the box below.

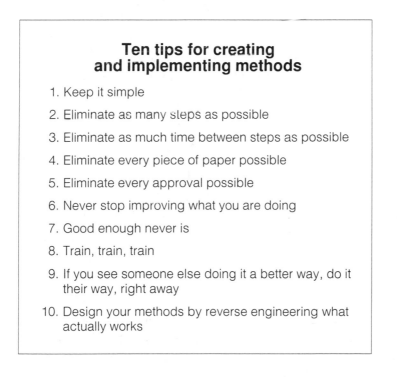

Ten tips for creating and implementing methods

1. Keep it simple

2. Eliminate as many steps as possible

3. Eliminate as much time between steps as possible

4. Eliminate every piece of paper possible

5. Eliminate every approval possible

6. Never stop improving what you are doing

7. Good enough never is

8. Train, train, train

9. If you see someone else doing it a better way, do it their way, right away

10. Design your methods by reverse engineering what actually works

Do not overlook the details. Deciding what your receptionist is going to say when answering the telephone is an important element of your communications system; it creates the first impression many will have of your company. Also, don't under-estimate the value of standardization. One way to leverage and manage know-how is to train people in the use of standardized procedures. And don't forget technology. Look for activities that are being performed by hand and ask yourself if it would save time to adopt a computerized system or a computer-assisted approach.

New methods will always be met with some resistance

Individuals respond three ways to new methods: as eager beavers; middle-of-the-roaders; or change resisters.

Eager beavers represent approximately 5% to 10% of any given population, whether they are employees, members of a professional association, or students in a biology class. These individuals enthusiastically embrace everything new that comes along. They are eager to experiment and begin using new methods immediately, even if they don't fully understand them.

Middle-of-the-roaders represent the bulk of the population, perhaps 70% to 80%. They approach new methods slowly and cautiously. They come around and try new methods, but they won't be first in line. Middle-of-the-roaders want to make sure that new methods work before they use them. They respond to reasonable amounts of encouragement, reinforcement, and proof that the new methods are worthwhile.

Change resisters represent the remaining 10% to 15% of the total population. These are the ones who won't try anything new without considerable effort, encouragement, and perhaps even insistence. They live and will die by, "If it ain't broke, don't fix it." They will spend time and energy resisting change, innovation, and the adoption of new methods.

Most of us are middle-of-the-roaders, but each of us has some eager beaver and some change resister tendencies in certain areas. I am an eager beaver when it comes to employing the latest and greatest computer hardware components, but I am a change resister when it comes to switching from a software package I know and like to one that is more powerful, but has a learning hurdle I have to climb over.

Each of these types should be handled differently when you are implementing new methods.

Eager beavers should be given what they need to learn and use the new method. After that, get out of their way. Make sure there are resources available so they can use the new methods. If eager beavers can't get access to the tools or information they need, they may become frustrated and move on. The time and effort necessary to support eager beavers in implementing new methods is usually minimal. Let eager beavers experiment and develop their skills so they can train others. However, if they are so smitten with new methods that they become overbearing crusaders, don't use them to train others. The last thing middle-of-the-roaders or change resisters need to motivate them is overzealous cheerleaders.

Middle-of-the-roaders require moderately paced, deliberate, and sustaining efforts to get them to experiment and adopt new methods. This means training, reinforcement, encouragement, *and time for the methods to be absorbed.* One entrepreneur who was trying the *GOAL-DRIVEN MANAGEMENT* method for the first time went out of his way to tell me he was only going to write his action plans in detail *for my benefit* since he thought it was a waste of time. "I'll give it my best shot, for your benefit," he said. After experimenting with several action plans over a two-week period this man became an evangelist. Now he requires detailed action plans from all his associates. Middle-of-the-roaders become loyal to new methods once they are convinced of their effectiveness.

Change resisters should be treated as middle-of-the-roaders *except* that steps should be taken to neutralize any of their proactive negativity. Individuals in this group should not be given the opportunity to sidetrack the main implementation efforts.

I worked on a project with Joe, a negative individual who was a limitation thinker every way imaginable. For each new idea advanced Joe provided six reasons it wouldn't work. To minimize Joe's rhetoric, the project leader began asking him to provide suggestions to overcome the concerns he raised.

For example, Joe said he thought the timetable for the project was too tight, if not impossible to meet. "Well, what would you recommend we do to move things faster?" the project leader said. Such comments were not confrontational. The project leader sincerely wanted Joe's positive input.

Joe, challenged in a positive way, gave the project some serious creative thought and came forward with several suggestions that advanced the effort—all because of careful handling.

Methods take time to learn and implement

A key aspect of implementing any new method is absorption time. You can't make a good stew fast. It takes time for people to absorb new methods so that the methods become ingrained as part of the organization's DNA.

There are four stages of development in any learning situation: creation of the desire to learn; acquisition of the necessary information; experimentation; and refinement. They are depicted by the chart on the next page.

When Arthur Andersen introduced Transaction Flow Auditing (TFA), its then new methodology for performing examinations of financial statements, it took more than two years to instill the methodology firmly within the organization. The company went through each of the four stages of development:

Stage 1: Creation of the desire and attitude to learn: Early in the first year there was an all-out launch campaign. We held meetings with partners and managers to tell them what would be coming and how good it was going to be. This was a rah, rah presell effort to warm everyone up to the idea of TFA. At

Four stages of learning

this stage, the eager beavers were leaning forward on the edge of their chairs raring to go and the change resisters leaned back in their chairs with their arms crossed.

Stage 2: Acquisition of information and know-how: During the remainder of the first year we scheduled hundreds of training sessions across the firm to teach everyone the new method. This was a one-fell-swoop approach, but the firm was so large that it took several months just to get through the introductory training. At this stage, the eager beavers were off and running, the middle-of-the-roaders were warming up to the idea, and the change resisters still had their arms crossed.

Stage 3: Experimentation, trial and error, and practice: After all personnel were trained, they were asked to use TFA on one or two engagements to gain experience. Everyone was repeatedly told, "There are no sacred cows. Use the methodology and try new techniques." This trial-and-error effort began during the latter part of the first year and extended into the second year.

During this period we held workshops where individuals shared their experiences. By now, several eager beavers had established themselves as gurus in the new methodology, the middle-of-the-roaders had bought in and were pleased with the approach, and the change resisters were starting to feel left behind.

Stage 4: Creation, refinement, and reinforcement of habits: During the second half of the second year, individuals began using TFA for the second and third times. As they refined their approaches, they began to use the methodology as a matter of rote. By the end of the second year most individuals had integrated TFA into their daily work habits. TFA was no longer talked about as our powerful new tool. It was simply the way we performed examinations of financial statements. The eager beavers were now searching for the next new innovation, the middle-of-the-roaders couldn't remember when they did *not* use TFA, and the change resisters had either become converts or had left the firm.

Absorption time for GOAL-DRIVEN MANAGEMENT

GOAL-DRIVEN MANAGEMENT will take time to learn and acquire as an integral tool in your business and personal goal-achieving activities. You will have to invest a few days to read the materials and learn the techniques either in training sessions or on your own. Then it will take most individuals several weeks of experimentation and trial and error to get used to employing the comprehensive approach the methodology requires.

During this period, most everyone will realize some immediate results, but it will take a few months before the methodology and its related processes and techniques are ingrained and improved results are being realized throughout a company.

An example is a sales associate in the financial services field who learned these concepts in September. He began applying them and immediately produced more sales. He continued refining his use of the principles through the year-end and by the end of January his sales results had doubled. "The big difference, for me," he said, "is I'm focused and I'm working smarter, not harder." He says he isn't working as many hours as he had been.

It is better to begin small and ensure consistency and repetition of the techniques than to start big and not sustain anything. For example, to start using the *Action Plan Recap* sheet technique, experiment with one sheet for one goal and begin implementation of the action steps on that sheet. Once that becomes familiar, prepare sheets for other goals.

In addition to the GOAL-DRIVEN MANAGEMENT method itself, implementation of the fifth key to the process, *SYSTEMATIZE your efforts,* involves creation and use of methods for the primary "must do" action steps to achieve your goals. This process is ongoing and requires time and effort, but the rewards of adopting this approach are lifelong.

In business applications, it is essential to have a deliberate and planned approach. There is nothing worse for a business than to start something and not reinforce and finish it. This establishes a negative example for the acceptable way of doing things. A start without a finish does more damage than good.

You can't break old methods or habits; you can only exchange them for new methods and habits

The first step is to recognize we don't adopt or break our methods and habits; we *exchange* one method or habit for another.

For customer service representatives to develop the habit of answering the customer service lines by the second ring, they must abandon the habit of letting the telephone go for someone else to get. If service station employees are going to acquire habits that keep the rest rooms clean, they need to discard habits that leave the rest rooms in sad shape. If account representatives are going to acquire the habit of giving major accounts a call twice a month to touch base, they need to discard the habit of allowing distractions to divert their attention and keep them from making the calls.

To get *into* the habit of spending your time in chunks, you must get *out of* the habit of spending time in drabs and dribbles. To lose weight, you must replace a habit of eating junk food with a new habit such as reaching for a piece of fruit. To cultivate the habit of writing in your journal each night to clear your mind and plan your tomorrows, you may have to weed out a current evening habit such as watching television.

It would be easy to read this chapter, agree that the concepts make sense, and then change nothing in your approaches to setting and pursuing your goals.

But don't do it. This is important information. The chapter's opening section is vital: The greatest secret of successful individuals and businesses is they have a method for everything they do.

It takes effort and time to create new methods and habits, and discipline to reinforce them. Creating methods and habits and becoming systematic is not the easiest way, but it is the most reliable way to achieve your goals. If you want to achieve more goals and greater goals, become systematic and habit-driven.

22

SYSTEMATIZE
your efforts—
Success strategies, tools,
and techniques

The success strategies, tools, and techniques for systematizing
your efforts are discussed in this chapter under these headings:

- Make developing, enhancing, and using methods both
  organizational *and* individual responsibilities

- Teach people what they need to know about methods
  and related systems and procedures

- Create a systematic environment

- Flowchart your methods so you can see them

- Use these tips to make the best systems possible

Make developing, enhancing, and using methods both organizational *and* individual responsibilities

There is a paradox about methods and systems. On one hand,
users of systems are the most critical persons because they are in
the position to observe how the systems are working and to identify opportunities for improving them. On the other hand, users

don't always have the requisite skills, expertise, and knowledge to design procedures and techniques that constitute the best possible methods.

Consider the space shuttle. There would be no space shuttle if NASA didn't have engineers and scientists with the expertise to design and build the myriad of electrical, mechanical, and computer systems and methods. But, where would the program be without the skilled astronauts who pilot the shuttle and provide critical feedback as to how the systems function? It would be nowhere, that's where. Both groups are essential. To achieve success, designer and user collaboration is required.

A collaborative approach embodies the essence of *DNA Leadership*. Each individual has a unique role, but all roles must come together in a coordinated and harmonious manner toward the same goals.

In business, there must be top-down coordination and centralized influence over the creation, adoption, sharing, and training of methods and systems. This ensures that the best expertise available is brought to bear, and it enables companies to take advantage of uniformity, standardization, and economies of scale. At the same time, business applications must *not* be designed in the vacuum of an ivory tower. Users must provide their real-world expertise and know-how, or the systems are going to end up being ineffectual, inefficient, and impracticable. And very costly.

At one store of a national chain my wife, Dolly, tried to purchase a pair of black shoes, but her size was not available. "No problem," the sales clerk said. "I can order those for you through my register and ship them to your home. Plus, we'll pay the shipping since we were out of stock on a standard item." Fantastic service, right? My wife was amazed. So was I. When the shoes arrived in a few days as promised, we were astonished.

Dolly liked the shoes so much that while at a different, but bigger, store in the same chain she decided to purchase a second pair in brown. Again, they didn't have her size. "That's okay,"

Dolly said. "Can you just order me a pair through your register?" The sales clerk frowned. Then she said maybe it was possible, but she didn't know how, so she called her manager. The manager told Dolly that he, too, thought it was possible to order the shoes through the register, but he also didn't know how. He suggested Dolly go upstairs to the customer service department. "Maybe they can help you," he said. Instead of going upstairs, Dolly purchased the shoes from a competitor.

That chain of stores has a centrally developed method that provides a neat feature. It allows customers to order items through the sales register. A sales clerk in one decentralized store was on her toes. She offered and used the feature as it was intended. Yet in another store, not even the department manager knew how to effect the transaction. Thus, the time and effort expended centrally to create the special customer service feature was a wasted investment in the second instance.

Where was the breakdown? Were the shortcomings in the second transaction the fault of the department manager and the employee? Was it their job and responsibility to know the capabilities of their systems? Or were the individuals who designed the system at fault? Should they have taken steps to make sure everyone was adequately trained on use of the system? Dolly couldn't care less who was at fault. All she knows is she was frustrated and disappointed at the second location. And she bought the shoes somewhere else.

For many years, we received a booklet annually that contained coupons to send in with our monthly mortgage payment. This past year we did not receive one, so I called the mortgage company. The service representative explained, "The company decided to send out a statement each month instead." I related that the last thing I was interested in was more mail, and I asked if I could just have the coupon book. The service representative told me the booklets were no longer available. She told me I should not feel bad because I wasn't the only one who complained. "I've tried to get my customers their coupon booklets, but *they* won't print them for me," she said. "I don't know why *those people* do things like this—going off changing things without asking anybody what they think." This is the same situation in reverse. Here the people in the field know what to do to keep their customers happy, but they are losing the battle to someone or some group in a centralized control position.

It isn't centralized or decentralized control over the development and use of business methods that is needed. We need a DNA approach where individuals work together. Here are several ways to foster collaborative efforts:

- Assign a representative sample of users to the design teams for all systems efforts

- Use surveys or other input devices to solicit input from users who are not on the design teams

- Have users sign off on the practicality, efficacy, and usefulness of systems designs or modifications before they go beyond the design stage and again before they are actually implemented for full-scale use

- Periodically ask users for their input and suggestions for improving systems and procedures

- Have systems designers go into the field and use the systems on a hands-on basis

- Provide incentives and other programs to recognize individuals who make suggestions for enhancing systems

In addition, everyone should be encouraged to periodically ask themselves why they are doing what they are doing the way they are doing it. "We've always done it this way" is not acceptable. It shirks the responsibility to constantly improve.

Teach people what they need to know about methods and related systems and procedures

Individuals avoid responsibility for developing and enhancing methods for many reasons including: poorly defined responsibilities; lack of training; lack of incentives; and a lack of structure to share methods.

Four reasons individuals don't accept responsibility for developing and improving business methods

1. The responsibility for methods is ill defined.

2. Individuals have not been trained how to develop, improve, and implement methods.

3. There is a lack of incentives to encourage individuals to develop, improve, and implement methods.

4. There is no infrastructure that provides for the sharing of methods throughout an organization.

---

1. The responsibility for methods is ill defined

If people are unclear who is responsible for a particular method, rest assured, they are not thinking of themselves as having the responsibility. This problem can be addressed by adopting programs to educate individuals about their responsibility to identify improvement opportunities and to reward and recognize them for accepting and discharging this responsibility.

2. Individuals have not been trained

Only a small portion of employees have had any training in

the development, improvement, and implementation of methods. Most employees don't understand the importance of methods or how pervasive methods are throughout their organization.

This presents an opportunity—to provide employees with skills and tools in methods and systems development processes so they can think on their own and do their jobs better. Developing systems and methods is a primary skill necessary for success. Companies should provide introductory training programs that explain: what methods and systems are; the benefits of using them; how they are used; the processes for developing methods and systems; and techniques for continually enhancing them. All associates should have a basic appreciation for the roles they play in learning and implementing methods and in identifying areas where methods can be improved.

As associates advance into supervisory and managerial ranks, they should receive additional training in methods and systems development skills. Programs should be created to expose them to systems and methods used by other organizations. The degree and nature of these advanced programs would vary depending on the job responsibilities and experience levels of the individuals.

3. There is a lack of incentives

Incentives encourage individuals to develop, improve, and implement methods. Without incentives, these processes suffer. The concepts and rationale for providing incentives are discussed in *Chapter 12*. Those concepts are applicable to methods. Businesses must reward and recognize individuals who develop, improve, and implement the methods of the business.

4. There is no infrastructure

When I worked at the steel mill while in college, we received a $100 spot bonus for any idea we provided that the company adopted to improve performance or profits. We submitted ideas on a three-part form that shift supervisors initialed. We placed two parts of these forms in a suggestion box and kept the third copy. Once a month the plant manager climbed up on a stack of pallets in the center of the loading dock. When everybody had gathered around, he announced the month's winners and handed out the awards: crisp $100 bills. The shouts and hoopla were tremendous. I received three crisp $100 bills, and I will never forget them. After receiving my first award, I began submitting ideas at the rate of about one a week.

The plant had a specific and effective infrastructure to solicit and use ideas for improving operational methods. It wasn't fancy, but it worked. There was a three-part form. A suggestion box to put them in. A group of individuals who met once a month to evaluate the suggestions and decide which ones would be implemented. And a few crisp $100 bills.

All businesses should provide an infrastructure for creating and improving methods. Some companies receive thousands of suggestions a year from their employees—because they have systems and procedures to solicit the suggestions and reward those who provide them. What is the infrastructure in your business? Where is your suggestion box? What form do people use to submit ideas on? How are individuals rewarded and recognized?

Adopt procedures to continually improve methods. Those firms that take the time and make the effort to do so will be tomorrow's leaders; those that do not will be less successful.

Create a systematic environment

If there was an award for productivity czar, I would nominate Dottie, the bookkeeper for a manufacturing company I did some work for years ago. Each year when Jeff, the owner of the company, was preparing Dottie's performance appraisal he would call me and ask what I thought Dottie's raise should be. My comment was always the same: "Well, look at it this way, Jeff, if Dottie ever leaves, you will have to hire three people to replace her."

Dottie's most valuable characteristic was her innate ability to organize her work into highly effective action steps. Dottie created a mini-system, method, or form for every task she performed.

As a result of her organizational propensity and her attention to details, Dottie got more done in a day than other individuals in similar positions. The quality of her work was superior—virtually error free. Plus, Dottie made money for her company because of her high performance and effectiveness. She got her billings out faster than most bookkeepers do and she was on top of back charges to vendors. Dottie was a finely tuned, high-performance engine. She never missed a beat.

While her performance was of great value, Dottie's greatest contribution was that she was a catalytic cornerstone to the company's overall systematic environment. Her organization and systemization permeated the DNA of the entire company. Whenever anyone in any area of the company was going to tackle a new task they would say: "How do you suppose Dottie would approach this?" Or, "What would Dottie think of this?"

It has been said that no one moves in the military until they first check with the sergeant. That is the way it was in this manufacturing firm. No one moved until they checked with Dottie—if not literally, figuratively.

I remember asking Dottie where she learned how to be so systematic. "From my grandmother," Dottie said. "My grandmother owned her own farm and she told me to find a place for everything and put everything in its place."

That is good advice for anybody or any business. Have a place for everything. Also establish an environment where everything is systematically placed and performed. This avoids wasted time and effort re-creating the wheel and it provides a basis for training people and transferring skills.

A great technique for systemization is to identify and copy those people in your company who, like Dottie, have a natural tendency toward systemization and organization. A sales manager

I know tells his people to see how Fred is handling things—because Fred has a natural knack for cutting through minutiae and organizing his work systematically.

I have observed firsthand that companies that tend to be the most successful in their industries also tend to have systematic environments. This means the better performing companies have a more disciplined and defined approach to their work.

Flowchart your methods so you can see them

A technique for developing or refining methods is to flowchart the components so you can see and evaluate them. A business could flowchart activities within operating functions such as customer services, sales, marketing, administration, and finance. Sketch out the major steps in a flowchart. List all forms or documents. Write a description of the procedures. Then step back, evaluate, and ask: What could be altered to improve the process?

Suppose a company wanted to improve its sales results by acquiring new clients. The sales team could flowchart and analyze each of the aspects of their selling method, which might include these components:

- Identifying prospects

- Soliciting and cold calling

- Qualifying prospects and preselling

- Preparing proposals

- Negotiating and developing financial arrangements

A company with a goal of reducing the time it takes to respond to customer requests could flowchart the steps in the process and the actions taken. Flowcharting and analyzing each of the tasks and actions would give the company a basis to evaluate the present system to determine what can be improved. Flowcharting is like taking an x-ray look inside methods to see how they work.

It might reveal that service representatives don't inform customers of options available. Perhaps it would illuminate the use of too many forms. See *Chapter 12* for additional discussion on flowcharting techniques.

Use these tips to make the best systems possible

Here are some tips and techniques to consider when designing and implementing systems to drive action steps.

- Keep it as simple as possible and make it practical
- Get a firm commitment from top management before the systems project is initiated
- Select a project team composed of both users and individuals with systems expertise
- Benchmark against existing internal and external systems
- Eliminate as many pieces of paper as possible
- Eliminate as many steps in the process as possible
- Keep the number of people involved to a minimum
- Reduce time between steps where possible
- Eliminate all unnecessary approvals
- Train all personnel on what they need to know
- Make sure the system provides feedback for how well it is functioning
- Provide the tools and resources necessary to use the system properly

23

SYSTEMATIZE your efforts— Implementation action steps

S*YSTEMATIZE your efforts* is the fifth and final key of *GOAL-DRIVEN MANAGEMENT*. The objective is to put yourself on autopilot toward your goals by making yourself *habit-driven*.

This is accomplished by designing, implementing, and continually improving systems that drive the "must do" actions necessary to achieve your goals.

These activities are summarized into the six major action steps to *SYSTEMATIZE your efforts* listed below and illustrated in the flowchart on the next page. The six steps are not necessarily performed in order; some are done simultaneously:

1. Administer the project

2. Collect data and define objectives

3. Sketch out an overall systems design

4. Finalize the design and develop subcomponents

5. Implement the system

6. Evaluate and enhance the system on an ongoing basis

Systems design and implementation are substantial topics beyond the scope of this book. However, everyone needs a basic

SYSTEMATIZE your efforts
Implementation action steps

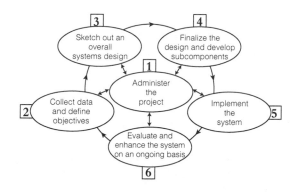

understanding of how to create methods and procedures to be able to begin to systematize their own goal-achieving efforts. The discussion below is intended to serve this purpose.

Step 1:
Administer the project

Project administration addresses the questions: Who is in charge? What is the plan? A variety of tasks are necessary to administer systems development efforts. These include:

- Obtain top level buy-in and commitment

- Establish project leaders and team members and specify their authorities and responsibilities

- Create communication and reporting conventions

- Determine interim milestones

- Establish an implementation timetable

- Determine, obtain, and manage financial, budgetary, and other resource requirements

- Develop a project plan

- Monitor and manage project implementation

Step 2:
Collect data and define objectives

This step addresses the question: What are the overall objectives of the system?

The primary purpose of this step is to determine the nature and scope of the overall system by gathering information, evaluating it, and making decisions. Tasks include:

- Obtain managerial and user input about the purposes and objectives of the system

- Define the primary systems components, processes, and deliverables. Answer the questions: What are the inputs? What are the outputs? What do we want the system to do, *exactly*?

- Obtain internal and external benchmark data for evaluating design alternatives and performance specifications. Ask questions like: What is possible? What is being done currently? How is it being done?

- Determine specific information needs through interviews with users and analyses of empirical data

Step 3:
Sketch out an overall systems design

The overall systems design addresses the questions: What do we want to accomplish? What is the best way to accomplish it?

During this step the system is preliminarily designed using flowcharting, storyboarding, critical path diagraming, or other techniques to document the action steps to be taken. This is where tasks, procedures, processes, and details are conceived, and the system is organized into a logical flow.

This step is comparable to an architect's rough sketches or preliminary design drawings for a custom-built home. At this stage the rooms are laid out and the exterior of the house is illustrated, but the engineering drawings are not complete.

One purpose of the preliminary design is to provide bases for user input. The types of questions to ask users are: How does this look? Does it make sense? What do you think? Will this do what you want it to do? How can we improve this? As these questions are addressed, the design is revised. Once the design is acceptable to everyone, detailed development can begin.

An easy way to start the preliminary systems design process is to refine the "must do" steps in *Action Plan Recaps*. As discussed in *Chapter 13*, *Action Plan Recaps* summarize actions to achieve goals. A salesperson has to make sales calls to generate sales. A delivery person has to make deliveries to get packages to customers. A doctor has to examine patients to determine their health.

In each situation, ask what methods will produce the greatest quantity and best quality of "must do" actions in the least time. What methods will enable the salesperson to reach the greatest number of people likely to buy in the shortest time? What methods can the delivery person use to pack the truck and select the best routes to expedite service? What methods can the doctor use to make sure blood samples are correctly interpreted?

A key aspect is to specify the performance criteria for the operational procedures to be performed. What are you really trying to accomplish? What is the purpose of the system? How is it supposed to help achieve your goals? What results do you want the system to produce? How do you define the levels of performance possible? (See *Chapter 4* for how performance levels are defined using the *MOSAIC* method.)

At the conclusion of this stage of design for a sales system, for example, the prospecting, presentation, and other subcomponents of the system would be outlined, but not all of the details would be completed. The project team may have decided to use telemarketers calling on small business owners. They may have decided to use a specific PC-based system to manage these efforts. But they would not yet have developed the calling scripts and related follow-through procedures.

To sketch out a systems design you brainstorm the action steps required to meet established performance criteria, and then organize those steps into a logical sequence. Use flowcharting or other techniques to illustrate the step-by-step processing so you can see how components interrelate. Once the big picture is satisfactory, create each of the components or subsystems in detail.

There are grey areas between this step and the next step. It doesn't matter what gets accomplished in which step as long as all the tasks are completed.

Step 4:
Finalize the design and develop subcomponents

This step addresses the questions: Who is supposed to do what? When are they supposed to do it? What exactly are they supposed to do? How are they supposed to do it?

Continuing the analogy of the new home, detailed designs and drawings would now be completed for all the subsystems and components such as the wiring, plumbing, framing, and construction. Samples would be provided so specific materials and components could be selected. The homeowners would choose kitchen cabinets, bathroom fixtures, carpeting, and other items.

In business systems, there is a tremendous amount of work to be completed during this step. In most cases this step requires the largest part of the resources and time. This is where forms are designed, procedures are documented, user instructions are written, and computer programs are coded.

The detailed design process works best using an iterative approach—components are designed, altered, and improved repeatedly as user input is obtained throughout the process and the system comes together.

Once all of the system components have been designed, they should be field tested with live transactions. Additional user input should be incorporated.

If you developed a method for teleselling, at this junction the telemarketers would make test calls following the established scripts and procedures. The results of these tests would be evaluated, and the telemarketers would provide feedback and suggestions for refinement and improvement.

Once all of the components are field tested, programs and processes should be debugged and procedures should be refined and completed.

Systems and methods then would be documented in a final form that could be used for training and ongoing operations. This systems finalization and the related documentation can take various forms. Keep it simple and to the point.

One of the final subsystems for assisting telemarketers in a direct selling business could be a computerized decision tree with additional menus as the telemarketers get further into their sales interviews.

Step 5:
Implement the system

Implementation addresses the question: What do we have to do to make this work in the real world?

Implementation involves three substeps: training, implementation, and ongoing reinforcement.

Training introduces users to the system in classroom or field sessions. Features of the system and techniques for using it are explained. Users experiment in a safe environment.

Implementation is when the system is used in real-time and real-world situations.

Ongoing reinforcement includes all efforts to encourage and assist users in implementing the system on an ongoing basis. This includes such activities as help desks, information hot lines, and user newsletters to promote awareness and use.

Step 6:
Evaluate and enhance the system on an ongoing basis

Ongoing evaluation and enhancement addresses the questions: How is it performing? How can we make it better?

This step involves soliciting and incorporating user input for improvements on a continuous basis and also for periodic overhauls and redesigns. "Users" include customers, associates, and others who directly or indirectly interact with the system.

All systems and methods degrade over time. Continuous enhancements and embellishments are essential. Put procedures in place to provide for these improvements before they are needed.

Systems for individual goals

The six steps above were described as they relate to substantial systems design efforts; however, the same steps are applicable for developing all systems and methods regardless of their size.

For example, a vice president of a real estate management firm had the goal of becoming a better mentor and leader. He created a series of programs where he would have more one-on-one "face" time with each associate and where he would help each associate develop and pursue a personal growth plan. The vice president blended the six steps of systems development together and created a single *Action Plan Recap* to manage his efforts.

1. **Administer the project** was taking the time to create, monitor, and enforce a schedule for his meetings with associates and his reviews of their performance results.

2. **Collect data and define objectives** consisted of identifying the areas he wanted to concentrate on for each associate. The vice president accomplished this by having a meeting with each associate where they worked together to develop mutual overall objectives.

3. **Sketch out an overall systems design** involved the

creation of an overall calendar and timetable along with several forms for use in documenting the goals and performance results of associates.

4. **Finalize the design and develop subcomponents** included finalizing the forms and specifying the exact meeting dates for each associate.

5. **Implementation** consisted of holding performance review and coaching meetings with the associates. Training was a general meeting where the vice president met with all associates and explained what he wanted and how he was going to accomplish it.

6. **Evaluate and enhance the system on an ongoing basis** included follow-up group meetings and use of an upward evaluation form where the vice president solicited input.

Part
Three

Success summary
and executive
recommendations

Part Three Overview

Chapter 24, Twenty-one myths and misconceptions about goals and action plans, provides insights into common misunderstandings which prevent businesses and individuals from using the power of goals to their full advantage. Examples are provided to illustrate and shatter the myths and misconceptions, and suggestions are provided to overcome them.

Chapter 25, Twenty-five do's and don'ts when selecting and pursuing goals, is a fast-paced summary you can use to review twenty-five important points covered in this book.

Chapter 26, Ten reasons individuals don't establish and achieve their goals, describes ten pitfalls you should avoid when setting and pursuing your goals and provides techniques for overcoming those pitfalls.

Chapter 27, Fourteen recommendations for executives, offers business leaders suggestions for getting the optimum benefits from the concepts in *DNA Leadership through GOAL-DRIVEN MANAGEMENT* in the least amount of time.

24

Twenty-one myths and misconceptions about goals and action plans

Myth #1:
Goals and planning are for use only in big corporate environments

Goals and planning are *not* just for large corporations. Setting and pursuing goals is a key to personal fulfillment and the fulfillment of business potential regardless of the size or nature of the business. Every business and organization should have goals and plans to achieve them. Every person old enough to read this book, regardless of occupation, social status, education, or origin, should have goals and plans to achieve them.

Myth # 2:
You can learn all you need to know about goals in a couple of hours

You can learn a lot about goals in a couple of hours. But, that's the tip of the iceberg. There is more beneath the surface to learn, absorb, and apply. Each investment you make to learn more about setting and achieving goals will reap a proportionate return. You can get started in a few hours, but the learning process should be lifelong. The more you know about goals and how to achieve them, the better you will become at setting and achieving them.

Myth # 3:
Real entrepreneurs don't plan

Not true. Real entrepreneurs, the successful ones that is, have goals and well-thought-out plans of how they are going to achieve those goals. Entrepreneurs who fail to plan may fail completely and they are limiting the success of their businesses.

Myth # 4:
All it takes to get ahead and achieve your goals is hard work

Hard work is important, but it is *smart* hard work *toward the right goals* that is required. As Peter Drucker said, "It is more important to do the right thing, than it is to do things right." The right thing to do is create a plan and work it.

Myth # 5:
The secret to success in business is to have a good idea

Good ideas are not a license to print money. Sound goals and solid execution are more important than a great idea poorly pursued. People who are successful in business have specific goals, and they execute extremely well to achieve them.

Myth # 6:
CEOs and senior executives are experts at setting and achieving goals

Many CEOs and executives are experts at setting and pursuing goals. But the title of CEO or executive does not mean those individuals know *all* they need to know. Successful executives study the processes for setting and achieving goals throughout their careers. Everyone can learn more.

Myth # 7:
Successful people can tell you what it takes to set and achieve goals

Ironically, some successful people are *not* particularly good at telling others how to set and achieve goals. They instinctively know what to do. They can provide valuable examples, anecdotal information, and advice from their experiences. But there is a difference between hearing about experiences and having someone analyze the fundamentals so they can teach them to you.

Myth # 8:
The key is to concentrate on your current goals

It is important to concentrate your energies toward your current goals, but you should not stop there. You should also focus on goals *beyond* those you are pursuing. To maintain momentum, you must know what you are going to do next. You can lose momentum just before achieving your goal if you don't know what you are going to do immediately after it is accomplished.

Myth # 9:
Successful people accomplish all their major goals in their lifetimes

Nothing could be further from the truth. Successful people establish more goals for themselves than they could possibly achieve in a lifetime. When we've achieved all we set out to achieve, or all we want to achieve, we begin to die.

Myth # 10:
Most people achieve all the goals they have the ability to achieve

This may be the most harmful myth of all. People do not achieve what they have the ability to achieve. Rather, they achieve what they *think* they have the ability to achieve. Most people underestimate their abilities and potential, and therefore underachieve.

Myth # 11:
The time to start learning about goals is when you start your adult career

Not true. The time to start learning is now—regardless of how old you are or how much you know. Don't wait to start your education and don't ever finish it. Learning is a lifelong process. When you stop learning, you stop growing.

Myth # 12:
The best time to plan goals is right after the first of a new year

January, or the first month of any fiscal year, is *not* the best time to establish goals and create action plans—because by the time you get your planning done, you are well into the year. The time to plan for a new calendar year is in October and November. December could be good too; however, December often is a busy month. But goal planning is not a one-time annual event. Goal planning should be continuous throughout a year—weekly, monthly, quarterly, and annually.

Myth # 13:
The way to accomplish your goals is to prepare a "to do" list each morning

This is half right. A daily action plan, which I call a *Thunderbolt* list, is essential. But to benefit from mental imprinting and improve your focus, your daily action plans should be prepared *the day before*, not the morning of the day the items are to be accomplished. Daily planning works best when it is part of a weekly, monthly, and quarterly planning approach.

Myth # 14:
The way to establish goals is to develop them on your own

It is good to get away for quiet time to establish goals and plans, but it is also beneficial to get input from others. Individuals who have your best interests at heart can help you shape your goals and achieve them.

In business, everyone responsible for achieving goals should be involved in formulating them and developing the plans to achieve them. This does not mean that a company can have each of its employees provide input into corporate goals and plans, but it does mean that all employees can have input into their personal goals and plans that contribute to achieving corporate goals.

Myth # 15:
It only takes a few minutes to select goals

There is a risk to selecting goals too hastily. The selection of goals is important and a reasonable amount of time should be set aside for the task. Often your goals will sharpen if you establish them preliminarily and let them stew for a few days before you lock onto them permanently.

Myth # 16:
Forget ready, aim, fire—the best way to achieve a goal is to just fire

This is an out-of-context misinterpretation of otherwise excellent advice. It is always better to give thought to what is to be done before doing it. We think at the speed of light. We move at two to three miles per hour. You should pause before acting and use your brainpower. Taking action is important and it is essential to get in motion quickly—just not so quickly you don't think.

Myth # 17:
College graduates starting their professional careers know all they need to know about setting and achieving goals

I, for one, was a neophyte in understanding the power and value of goals and what it takes to achieve them when I graduated from college. No one sat me down and said, "Here's how you do it." When individuals start their professional careers they need skills on establishing and achieving goals because they are entering a competitive marketplace where these skills separate those who achieve success from those who don't.

Myth # 18:
On a scale of 1 to 10, goals are a 7 or an 8

Nope. Goals are a 10. Some people argue with this when they first hear it, but what they are overlooking is that everything we rank as a 10 in our lives is a 10 because of a goal we have with respect to it. (See *Chapter 3*.)

Myth # 19:
We don't have to have goals to be successful or happy

Whether you can be successful or happy without goals is not the point. The point is that your pursuit of goals and your achievement of them brings success, joy, and happiness. Goals increase your joy and success.

Myth # 20:
The key to achieving your goals is to establish them

One of the keys to achieving your goals is to establish them, but more is required. This book reveals five fundamental keys that constitute a method, along with a number of related techniques that are necessary for achieving goals.

Myth # 21:
All you need to do to achieve your goals is to visualize them being realized

Visualization is an important part of the goal-achieving process, but it is only one of many factors required. Visualization without action is daydreaming. No one ever said "ask and you will receive" is *all* that is required. To receive, you must act.

25

Twenty-five do's and don'ts when selecting and pursuing goals

1. Take time to plan

Don't pick the first goals that come to mind and pursue them. If you rush in and pursue the first goals you think of, you run the risk of being partway toward achieving them and then realizing there are other goals you wish you had considered. This can cause you to hesitate, falter, or lose zeal for the pursuit of your goals.

Do take time to think about the goals you want to pursue and do consider goal possibilities in all aspects of your business or life. This provides a balanced approach. It improves your chances of maintaining momentum and staying on track. Strong beginnings are important. It is also important to continue strong. Thinking through alternatives provides sustaining energy and drive.

2. Write out your goals

Don't fail to write your goals down, and don't rely only on your memory to provide the mental focus and conscious and sub-conscious reminders necessary for pursuing your goals. We live in a fast-paced world with many distractions and activities vying for our time and attention. Writing goals down provides a ready reference and reminder of your goals. In addition, the writing process sharpens your focus and improves your perspective.

Do make sure each of your goal statements is complete. Goals should be specific and measurable, and they should have a deadline. Your mind needs specific targets to focus on, so the more complete your goal statements, the better.

3. Make goal setting a continuous process

Don't view goal setting as an activity you do just once a year. Goals are tools for growth, and your goals should be continually growing and changing. An important aspect of setting goals is to drive your vision and plans for achieving them into your subconscious mind so you are on autopilot. Reflecting on your goals only once or twice a year will not accomplish this.

Do look at goal setting as an evolving process you will continue on a lifelong basis with ever-increasing and changing goals. Evaluate your major goals monthly, and once each quarter expand the process to a more thorough review.

4. Establish deadlines for your goals

Don't select goals without specifying a deadline and a timeline for completion. Our minds operate at the subconscious level with an undeniable and extremely reliable built-in clock and sense for time parameters. We generally put off things when there is no impending timetable or deadline.

Do specify deadlines and completion time frames in writing for each of your goals so you can see what they are. Because we tend to hit the targets we aim at, establishing your targets in time parameters is an essential step. Timetables and deadlines are tools for pacing your efforts and the efforts of others. They provide a ready reference for where you are and where you need to be next.

5. Be as specific as you can

Don't select generalized, non-specific goals. Our minds are biomolecular information processing miracles, but they cannot and will not process generalized information. Generalized goals such as "improve quality" or "get rich" are meaningless until you define the terms quality and rich. Similarly, we are not able to pursue goals such as "increase sales" or "lose weight" effectively because to our minds *any* increase in sales or loss of weight, regardless of how small, will satisfy the stated goal.

Do specify your goals in concrete and exact terms so you provide a *laser-clear* target for your brain. Specify the pounds you want to lose, the sales results you want to achieve, or the marathon races you wish to compete in. The specification of a goal clicks you into "on" and "forward" toward your goals.

6. Select *cause* goals as well as *end-result* goals

Don't select just *end-result* goals. *End-result* goals are important, but they are not all that is required because end results are not doable per se. You can't "do" a goal like "save enough money for a college education." You can establish a savings plan that will accumulate into the amount desired. The actions are *cause* goals or supporting action steps, and these are what you do.

Do break each major *end-result* goal into its subcomponent *cause* goals or action steps that when taken together will cause your *end-result* goals to be achieved. Like lining up dominos against a target, each of your *cause* goals will invoke a chain reaction resulting in the completion of your *end-result* goals.

7. Keep your goals to yourself

Don't share your goals or your plans for pursuing them with more people than necessary. Some people, family members and friends included, don't really want you to pursue and achieve your goals. This is not because they do not love you or think well of you, but because they are comfortable with you as you are and they are comfortable with their relationship with you as it is. When people become aware that you are pursuing goals that may separate you from them or change how they know you, they may unconsciously resist your efforts.

Do share your goals and your plans for pursuing them with the individuals who must know about your goals so they will support you in the process of achieving them. We each need help, encouragement, and resources others can provide. But others can't help you unless they are aware of your needs. Make your goals "participative" with a small group of people who should know about your goals so you can be successful. Share business goals with everyone who can contribute to their achievement.

8. Make yourself constantly aware of your goals

Don't write your goals on a piece of paper and stick them in a drawer. Repetition is the way you learn. To imprint your goals permanently on your mind so you can pursue them on autopilot, you must remind yourself constantly of your goals.

Do create a variety of visible reminders of what your goals and plans for pursuing them are. There is no one way to do this. It is better to use a variety of physical reminders than to select just one that can become so obvious you ignore it. Get creative in establishing your reminders so you see them often in the various environments you live in: at the office, in the car, at home, at school, and so on. Illustrate your goals graphically by preparing progress charts or posting pictures of completed goals such as your dream vacation home.

9. Choose BIG goals

Don't pick small goals that are easy to achieve. The biggest reason to have goals is to use them as tools for stimulating and guiding our business and personal growth and development. This means you must exert effort to stretch from where you are to where you want to be. Small goals produce small power.

Do pick big goals beyond your comfort zone so you can grow to new levels. Big goals force you to develop your skills and get better at doing what you have to do to achieve them. Big goals are inspiring. They provide pulling power and a targeted magnetic focus for your energies.

10. Start with a plan

Don't start pursuing your goals without a plan. Individuals without a plan run a great risk of not achieving their goals or they expend more energy, time, and resources in achieving their goals than individuals with plans. There is a natural tendency to want to get started quickly. But unplanned fast starts are more likely to fail than efforts pursued with a plan. Also, it is important to have an awareness of the progress you are or are not making toward your goals. A plan provides a ready reference as to where you are and how much further you have to go.

Do think through and prepare a plan specifying the major actions required for your goals to be achieved. In addition to increasing the effectiveness of efforts, a well-thought-out plan will create momentum because you will always know what to do next. Many efforts fail because individuals get partway to their goals and have to stop and think how to complete their journey. This can bring things to a complete stop; once stopped, progress may never begin again.

11. Make your plans the *best* plans possible

Don't adopt and follow just any plan to pursue your goals. The objective is not to have a plan; it is to have the *best* plan possible—so results are more assured and so the least amounts of energy and resources are expended in the least amount of time. There are many approaches to achieving any given goal, and by spending time at the front end identifying and evaluating these approaches you reap substantial rewards.

Do take some time to get away to a quiet place and give serious thought to how you can best achieve your goals. Identify alternative approaches. Consider possible resources or assistance you may be able to obtain. Gather fresh input. Ask others for advice. If you spend a little more time at the front end, you are more likely to achieve a better result.

12. Break big goals into smaller goals

Don't try to pursue big goals without breaking them into manageable components. A big goal can become mentally overwhelming or insurmountable because of its size. When this occurs you can get disappointed and frustrated, and you can lose interest and stop pursuing your goals. It is easier to pursue action steps if they are small enough that you can literally "see" their accomplishment and get a feel for the time parameters involved.

Do break big goals into small, manageable segments that can be pursued on a monthly, weekly, daily, and hourly basis. Restate a goal of exercising five hours a week as "exercising 45 minutes six days a week and 30 minutes one day a week." You are more likely to take one small step and continue with another step than you are to begin projects you know will require tremendous efforts.

13. Begin each day with a plan

Don't ever begin a day without a plan. Individuals who begin their days without a plan only achieve a fraction of the results individuals who begin with a plan achieve. Without a plan you are open to whatever comes your way and you run a great risk of having others spend your time and energy the way they want you to versus the way you want. Without a plan to work on *your* goals, you will be working on somebody else's goals.

Do begin your day with a plan that specifies the five most important actions you intend to accomplish. Prepare your plan the day before by listing the actions you intend to take in priority order. After your plan is written, take a few minutes to see yourself completing the actions. Begin each day by starting your plan immediately. Complete the first item as far as you can before going to the second item. Do this until each item has been completed. While you will not always get all items completed, many times you will. In addition to beginning each of your days with a plan, begin each of your weeks, months, and years with a plan. It is essential to make daily progress, but it is also important to keep daily progress in line with your longer-term goals.

14. Make *daily* progress your number one priority

Don't let a day go by without making progress toward your major goals. If you don't make *daily* progress, it is difficult to continue momentum and sustain energy. One day without progress leads to two days without progress, two days leads to several days, and several days lead to weeks. Suddenly you look back and realize you have made no progress for months.

Do make achieving *daily* progress toward your major goals a high priority. Do whatever you can to achieve tangible progress daily. Use a daily plan to monitor and focus yourself. Highlight action items you will pursue that relate to your major goals. Make sure you have at least one action item for at least one major goal each day. Some days you won't be able to take substantive, tangible steps toward your goals, but at a minimum each day you can review where you have been and where you are going and reorient your thinking. Just taking ten minutes a day to think about your progress can sustain momentum.

15. Periodically evaluate how you are doing

Don't keep working your original plans to achieve your goals without periodically evaluating how well you are doing and whether you can improve or accelerate your progress. There is no such thing as a perfect plan, only plans that are continually improving. Plans should be evaluated because events and circumstances change. We continually learn more about what works, doesn't work, and what works best. Don't let weeks and months go by without evaluating your progress and reorienting yourself.

Do evaluate your plans and progress on a systematic, periodic basis. Begin with a daily appraisal of your daily progress and a weekly appraisal of your weekly progress. Establish milestones at the outset as to when you will more formally take a hard and objective look at where you have been and where you are going.

16. Seek assistance from others

Don't be a loner in pursuing your goals. No one ever achieved a significant goal alone. We all need help, assistance, and support in pursuing our goals—even if they are personal goals.

Do give some thought to the help and support you will need to achieve your goals and then ask for help and assistance and persist until you get it. People won't always do what you want them to do when you want them to do it. Persistence on your part in making and pursuing your requests is required. When you are thinking about getting assistance, think big. Who could help you best? How can you get them to help?

17. Use a method for pursuing goals

Don't try to select and pursue your goals without using a goal-setting and pursuing method. Without a method our efforts are ineffectual and inefficient. This can delay achievement of goals or jeopardize them entirely.

Do establish and follow a systematic method for selecting and prioritizing your goals and for developing and implementing action plans to achieve them. Methods are the best kept secrets of successful businesses and individuals. A good method will serve as a solid bridge between you and your goals—one you can rely on to produce the results you want. A key to success is putting yourself on autopilot. A method you can internalize at the subconscious level enables you to do this. Without a method you must rely on brute force and your continuous conscious efforts. This is hard to do. A method gives you an edge.

18. Pursue goals you believe in and want to pursue

Don't pursue goals you don't believe in or don't earnestly want to pursue. Unless you believe in a goal and personally want to achieve it, you will put forth less than your full efforts. Goals pursued with less than our full efforts may not be achieved or they can become abandoned. When we don't have desire, we don't have energy, and when we don't have energy, we procrastinate.

Do select goals you personally want to pursue. Desire is the engine that drives our motivation, which in turn drives our actions. To get the most benefit from the personal growth factor of goals, select goals that are appealing to you. When you really want a goal, you create an inner power. Power is necessary to propel you through obstacles and to sustain your energy.

19. Keep your goals in a *Goals Journal*

Don't be casual or careless about where and how you treat your goals and your plans to achieve them. If you are casual and careless in recording your goals and plans, you send a message to your subconscious mind that says, "This stuff is not that important—because if it was, I would take more care in writing my goals and plans down."

Do formalize your goal writing and action planning activities. Establish an official *Goals Journal* for goals and adopt official *Action Plan Recaps* for action plans. In addition to sending a message to your subconscious mind that your goals and plans are important and to be taken seriously, carefully prepared goals and plans are easier to review and use as tools for guiding progress.

20. Pursue only one or two major goals at a time

Don't try to pursue a number of major goals at any one time. People tend to spend their efforts in drabs and dribbles trying to do too many things at once. When they do, they diffuse their energies and become less effective than they could be otherwise. As a result of pursuing more goals, they achieve fewer goals.

Do prioritize your goals. Select no more than one or two major goals to be pursued at any one time. When you narrow

Twenty-five do's and don'ts
when selecting and pursuing goals
365

your focus to one or two goals you increase your concentration, your physical power, and the resources you can bring to bear. Big goals require big power, and concentration of power is essential to achieving them. Many big goals can be achieved, but not at once. To achieve many big goals pursue them one at a time.

21. Accept responsibility for achieving your goals

Don't expect someone else to achieve your goals for you. Other people are too busy to accept your goals as their priority. If you want to achieve your goals, you must be responsible. This doesn't mean you shouldn't get help. You should. But it is foolish to wait for others to volunteer.

Do take responsibility for your goals. Act to achieve them. It is not just "ask and you will receive." You must act. Force daily action and daily progress. The person who must pursue your goals is you. The person who must act on your behalf is you. You are responsible for your goals. You must be the one to act.

22. Get back on track fast when you get diverted

Don't stay off track. If you are going to pursue big goals, you are going to get off track many times. This is natural. Unplanned obstacles will appear. Other priorities will arise. You will have setbacks. These are to be expected. What you do about them is the key to your success. If you allow yourself to stay off track knowingly, there is a tendency to continue to allow this of yourself. It is easier to be easy on yourself than it is to be disciplined and persevere. But this is what you must do.

Do get back on track fast when you know you are off track. It is important to let your subconscious mind know you will not knowingly tolerate mediocrity or less than satisfactory results. Making a concerted effort to remedy or correct your progress right away provides this message.

23. Strive for consistency and persistence

Don't pursue your goals in a herky-jerky manner. When you begin in a start-again, stop-again manner, you miss the opportunity to create momentum. To get momentum, first build critical mass. Then drive it like a freight train down the right set of tracks toward your goals. This force will propel you through obstacles. If you begin to pursue your goals, then stop in mid course, you bring everything to a standstill.

Do wait until you are committed to your goals and ready to pursue them to completion before you begin. When beginning, keep on going with steady and growing effort until your goals are realized. Often you will have to persist until you break through barriers. This requires a steady, sustained effort.

24. Get all team members to buy in to team goals

Don't mobilize a team to pursue its goals unless all team members have bought into the goals and the team plan to achieve them. The value of team effort is the synergy and multiplying power teams can produce. Joint efforts are not maximized unless team members are pulling together toward the same goals at the same time in the same manner. If teams begin or continue their efforts on a non-unified basis, the value of having the team is lost.

Do take whatever positive, proactive steps are necessary to unify your team in pursuit of its goals. Begin with a *laser-clear* statement of the goal. Get individual team-member buy-in by making them aware of what achievement of the goal will mean to the team and to them personally. Address any misgivings or concerns. Provide incentives and motivational prompts. Make sure each team member understands the overall action plan to realize the team's goals and the integral part of the plan each is responsible for implementing. Make sure team members know what is to be done, when it is to be done, and who is to do it.

25. Learn from your mistakes

Don't make a mistake, big or little, and not learn from it. Mistakes, short-term setbacks, and other difficulties are part of life. You are bound to make some mistakes or errors in judgment in pursuit of your goals. It is not possible to avoid all mistakes, but it is possible to avoid making the same mistake twice.

Do learn from your mistakes when you make them. Most people know this is important to do, but few individuals take steps to identify mistakes or errors made, consider how they could have been avoided, and then develop strategies or plans to avoid making the same mistake twice. The way to learn from your mistakes is to ask questions: What went wrong? Why did it go wrong? How could it have been prevented? What can be done to preclude it from occurring again? Who needs to know about the mistake so they can avoid making it?

26

Ten reasons individuals don't establish and achieve their goals

Ten reasons individuals and organizations don't achieve their goals are described below. Each of these is a pitfall to be avoided.

1. Failure to establish goals in the first place
2. Fear of failure *and* fear of success
3. Error of thinking you know more than you do about setting and pursuing goals
4. Lack of training in pursuing goals
5. Absence of a method, or use of a method that does not work
6. Failure to accept responsibility or be held accountable
7. Incongruities between goals and beliefs
8. Insufficiency of desire
9. Lack of realistic goals or expectations
10. Underestimation of the effort involved

1. Failure to establish goals in the first place

The biggest reason organizations and individuals don't achieve the goals they would like to achieve is that they don't establish the goals in the first place.

More people fail before the starting line for their goals than after it. How many firmly established goals have you *not* achieved? Most people can't provide a big list. But we all have dreams that have faded unfulfilled because we never pursued them.

To overcome this pitfall, treat goal-setting as a serious and important effort. Make time to establish your goals.

2. Fear of failure *and* fear of success

Many people don't establish goals because they are afraid to fail. They don't want to risk disappointing themselves and they don't want others to think less of them. So, they establish goals that pose little challenge or they don't set any goals.

Ironically, what may sound like the safest approach is the most dangerous. The bigger disappointments come not from trying and failing, but from not trying. A key to success is to try more often. Some of my greatest successes have been realized not because I achieved a stated goal, but because I made the effort, and realized other accomplishments in the process.

In addition, as strange as it may sound at first, many individuals do not establish goals because they are afraid to succeed. They feel their success will betray the image of what they are supposed to achieve based on expectations others have for them. While this fear may exist at the conscious level for some people, more likely it is locked away in their subconscious minds.

In my book, *Soar . . . If You Dare*®, I called this phenomenon the *Anaconda of Undeservedness*. At the subconscious level many individuals have a limiting view of what they believe they deserve—based upon who their parents were, where they grew up, where they went to school, who their friends were, and so on. Like an invisible *Anaconda* snake, these limiting thoughts wrap around us and constrict our dreams to the "station in life" we were born into. An example is the business owner who doesn't believe, at the subconscious level, that he deserves to own a business of a certain size because no one in his family ever achieved that level of success. Another example is the young woman who subconsciously thinks, "If my parents weren't millionaires, why should I deserve to become one?"

This doesn't mean individuals who have a *deservedness* limitation can't achieve goals beyond those realized by their role models, but it does mean they may be handicapped by significant mental obstacles.

To avoid this pitfall, you must address these obstacles head-on before greater goals can be established and pursued successfully. If you don't believe you deserve to achieve a goal, it will be impossible for you to imagine achieving it, and imagining goals being realized is an integral part of the overall goal-achieving process.

3. Error of thinking you know more than you do about setting and pursuing goals

Most people think they know more about setting and pursuing goals than they actually know. As a result, they have misconceptions or an incomplete understanding of what it takes to set and achieve their goals. That's one reason this book was written.

Virtually everyone knows something about goals and has achieved goals. However, few people have spent time studying the *process* of setting goals and the principles.

To avoid this pitfall, commit to learning all you can about goal-setting—by reading, studying and observing others, and by discussing the process with friends and advisors.

4. Lack of training in pursuing goals

Have you ever had a comprehensive course on setting and pursuing goals?

Most people haven't—not in high school, college, or in any career or business experiences. You learned what you know about goal setting through your experiences.

One way to improve your skills in this area is to read and study the materials in this book. Another step is to apply the principles and learn by trial and error.

5. Absence of a method or use of a method that does not work

Only a small percentage of individuals and organizations have thought through and adopted a method to guide daily actions and progress toward their goals. Yet, without methods we become distracted and ineffective; there is no basis to evaluate and improve; and we have difficulty concentrating on activities that will yield the results we want.

Most people have not been taught how to create systems and methods. They do what they do because of habits created without the benefit of forethought and evaluation. This produces some results, but not necessarily reliable, predictable, and consistent results.

Successful individuals design their own methods or refine methods others have created. What successful companies do best is create and use methods to establish and achieve corporate goals.

To avoid proceeding without a method, use *MOSAIC* and *GOAL-DRIVEN MANAGEMENT.*

6. Failure to accept responsibility or be held accountable

Many individuals don't achieve their goals because they don't accept the responsibility to do so. In business environments, goals often are not achieved because the individuals pursuing the goals have not bought into the goals and are not held accountable for their actions to realize them.

To avoid this pitfall, be responsible and hold people accountable.

7. Incongruities between goals and beliefs

You cannot and will not achieve more than you believe you *can* and *will* achieve. Trying is not enough. If you express a goal of doubling your sales next year, there is little chance you will achieve this goal until you believe it is possible, believe you will accomplish it, and pursue it as though you will. A goal thought of as impossible or unlikely is not a goal; it is an impossibility.

To make physical progress toward your goals, first make mental progress. We accomplish everything first in our minds, then in physical reality.

This principle is often overlooked when people are setting goals—they do not realize they are mentally at point A, when their goals are at point B. You cannot move from where you are to where you want to be until you do so mentally. You cannot achieve goals physically until you believe you can mentally.

Consider the business owner who says she wants to build a $10,000,000 per year business, but who remains thinking and acting like a person running a $2,000,000 business. To get to $10,000,000 she must first move there mentally. As Emerson said, "You are what you think about all day long."

8. Insufficiency of desire

Often individuals do not have a sufficient desire and underlying motivation to achieve their goals.

Desire is the engine for all accomplishment. If your desire is too small for a goal, that goal will never be achieved. You will not put forth the effort required and sustain it.

There is no power to goals unless you have bought in to them and established them as your personal wants.

You achieve only what you want to achieve. If you have not bought in to a goal, you want to maintain the status quo, and that is what you will do. You will always remain or move to where you are the strongest mentally, at the subconscious level. This applies to business and personal goals.

The first step for overcoming insufficient desire is to match your motivation with your goals.

The question to ask is: *Why?* Why are you pursuing the goals you are pursuing? Why is your team or company pursuing the goals it is pursuing? What will accomplishment of your goals do for you? Do *you* want to achieve your goals or are you pursuing them because they are being forced upon you? Are you pursuing your goals because you *have* to? How important is it that you achieve your goals? If there were no outside forces to consider, would you still pursue the goals you are pursuing now? Why?

No one can motivate another human being or create desire in another person. The switches for motivation and desire are inside, in our subconscious minds. Each of us must click them into the "on" position, from the inside.

If you want to be motivated, you can take steps to get positive stimuli and change your mental frame of reference. You can start by reading books, listening to tapes, or going to hear a speaker. You can visit some new locations or meet some new people. You can seek out mentors. You can strike up relationships with the kinds of people you might like to emulate. There are many things you can do. Pick one and do it.

9. Lack of realistic goals or expectations

We sometimes set unrealistic goals. And, sometimes we expect to accomplish too much, too fast. Most of us are susceptible to a little overstatement or exuberance now and then. When you set unrealistic goals, you don't really fool anybody, including yourself. Big stretch goals are important. But you must believe your goals are possible or they are pipe dreams.

To avoid the pitfall of establishing unrealistic goals, write them down on paper as *laser-clear* goal statements. Prepare an action plan to achieve the goals. Leave them for a week or so. Then come back and see how they sound and feel. If they still sound and feel good and realistic, trust your gut. Go for them.

10. Underestimation of the effort involved

Most of us underestimate the effort, time, and resources required to achieve our goals. If you underestimate too much, this can be a problem. What happens to some people is that halfway on the way to realizing their goals they become tired, frustrated, and disappointed. If these conditions persist, they may possibly give up the effort and quit altogether. It is important at the outset to have a realistic appraisal of the efforts and sacrifices required.

The way to estimate correctly is to prepare a good plan that spells out the major steps required. A good plan will show the effort required to achieve your goals.

27

Fourteen recommendations for executives

While anyone can benefit from the concepts in this book, firms can get more out of *MOSAIC* and *GOAL-DRIVEN MANAGEMENT* when their executives consider the recommendations below. Some, which are included elsewhere in this book, are reiterated here because of their importance.

1. Implement *MOSAIC* and *GOAL-DRIVEN MANAGEMENT* on a "total unit basis" to realize maximum benefits

Remember the tower of Babel?

According to the Bible, the descendants of Noah were trying to unite all peoples by building a tower in Babel, a city on the plains of Babylonia, that would reach to Heaven.

God thwarted the tower-building efforts by causing each person to speak a different language. Reduced to babblings, the people could not proceed with construction.

Without a common language and a common systematic approach, our efforts to achieve our business goals would be reduced to the level of the people trying to build the tower of Babel when they discovered they couldn't understand each other.

Conversely, as we improve our communication, coordination, and methods for working together toward common goals, we improve our results.

MOSAIC and *GOAL-DRIVEN MANAGEMENT* serve as a common language and approach for systematically selecting and pursuing business goals. When learned and applied properly, these methods can guide the way people think and communicate with each other about goals and their plans to achieve them. They can become ingrained into the DNA fiber of every associate and fused into an integral part of your culture and framework for achieving results.

To maximize *MOSAIC* and *GOAL-DRIVEN MANAGE-MENT*, all members of the same team, workgroup, or business unit should learn and apply the concepts at the same time—so they can communicate with each other and share and build upon their collective experiences.

2. Establish goal-setting and goal-achieving processes that foster teamwork at the DNA level

People are individualistic. It is not natural to come together, agree on mutually beneficial goals and plans, and then pursue those goals in a unified manner.

In his book, *I Can't Accept Not Trying,* Michael Jordan, the famous basketball player, wrote, "Talent wins games, but teamwork and intelligence win championships. . . . It took us a period of time to understand that. It's a selfless process and in our society sometimes it's hard to come to grips with filling a role instead of trying to be a superstar. There is a tendency to ignore or fail to respect all the parts that make the whole thing possible."

One of the most fervently protected sanctities at Arthur Andersen was Andersen's *One Firm* concept. This meant that all decisions and actions were to be taken, not in the best interest of one individual, group, or office, but with the firm's overall worldwide best interest in mind.

One Firm is an incredible concept. A number of companies

have a one-firm philosophy. Lehman Brothers, for example, describes their "One Firm" philosophy in their annual report.

The one-firm concept promotes the long-term mutual best interests of everyone as a whole while dissuading short-term and self-serving decisions and actions. For example, at Andersen any partner or manager in the Washington office could refer work for a local client to a partner-manager in the Hong Kong office and know unequivocally that the team in the Hong Kong office would perform the work as though the client was their client, which it was. It also meant no cutting back on staff training to boost short-term profits, because everyone understood the long-term, essential nature of the ongoing investment in personnel.

The championship teamwork Michael Jordan seeks and the one-firm behavior Andersen strives for can be created only by implanting the concept of teamwork at the individual DNA level throughout an organization. This results in true *DNA Leadership*. Central to this are the processes an organization uses to achieve the unified adoption and pursuit of common goals.

To ensure teamwork over the longer term, involve everyone in the goal-setting and goal-achieving processes. Teach individuals and teams the skills required and encourage them to *plan and pursue* their goals with their teams. No team member should go it alone. No one should be out there alone setting individual goals, objectives, and plans. We must plan and work together.

3. Use a combination top-down, bottom-up approach to set realistic goals

Martin called to say that he had been promoted to area manager. Now he had to prepare a marketing plan. Martin wanted to discuss with me the logic he was using for his projections. The approach he explained was what I often refer to as the Chinese Coca-Cola® theory.

I encountered this theory repeatedly in my venture capital business. It goes something like this: Let's see, if there are a gazillion people living in China and we can sell just one Coca-Cola® to every 20th person there, then we can capture 5% of the market and build a business that will have revenues of . . . that's right, 5% of a gazillion.

This approach is sometimes useful for getting a ballpark estimate to evaluate a market. But it doesn't establish realistic goals someone actually intends to achieve.

What people forget when they take the Chinese Coca-Cola® approach, especially when sales results are being projected, is that in order to sell 5% of a gazillion-sized market, you have to be able to afford to address a market that large.

Goals are more often limited by the resources that can be brought to bear than by the magnitude of the opportunity. It is not impossible to achieve 5% of a gazillion-sized market if you can obtain and afford the resources required. The problem is not with the goals; the problem is with the shortfall between the goals and the resource cost of achieving them.

Unfortunately, many businesses and individuals use only a macro or top-down approach to setting goals. A result is imprecision or softness in the goals at each level because individuals tend to push their goals up or water them down to match the top-down influence.

Ideally, for establishing goals use an iterative approach that is both top-down and bottom-up. Establish top-down parameters as generalized working guidelines and concurrently build goals from the bottom up based on planned actions that will drive realization of the goals at each level. Once you know and compare these two parameters, you can consider further analyses and planned actions back and forth iteratively until you establish realistic and achievable goals and action plans.

For Martin's marketing plan, I recommended he evaluate the realism of his macroestimates by building a market-segment-by-market-segment plan based on the resources available and the marketing and selling activities he could implement. I told him to estimate the success rates and results of the selling activities, based on his prior experiences. Then I said that he should accumulate his results and compare them to his macroestimates. That done, I told him to evaluate the gap between his macroestimates and his bottom-up estimates and determine whether to adjust his approach, add more resources, or create other actions to close the gap. Martin ended up with realistic stretch goals and a solid, workable plan to achieve them.

4. Stop and consider quantum leap possibilities

Webster's defines quantum leap as "an abrupt change, sudden increase, or dramatic advance."

An example of a quantum leap is the rapid growth of U.S. Office Products Company. Jonathan Ledecky founded the company in 1994. By the end of 1996, just three years later, the company had made more than 110 acquisitions and had achieved annualized revenues in excess of $1 billion.

That is a quantum leap.

A quantum leap on a smaller scale is the results Blair Reischer achieved. Blair owns a firm that installs software. He established his business eight years ago and it remained a one-man operation. After learning the *GOAL-DRIVEN MANAGEMENT* principles, Blair decided to raise his sights and also to narrow his business focus to concentrate on sales support software. In less than one year Blair's business doubled and he hired an associate.

That, too, is a quantum leap.

Do you know what the main ingredient was in both Jonathan's and Blair's situations that enabled them to produce their quantum leaps? Do you think Jonathan is ten times smarter or works ten times harder than other executives? Do you think Blair suddenly got twice as smart or started working twice as hard?

Not really. It wasn't raw intelligence or Herculean efforts that enabled Jonathan's and Blair's quantum leaps. It was that they *thought bigger.*

Jonathan set a goal in 1994 to build a billion dollar company by 1999. He did it two years sooner than even he had planned. Blair decided to build a business that generates enough income to improve his lifestyle and financial security. He, too, had rapid results and surprised even himself. Of course, there are significant differences in these two examples, but on a relative basis, both Jonathan and Blair produced quantum leaps.

As explained in *Chapter 7, Limitation thinking keeps us from choosing big goals.* Knowing this, and also knowing that quantum leaps are possible if we raise our sights and the sights of the people in our companies, business and other leaders should stop and consider the possibilities that might be before them.

Don't be satisfied with the so-called "big" goals that first come to mind when you are considering the goals for your organization or yourself—because they may be below the potential of your business or your potential. Ask yourself: What's possible? What goals would you pursue if you could get the help and resources you need to pursue them? And don't be willing to wait to achieve your goals. Ask yourself: When is the earliest this can possibly be accomplished? Then ask: What can we do to achieve our goals sooner?

5. Establish goals that have real-world reference points

While it is important to consider quantum leaps and select stretch goals that stimulate growth, overly aggressive or unrealistic goals can be detrimental. They can depress morale, deflate enthusiasm, and lower self-esteem. Worse, they can establish a pattern for not achieving goals—the exact opposite of the pattern that should be created.

There is no power in *not* achieving goals. Goals create power only if you are in the habit of setting and achieving them.

To make sure goals are realistic, find real-world reference points that support achievability of the goals. The process of finding these real-world reference points is sometimes called *bench-*

marking. It involves evaluating results that a third party has achieved in similar circumstances.

The third party could be other companies, such as when one company compares its profitability or performance data to other companies in its industry; or it could be internal third-party data, such as when the results of one associate are compared to another.

6. Identify action steps at a sufficiently detailed level

When I was a new staff accountant at Arthur Andersen, I thought I was going to be fired many times during my first year. I am not saying this in jest. It was a somber secret I kept to myself.

A common criticism I received that first year was that I began my work before I thoroughly understood the objectives and the action steps I should take to achieve them. I recollect those comments well. I vividly recall my frustration in not understanding what was meant by the need to "understand my objectives and plan of attack better before I began my work."

Soon, I thought, at twenty-three years old I would be washed up and asked to leave. It was only a matter of time.

Sometime during my second year I woke up. Like a block of granite being hammered on, my brain finally cracked open, and I realized that I had not *really* been thinking through my objectives and plans before I began my work. Instead, I had been reading the programs (action plans) someone else had written and trying mechanically to implement them perfectly. What was missing was my own thinking about what we were trying to achieve and how we were trying to achieve it.

Once I had this revelation, I began to modify the programs that others wrote to include additional and different action steps that *I* believed were essential to achieving the objectives.

I began to think things through before I acted them through. Instead of bellying up to the desk and starting my work, I *imagined* starting the work. I thought through the steps I would take and envisioned the results. Then I asked myself whether those results would be adequate, and if they were not, what would I do differently. Then I did that, in my mind.

After I adopted this new approach, my performance evaluations improved immediately. After my second year at Andersen I never again worried about losing my job—because I felt in control of what I was doing and the results I was achieving.

A key to my self-confidence is that I moved my thinking and writing of action plans to achieve goals from a generalized level to a specific, detailed level. For example, instead of just writing, "Meet with the vice president of operations and discuss year-end results," I would add a supplemental checklist of questions I wanted to cover and areas I wanted to discuss during the interview. That gave me a specific, detailed action step.

A comment some individuals make when they are exposed to *GOAL-DRIVEN MANAGEMENT* for the first time is: "I had no idea how detailed I had to be in developing my action plans."

It is true that you have to think in details and specific terms to use the approach in this book, and this will take time and effort. However, deciding in advance what actions to take, one-after-the-other, avoids dead ends and wrong turns, and it minimizes the need for seat-of-the-pants or makeshift alterations after you start. The net result is that you will save time and resources and improve your overall results.

7. Empower associates by adopting crystal-clear mission, vision, and philosophy statements and *laser-clear* goals

The word *empowerment* has reached buzzword status, particularly in reference to individuals and their empowerment to pursue corporate missions, visions, philosophies, and goals. A problem with empowerment is that it can be misinterpreted to mean more than was intended. And empowerment doesn't work well unless care is taken in developing the framework in which individuals are to be empowered.

Jim Ferrell, Chairman and Chief Executive Officer of Ferrellgas, put this in perspective at a company retreat. Approximately two hundred executives had gathered to develop their respective operating plans for the company's future. This is what Jim told them, paraphrased from the notes I took at the meeting:

"There has been a lot of talk recently about empowerment and I want to comment on it.

"If you interpret empowerment to mean that an individual has to act responsibly and professionally and use his or her best judgment to do what is right for our customers, our employees, and our company, then you and I agree with what empowerment means and you, indeed, are empowered to do what I just said.

"But, if you think empowerment means individuals are supposed to go out on their own, with their own agendas, setting their own goals and developing their own plans, and doing things their own way, then we don't agree and we need to talk about it.

"We are all in the same company, and we must have a team effort toward the same vision and the same goals."

Employees are empowered when their DNA is aligned with the DNA of the company they work for. This means they understand the core values and strategic direction of the company; think they are part of an overall plan; know their required contribution to achieving that plan; and have the ability to make decisions and take actions to produce results within this framework. The way to accomplish this is to develop crystal-clear mission, vision, and philosophy statements and *laser-clear* goals throughout an organization so the goals and actions of individuals are aligned with corporate goals and philosophies. (See *Chapters 1* and *2* for additional discussion on these topics.)

8. Review and reconfirm your company's mission and vision periodically

"Well, it's official," said Mike Soignet, Vice President of Distribution at Domino's Pizza, Inc. "We are going to continue to be in the pizza business—the *home-delivered* pizza business."

Domino's has been in the business of selling home-delivered pizza for many years, so Mike's comments at the conclusion of an executive retreat may not seem important. He certainly wasn't announcing a revelation. But what Mike was saying was very significant.

At the retreat, one of the topics Domino's executive team considered was the business the company was in. The question was: Should the company continue in its present business, or should the company begin offering other products and services and thereby turn the business in other directions? Mike was saying that the executives came together, weighed the alternatives, and decided to stay in the same basic business they were already in— the business of serving pizzas to people who want them delivered to their homes, places of work, college dormitories, hotel rooms, or wherever else they might be when they get the urge for pizza.

This exemplifies the ongoing process for developing mission and vision statements—periodically pausing to reflect on what is important and what has been accomplished, and reaffirming the purposes, objectives, and strategies of the business. This is a critical exercise. It reconfirms what the business is and is becoming and it establishes parameters for the allocation and expenditure of resources to achieve goals.

9. Use the *MOSAIC* method to adopt a balanced approach for balanced growth

A shortcoming of many businesses is that they do *not* do everything required for success. Rather, they do some things very well, but ignore or slight other important aspects.

Joe Mancuso, founder and president of the Chief Executive

Officers Club, puts it this way: "To be successful, businesses don't need to be perfect or do *some* things 100%. What they need instead is to do *all* things pretty well at 80%." In other words, businesses must have *balance* among their important operational functions.

I learned this lesson in my venture capital business: To have a solid foundation for growth, businesses must have balance among their core operating components. On more than one occasion we found ourselves with an investment in difficulty because the technological strength and emphasis of the management team was so strong it overshadowed and drained resources from other key areas of the company. An example is the company that created the "perfect product" no one in the market wanted. The focus on marketing was short shrifted. The company we invested in was not unique in this respect—there has been more than one venture capitalist who had a great technological product with no one on the management team capable of selling it.

Repeated on the next page is the *Current MOSAIC* for the Jones Insurance Agency which was explained in *Chapter 4*. This points out the need for the company to round itself out. It also shows that the company is *not* presently a stellar performer. Simply becoming aware of these performance assessments will help Mr. Jones focus himself and his business on important areas.

Businesses should also strive for balance in the development and growth of individuals.

Consider this headline in an issue of *Fortune* magazine: "This tough guy wants to give you a hug." The tough guy is Les Alberthal, the CEO of EDS. The gist of the article is "Alberthal has decided to do nothing less than remake the souls of his 95,000 troops." Alberthal "has gone touchy feely," the article says, because he sees where EDS is headed—to a future where EDS employees will have to be more sensitive to customers, employees, and colleagues. Analysts apparently are raving about

Jones Insurance Agency
Step 3: *Current MOSAIC*

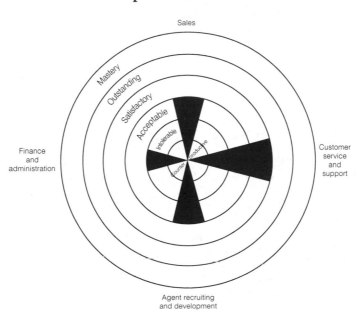

Alberthal's approach because they know how important it will be in the years ahead for EDS to "nurture and care for their clients."

Mr. Alberthal is saying that his associates can't just be technologically strong. Their strength must be balanced with well-rounded people skills.

Richard C. Bartlett, vice chairman of Mary Kay Holding Corporation in Dallas, Texas, made this comment in a recent issue of *Executive Excellence*: "The more employees you have living full, rich, contributing lives, the stronger your culture of success." Mr. Bartlett's comment was in reference to the importance his company places on individuals leading "balanced lives, with family, faith, and career in harmony."

Balance is also important on a personal level. Consider Rafeo, the owner of a little Italian eatery. He was successful in establishing and growing his business. But his efforts became all consuming, and he destroyed his marriage and distanced himself from his children in the process. While it *is* possible Rafeo knew his life was out of balance and didn't care, it is more likely that he didn't know how out of balance his life was or didn't take steps to put himself in balance until it was too late to remedy the situation.

We become more interesting, more creative, and *more valuable* to ourselves and the companies we work for when we expand our horizons and experiences instead of being narrowly focused on the same experiences all the time. For example, a vice president remarked how she has been transformed into a new person with fresher ideas and a brighter outlook—because she has begun taking tap dancing lessons. The exposure she is getting to new people, surroundings, and activities have uncaked her thinking and set her mind in new directions.

We can find ourselves or our businesses in need of some rounding out at any age or stage of development. In the book *Late Bloomers*, Brendan Gill provides an insight into one of the great thinkers of all time with this quote credited to Montaigne: "There is nothing more remarkable about the life of Socrates than that he found time in his old age to learn to dance and play on instruments and thought it time well spent."

MOSAIC is an excellent tool for identifying the areas where companies or individuals may be out of balance. Use it as an integral part of your overall goal-setting process. I am reemphasizing this because once exposed to the concepts in this book, some firms and individuals are so anxious to begin selecting and writing *laser-clear* goals and developing their *Action Plan Recaps* that they may bypass the *MOSAIC* process. They think they already know their priorities and where they are and are not out of balance. But my experience is that people and businesses do *not* have a clear assessment of themselves and implementation of the *MOSAIC* method is always beneficial and enlightening.

10. Use *Action Plan Recap* sheets to establish a library of best practices or best methods that can be shared by all associates

The real asset in a company is more than its people—it is the collective *know-how* of the people: how they apply that know-how and how they share that know-how. This includes their collective ability to increase their know-how by innovating and learning new methods and techniques, and adapting to and using new technologies. Many corporations have programs to establish, improve, and capitalize on corporate know-how and this is a frequent topic in many board rooms.

As discussed in *Chapter 13*, *Action Plan Recaps* are a tool that can be used to create and employ the best practices or best methods throughout an organization. Once *Action Plan Recaps* are adopted as a standardized convention for documenting action plans, the completed recaps can become a library of know-how that is easily transferred and shared among associates.

Do consider this concept in one form or another. There is more to this idea than initially meets the eye.

11. Incorporate *MOSAIC* and GOAL-DRIVEN MANAGEMENT into performance appraisal and coaching systems

People do not know how they are doing. That can be a big problem in business. Another problem is that people in business don't always plan from year-to-year for personal growth.

Evaluating personal performance is not the objective of personal performance management. Improving the quality and effectiveness of personal performance while improving the capacity of individuals is. Aligning their efforts with company objectives and purposes is a part of it, too.

In order to guide and energize people so they meet their goals, business leaders must first make sure people have goals and workable plans to achieve them.

MOSAIC and *GOAL-DRIVEN MANAGEMENT* provide an opportunity to do this. These methods guide individuals in their personal development, performance, and growth. In a financial services firm I have worked with, associates work with their respective managers to develop their own *Personal Performance Plans,* setting forth their individual goals and action plans on a month-by-month basis throughout the year. The individual plans are summarized and become a core element in the regional plans of the company.

There is nothing quite like having associates participate in the development *and documentation* of their own *MOSAIC Performance Assessment,* their own *laser-clear* goals, and their own *Action Plan Recaps.* This participation drives home the responsibilities of individuals and the performance criteria upon which they will be evaluated. The benefit is they know their responsibilities and the performance criteria at the DNA level. Plus, these mechanisms are tools for monitoring performance and for coaching and mentoring individuals in their personal growth.

In the financial services firm above, for instance, the associates and their managers meet weekly to review the *Personal Performance Plans* of the associates and the results they are realizing. There is no beating around the bush in these discussions. The goals and plans are laid out on paper. The positive candor and accountability this creates on a timely basis are enormous.

12. Begin implementation with top-level commitment and buy-in

To achieve the optimum results from *DNA Leadership* using *MOSAIC* and *GOAL-DRIVEN MANAGEMENT,* begin only after top-level management is fully committed and prepared to support the program continually.

People pay more attention to what leaders do than to what they say they are going to do. If a CEO says, "We're going to adopt a goal-setting program throughout the company," and takes no actions to establish corporate goals and plans to achieve them, then it's hard for associates to understand why they should improve their individual approaches to setting and achieving goals.

I worked on a project years ago for the Business Roundtable (BRT). The first action we took to ensure success of the project was to make sure Frank T. Cary, then CEO of IBM and Chairman of a BRT taskforce, knew the key aspects of the project and supported them. To demonstrate his support, Mr. Cary's first actions were to commit IBM to the project and get the project underway at IBM. Then he called the CEO of General Motors and secured GM's commitment to participate. Once these two industry giants were in place and committed, selling participation in the project to other companies in the BRT was straightforward and easy—because we started at the top. The project never would have gotten off the ground without this strong and open top-level support.

Top-level commitment must come in both words and actions. CEOs and other leaders must communicate what they are going to do and what they want their associates to do to implement *MOSAIC* and *GOAL-DRIVEN MANAGEMENT*. They must also take steps to implement the concepts themselves.

Once the executive team understands and begins using the concepts and establishes corporate goals, the methods and processes can be rolled out to the entire company.

When executive education and training fail in the corporate world, it usually is not because the content or materials are deficient, but because too little attention has been paid to the actual implementation and reinforcement of the process. "We gave them the tools. Why did they fail?" is a common comment.

We all need constant reminding and reinforcement in learning new skills. People don't get it, whatever "it" is, the first time around, and it is unrealistic to think they can or will.

For these reasons, it is important to view the implementation of *MOSAIC* and *GOAL-DRIVEN MANAGEMENT* as a long-term commitment. The methods and techniques won't become firmly established in an organization by offering a few courses and then forgetting about it. More effort and reinforcement are required. But once the methods are in place and functioning, the benefits of increased productivity, profits, growth, innovation, job satisfaction, and individual development of associates can be enormous. These methods do produce power—*Goal Power.*

13. Create a goal-achievement environment

I recently interviewed the founder and president of one of the most successful agencies within a large, successful financial services company. A millionaire many times over, this man has a vibrant and growing business, and his team of associates and business partners is superb by every standard.

When I asked him what he attributed the success of his business to, he fired back: "I manage our *environment.*"

I wasn't sure I had heard him correctly. "You manage your environment?" I said.

"That's right," he said. "My number one most important job is to manage the environment our people work in."

He went on to explain how he creates a motivational climate that attracts and cultivates "eagles," as he calls them—people who generate their own ideas and make things happen by establishing and pursuing big goals day-in and day-out.

The simplicity of this concept is so obvious that it may be overlooked. Many leaders in companies overlook the importance of creating an environment where the habits of setting and pursuing goals as a way of life become ingrained as part of the DNA fabric of everyone throughout the organization. All too often individuals come to work just to put in their time and go home. While this may seem like the easy way out, it is not.

One of the biggest reasons people leave organizations is that they are not held accountable for results. Individuals become disenchanted when they don't know how they are doing and when they don't think that they are making a positive contribution. Without goals, there is no accountability and there is no identifiable contribution being made.

People bond together, communicate better, and help each other more when they understand why they are pursuing a common goal together. The pursuit of common goals in a goal-achieving environment is the engine that drove my entire career at Arthur Andersen. Everything we did at Andersen was viewed as a project of one kind or another—and every project had a goal, an action plan, *and* a team assigned to achieve the results. We ate, slept, and talked about achieving our results daily. The goal-pursuing DNA implanted into me at Arthur Andersen is one of the greatest benefits I obtained from my career.

The absence of goals and a goal-pursuing environment is a great disservice to employees. Leaders at all levels should take steps to create an environment where associates are encouraged and held accountable for significant goals they are pursuing.

14. Demand excellence and press individuals to fulfill their potential

Two of the greatest services leaders can provide to those they are leading are *not* to accept mediocrity under any circumstances and *not* to ask people to do less than they are capable of doing. Stated another way, the greatest services leaders can provide are to demand excellence and to press individuals hard to fulfill their potential.

Years ago Dr. Norman Vincent Peale coined the phrase: "You are greater than you think you are."

Dr. Peale's encouraging admonition is still applicable. Individuals are greater than they think they are, and they are capable of producing more results and achieving greater success for their companies and themselves than they think they can.

Most leaders and most people do not press themselves or the

people in their organizations hard enough for superlative results and superlative skills development. There is a tendency to accept mediocrity as the status quo.

One of the worst things leaders can do is tolerate mediocrity or marginal effort. When they do, they condone a false limit of an individual's performance potential, which has a way of becoming fixed as an immovable, concrete belief.

I often am asked what criteria I use for evaluating leaders. My answer is to ask myself this question: Would I want either of my two daughters to work for this individual?

For me, the answer to my question says it all since I want the very best for my daughters. I want them working with competent, value-based individuals who have the wherewithal, know-how, and the desire to bring out the best in them. This requires an impeccable value system, tremendous desire, willingness, commitment, and other similar personal attributes in the individuals involved. It also requires that they demonstrate structure, attention to detail, discipline, pursuit of specific goals, and an understanding of excellence and the courage to demand it.

The greatest impact leaders have had in my life is that they have seen, encouraged, and demanded strengths in me that I myself was not aware of. These leaders became mentors or role models, and they planted in me seeds of expectancy and belief.

My Uncle Emil, a fireman by profession, planted *expectancy* in me to become a businessman even before I knew what a businessman was. My uncle called me "JB" and when I was just a boy he repeatedly told me that I would be in business some day. "A big shot with his feet up on the desk smoking a cigar" was the vision he painted.

I don't smoke cigars or prop my feet up on the desk thinking of myself as a big shot, but in a real way my Uncle Emil influenced what I have become and what I have accomplished. (For readers who notice the coincidence, yes, I had two mentors named Emil in my life—my uncle and the one in the steel mill mentioned in *Chapter 19.*)

The value of bringing out the best in people becomes apparent when we aim the spotlight on the cliche: "People are our most important asset."

If this is true, and I believe it is, then the greatest opportunity in business today lies in helping individuals find and achieve their potential. Therefore, a primary responsibility of leaders is to bring out the best in people and motivate them toward mutually beneficial goals. To optimize the return on their people assets, leaders must put mechanisms into place that will allow their people to identify and realize their capabilities—they must institutionalize *DNA Leadership.*

One way to challenge individuals and help them fulfill their potential is to define and demonstrate excellence in specific, understandable terms. Unfortunately, this is rarely done as well as it could be. The *MOSAIC* method was developed with this important element of *DNA Leadership* specifically in mind. Instead of defining tasks and communicating in broad terms, *MOSAIC* requires individuals to define superlative performance criteria.

Another way to help individuals achieve their potential is to teach them how to set and achieve goals that will develop them into something greater than they were before they had the goals. This is a primary purpose of *GOAL-DRIVEN MANAGEMENT,* the other key method in *DNA Leadership.*

In a very real sense every true mentor along my path in life has thought more of me than I did, and every true leader I have had the good fortune of meeting has inspired me to greater heights than I had been targeting. My many mentors and all of the great leaders I have encountered are as much responsible for what I have become as I am—because they helped me see the goals that I could achieve. They helped me see what I could accomplish and become and then helped me fulfill those desires. I am very pleased and grateful they have been there for me.

I wish for you great joy and the best of success in life. I hope you are inspired and challenged by the leaders and the mentors in your life and that you will return the favor by inspiring and challenging others. Good luck and God bless you.

*"A man of talent has only to name any form
or fact with which we are most familiar, and
the strong light which he throws on it
enhances it to all eyes. People wonder they
never saw it before."*

—Ralph Waldo Emerson

Glossary

See Index for page references to these terms

10 Elements See *ten elements.*

100-Idea approach A technique used to think "out of the box." You press yourself or others to come up with a hundred ideas to overcome obstacles or achieve desired results. The challenge of the task forces a paradigm shift in thinking.

Action Plan Recap A simple-to-use format for summarizing goals and action plans to achieve those goals.

Action Plan Workbook A workbook used to file *Action Plan Recaps* and supporting information pertaining to goals being pursued. The purpose of the workbook is to keep everything in one place.

Action plans Plans containing the "must do" actions that will result in achieving one or more goals. Action plans are summarized onto *Action Plan Recaps* for ease of reference.

Action-driven Refers to O, OUTLINE *a plan.* Plans are *action-driven* when they drive actions that will result in the realization of desired goals.

Alignment Unity when everyone is working together harmoniously as a unit toward the same common objectives and purposes. Alignment is achieved in *DNA Leadership through GOAL-DRIVEN MANAGEMENT* when corporate missions, visions, philosophies, and goals are in line and harmonious with the missions, visions, philosophies, goals, and action plans of the groups and individuals in the organization.

Anacondas in Life Negative people, negative information, negative beliefs, and negative circumstances that limit the goals we pursue and the results we achieve in our business and personal lives. The *Anacondas in Life* is a term James R. Ball coined in his book, *Soar. . .If You Dare®*, first published in 1992.

Autopilot A mechanical device for automatically steering ships and aircraft toward a desired destination without intervention required by the pilot. We can place ourselves on autopilot toward our goals by establishing goals that contain the *10 Elements* every goal must have and by developing detailed action plans that we have internalized so completely that they are a part of our subconscious thinking.

Backwards planning A planning approach in which you visualize realization of a goal desired and work backwards to where you are now to determine the steps you would have to have taken to achieve your goal. James R. Ball coined the term *Backwards Business Planning* in the first edition of *The Entrepreneur's Tool Kit,* a guide for business planning published in 1985.

Ballgrams Short notes to associates on special *Ballgram* stationery that James R. Ball uses for internal communications regarding special events, special recognition of individuals, and other flash-type announcements.

Beginning, middle, and end approach A simple three-step approach where action plans for larger projects are divided into three parts—a beginning, a middle, and an end—to create more easily manageable segments.

Benchmark A reference from which measurements may be made.

Benchmarking The process where individuals or firms compare their performance results or processing methodologies with third-party "benchmarks" and then take actions to achieve results or implement systems similar to or better than those of the third-party. An example of benchmarking would be Firm A comparing its manufacturing processes and resultant error rates to those of Firm B and then taking steps to achieve the results Firm B is achieving.

Best methods or **best practices** The process of identifying and implementing on an ongoing basis the best methods or practices for achieving a desired result. The "best methods" are those that comprise the ideal or optimum approach when all criteria have been taken into account.

BHAG An acronym for *Big Hairy Audacious Goals* used in the book *Built To Last,* by James C. Collins and Jerry I. Porras.

Bite-sizing A technique for overcoming procrastination and creating momentum. Bite-sizing refers to dividing big, multifaceted, and long-term goals and action plans into small segments individuals and groups can mentally and physically "chew" on and accomplish.

Brainstorming A group problem-solving technique that involves the spontaneous contribution of ideas from members of the group. The primary objective of brainstorming is the generation of ideas, not the evaluation of them. Brainstorming is used in *GOAL-DRIVEN MANAGEMENT* to identify possible goals, obstacles that must be overcome, strategies, and action steps.

Business Advisory Board A group of individuals who provide advice and serve as a sounding board for the evaluation of strategies, tactics, and operational matters. This is different from a formal board of directors, which has legally defined purposes, authorities, and responsibilities.

Buy in A state of mind that occurs when an individual or group of individuals understand and commit to a goal or an action plan so intently and emotionally that they proceed toward accomplishing the goal or implementing the action plan as if they were their own goals and their own plans.

Cascading process A process to provide for the alignment and linkage of purposes, values, philosophies, goals, and actions throughout an organization. Cascading is used to regenerate DNA fabric throughout an organization.

Cause and effect A core principle upon which the *GOAL-DRIVEN MANAGEMENT* method is based. It states: *Effort, that is work, is required to produce results*. This means that there is a direct relationship between the effort we make and the results we can expect.

Cause goals The supporting goals or action steps that, when taken or achieved, will produce the effect or *end-result* goal we desire.

Change resisters People who vehemently resist change.

Chunking your time A productivity and performance technique of spending as much of your time as you can in one-hour uninterrupted chunks. It is particularly important to chunk time on the actions that will yield the greatest results toward your desired goals.

Chunking time activators (CTAs) Friendly door-hanger reminders that can be placed on the knob of a closed door to notify others that you do not want to be disturbed because you are *chunking your time.*

Command language   A technique for writing action steps so that each step begins with a command verb that describes what is to be accomplished. For example: *Develop* procedures for a customer hot line.

Congruency between goals and beliefs   This occurs when an individual or firm is pursuing goals that are harmonious and in line with the individual's or firm's beliefs, values, and philosophies.

***Continuing* goals**   Established goals already being pursued. Time and effort are required to achieve *continuing* goals, but the ongoing effort is not considered extreme or extraordinary, for example, calling on existing accounts once each month. *Continuing* goals are contrasted to *thrusting* goals, which are new goals requiring special effort, energy, and drive.

Corporate *Goals Journal*   A *Goals Journal* for businesses that contains a summary of *laser-clear* goal statements for all of the major goals being pursued by the company. See *Goals Journal.*

Critical mass   The fissionable material needed to establish and sustain a nuclear chain reaction. The critical mass concept is an important consideration in developing action plans to achieve goals. The question is: Does the plan provide for all essential actions necessary to establish and sustain momentum until goals are achieved?

Daily Journal   A record for making daily notations about progress toward goals, events, and other information—a written snapshot of your day.

Demons of Doubt and Despair   A specific type of *Anaconda in Life* representing individuals who cast doubt and promote despair with comments such as: "What if it doesn't work?" "You can't trust anyone." "No one wants to pay what our services are worth."

DNA bonded or **DNA transferred**   Terms referring to the integration of and buy in to cultures, missions, visions, philosophies, goals, and plans within an organization. DNA is bonded or transferred when the individuals in the organization think and act toward the missions, visions, philosophies, goals, and plans of the organization as if they were their plans—as if everything in the company were spawned from the same DNA.

***DNA Leadership*™**   A term coined in this book to describe a modern style of leadership based on a framework that creates motivation and guidance within individuals so they are internally driven and directed rather than externally controlled and managed.

***Doer-centered* goals**   Goals developed with direct and substantive input from the individuals responsible for taking the actions necessary to achieve the goals.

Eager beavers   Individuals who are highly receptive to change and eager to try new things.

Emotional linkage   A bonding between goals and emotions. It occurs when an individual or group has a strong emotional desire to pursue a specific goal or to take a specific action to achieve a goal. The "emotion" doing the connecting can be a powerful force such as love, but it can also be any emotion we experience through one or more of our senses.

Empower or **empowerment**   To give official authority or legal power. It refers to giving associates the power to do whatever it takes to get their jobs done. For example, retail clerks in many businesses are empowered to resolve customer complaints by doing whatever they believe is necessary—without having to get approvals from a higher authority.

***End-result* goals**   Goals represented by the actual, tangible end result achieved. For example: achieving a targeted sales level for a year; developing and introducing a new product; or completing a marathon. *End-result* goals are different from *cause* goals because *end-result* goals generally are not doable per se. The things we must accomplish are *cause goals*. They cause *end-result* goals to be realized.

Engine of desire   The internal motivation individuals have to achieve their personal hopes, wishes, wants, and dreams. The greater the size of the engine of desire, the greater the power there will be to achieve one's goals.

Five keys for selecting and achieving goals   The five keys in *GOAL-DRIVEN MANAGEMENT*: *G* stands for *GET a goal*; *O* stands for *OUTLINE a plan*; *A* stands for *ACT on your plan*; *L* stands for *LEARN from your progress*, and *S* stands for *SYSTEMATIZE your efforts*.

Five O'Clock Club   A club Mary Kay Ash, founder of Mary Kay Cosmetics, Inc., created in her organization for individuals who get up and get going at work by 5:00 a.m. with a short list of action items to accomplish for the day. By being in the club for three days a week members can stretch their week to eight days.

Flowchart   A diagram that shows the step-by-step progression through a procedure or system using connecting lines and symbols. Flowcharts are used in this book to illustrate the flow of the implementation action steps for *GOAL-DRIVEN MANAGEMENT*.

Four stages of learning   The four stages of development individuals go through when learning anything new. These are: (1) creation of the desire and attitude to learn; (2) acquisition of information and know-how; (3) experimentation, trial and error, and practice; and (4) creation, refinement, and reinforcement of habits.

Four levels of learning   The four stages of depth of learning: level one, unconsciously incompetent; level two, consciously incompetent; level three, consciously competent; and level four, unconsciously competent.

Fundamental principles   Comprehensive, original laws or facts supporting essential structures of cause and effect. By knowing the fundamental principles involved we can produce the effects we want by activating the causes. For example, *GOAL-DRIVEN MANAGEMENT* contains the principle of *Magnetic Attraction: firmly established goals will draw us toward them*. Thus, if we want to achieve our goals we must follow this basic principle and firmly establish them.

Gap of discontent   A gap that exists between our mental awareness of where we are and where we want to be relative to our goals. Knowledge of this gap creates internal tension. The tension is used as a positive force for achieving goals—once we are aware of the gap, we will consciously and subconsciously work to close it so we can alleviate the tension we are experiencing.

Genie Power   A term James R. Ball coined in his book, *Soar. . .If You Dare®*, first published in 1992. *Genie Power* is a technique to stimulate out-of-the-box thinking by using trigger phrases such as "What if" and "Just suppose" to introduce a presupposition into the thinking process. For example: "What if I gave you a million dollars to get this done by the end of the month?" or "Just suppose you were the president of the company, how would you approach the problem?"

Goal Power™ The power goals create for individuals and businesses to grow and achieve their potential.

Goal statement Declaration of a goal.

Goal Stimulators Lists of possible goals and written goal categories. These lists are used to stimulate thinking when identifying and selecting specific goals to be pursued.

Goals coach A competent, qualified individual who mentors, instructs, manages, and encourages individuals or firms in a professional manner toward establishing and achieving their goals.

Goals Journal A journal used to keep track of goals—goals being pursued currently, goals to be pursued at a later date, and goals that have been achieved. This is not a personal organizer or calendar; it is a record solely of goals. A *Goals Journal* is an integral part of the *GOAL-DRIVEN MANAGEMENT* method.

GOAL-DRIVEN MANAGEMENT™ A proprietary method developed by James R. Ball for establishing, pursuing, and achieving goals. This method is part of the core subject matter of this book.

Gravitational pull A principle in physics that is the measure of the attractive force one body has on another. We will be pulled toward goals that *we perceive* to have the greatest gravitational pull on us because of their size and closeness as measured by our ability to reach them.

Gyroscopic Planning™ A proprietary method developed by James R. Ball for use in developing business plans. *Gyroscopic Planning* refers to the *laser-clear* clarification of goals combined with the development of detailed plans and systems so completely that individuals and organizations proceed toward their goals on an error-free autopilot basis.

Habit-driven Refers to S, *SYSTEMATIZE your efforts.* Systems are *habit-driven* when they are developed and implemented so completely that the actions within the system become habits that are accomplished on autopilot.

Hideaway Anywhere you can retreat to be by yourself for some quality time without interruptions.

Hockey-Puck Management   A seat-of-the-pants management approach where little, if anything, is pre-planned. *Hockey-Puck Management* is the complete opposite of *Orchestral Management* where everything is planned in detail.

Imprinting   A learning process that establishes a behavior pattern by imbedding thoughts into our subconscious minds. When we have imprinted a goal or an action step, we will proceed toward the goal or the implementation of the action step on autopilot.

Improvement-driven   Refers to *L, LEARN from your progress.* Learning is *improvement-driven* when all actions to achieve goals are continually measured, evaluated, and improved.

Inertia   A property of matter by which it remains at rest or in uniform motion in the same straight line unless acted upon by some external force. Inertia in life represents an obstacle to change and goal achievement because people tend to continue doing what they have been doing.

Inside-out approach   The internal or self-motivation of individuals and organizations as compared to using external influences. See *DNA Bonded* and *DNA Leadership.*

Just-in-time learning   A technique where individuals can access the information they need when they need it or learn the skills they have to have when they have to have them; for example, help screens for software. Rather than taking the time to learn all of the nuances of the software, users access the help screens only when they need them to accomplish a specific task.

Know-how and **knowledge capital**   Knowledge, processes, systems, and procedures for doing something smoothly and efficiently. Know-how and knowledge capital in an organization refer to the intangible and tangible abilities of the people in the organization to do their work and to create and innovate. This includes all knowledge, skills, techniques, operations, and other factors that enable the organization to achieve its objectives. Know-how and knowledge capital are two of the greatest assets an organization possesses.

***Laser-clear* goals**   Goals that are clarified in writing and understood so clearly there can be absolutely no mistake as to what is intended.

Laser-clear goals meet all *10 Elements every goal should have* to maximize the power and benefits the goal can produce.

Limitation thinking When individuals or organizations allow mental limits or boundaries to be placed around their beliefs, expectations, or aspirations. These are not real limitations in the tangible sense, but because we perceive them as real they become real and tangible; for example, business owners who think that they cannot grow their businesses faster than 10% per year because that is what the best companies in their industry are able to achieve. The 10% is an imaginary limit which becomes real and realized because of the belief.

Linkage Refers to the linkage of corporate missions, visions, philosophies, goals, and action plans with individual missions, visions, philosophies, goals, and action plans. Also see *Alignment.*

Locomotive Leadership An authoritative style of leadership where leaders pull or push their organizations in a top-to-bottom approach.

Magnetic attraction A principle in physics that refers to the extraordinary power or ability that one body has to attract or pull upon another body. Magnetic attraction is achieved in the goal-achieving process by establishing a firm intent to pursue a specific goal. By establishing the goal, individuals or firms are drawn to it.

Mastermind group or **mastermind approach** A technique where an individual or firm arranges for several individuals to provide advice or counsel in the selection and pursuit of goals. The "Master Mind" concept was described in Napoleon Hill's book, *Think and Grow Rich,* first published in 1937. Hill described his Master Mind concept as "coordination of knowledge and effort, in spirit of harmony, between two or more people for the attainment of a definite purpose."

Method or **methodology** A systematic process or procedure for attaining an object of desire. The two primary methodologies contained in this book are *MOSAIC* and *GOAL-DRIVEN MANAGEMENT.*

Middle-of-the-roaders People who "go with the flow" when it comes to change. They neither resist change (change resisters) nor embrace change immediately (eager beavers); in time they will evaluate and adopt or respond to changes they deem appropriate.

Mission statement A statement that describes the objectives, roles, and responsibilities of a business, a group, or an individual. A business mission statement defines also the scope of the business—that is, what is included and not included within the intended operations.

Momentum   A principle in physics that represents the product of the mass of a body times its velocity. Momentum is gained in the goal-achieving process by developing a plan where you always know what to do next—this will increase your self-confidence in your actions and accelerate the speed at which you achieve results.

***MOSAIC*_{TM}**   A proprietary method developed by James R. Ball for regenerating DNA throughout an organization and for determining which areas to concentrate on when establishing goals and action plans so you end up with a systematic and balanced approach for growth. This method is included in this book.

***MOSAIC*_{TM} graphic**   The graphical display of a *MOSAIC Performance Assessment*—see below.

MOSAIC*_{TM} *Performance Assessment   A performance assessment based upon defining and evaluating six performance levels on a current and also on a desired basis. The six levels that comprise the acronym *MOSAIC* are: Level 6, Mastery; Level 5, Outstanding; Level 4, Satisfactory; Level 3, Acceptable; Level 2, Intolerable; Level 1, Counterproductive.

"Must do" actions   The actions that must be taken to achieve a given *end-result* goal.

Olympics in thinking   Refers to the fact that planning is a major event in thinking, not writing.

Orchestral Management   A professional and deliberate management approach in which everything is planned and orchestrated in detail and implemented with great precision. This contrasts with *Hockey-Puck Management* where little, if anything, is planned in advance.

Performance criteria   The six levels of criteria to be developed in the *MOSAIC* method. (See *MOSAIC Performance Assessment*.)

Performance Grid method   A method James R. Ball developed for coaching and mentoring individuals. A detailed *Performance Grid* is used to specify all criteria on which the individuals are to be evaluated. The "grid" aspect of this technique was a precursor to certain aspects of the *MOSAIC* method.

Personal Advisory Board   A group of individuals who serve as advisors to individuals in much the same manner as a *Business Advisory Board* provides advice to business owners or managers. (See also *Mastermind Group*, a similar concept.)

Personal Performance Plan   A written plan an individual develops summarizing his or her personal goals with the strategies and actions to be taken to achieve those goals. Individuals typically develop these plans annually and update them periodically throughout the year. The plans are used as tools for guiding personal growth and development as well as for monitoring and managing progress toward business goals. In *GOAL-DRIVEN MANAGEMENT*, *Personal Performance Plans* are documented using a series of *Action Plan Recaps* summarizing an individuals's goals and action plans.

Philosophy statement   A statement that an organization or individual develops expounding guiding ideologies with respect to ethics, quality standards, human behavior and relationships, work practices, values and beliefs.

Pocket Reminders   Written reminders of major goals being pursued. They are documented on a small card to be carried in your wallet or purse so they can be referred to periodically.

Postulate   A technique where you advance a hypothesis based on an essential presupposition or condition. Postulation is used in the *Genie Power* technique to stimulate out-of-the-box thinking. In "What if I gave you a million dollars. . ." the million dollars is the essential condition that forces a paradigm shift in your thinking, thus freeing up new thoughts.

Power   The measure of the amount of work that can be accomplished per unit of time; that is, the results we can achieve in a day, week, month, year, or lifetime. Goals have power (that is, *Goal Power*) because they increase the work we can accomplish and the results we can realize.

Power cycle for producing momentum   Thought→action→ thought→action. As our thoughts stimulate our actions, our actions reinforce and stimulate our thoughts. To produce momentum, we must think and then act, then we must think some more and take some more action.

Purpose-driven   Refers to *G, GET a goal*. Goals of individuals are *purpose-driven* when they are congruent and in alignment with the beliefs, values, and desires of the individual. Goals of businesses are *purpose-driven* when they are congruent with the mission, vision, philosophies, and the purposes and objectives of the business.

Reach and repeat   A technique used in advertising where the objective is to *reach* the right audience with the right advertising message and then *repeat* that message frequently enough to move the persons receiving it to action. This concept is used to imprint goals and action plans to achieve goals so that the goals and action plans are pursued on autopilot.

Relative improvement   A concept in economics and business where rather than striving for a precise targeted or standard performance level, you strive for continual, positive relative improvement. This approach can save time and yield better results over the long-term. The logic goes: don't take time to develop a performance standard that may be controversial anyway; just measure what the performance is currently and start improving it—continuously.

Resonance   The intensity and enriching of a musical note by supplemental vibration caused by vibrating molecules in the air. The greater the amplitude of the initial vibrating object, the greater the overall resonance or sound. This principle applies in goal-setting in that the drive, energy, and activity levels of individuals towards goals vary in direct response to the nature and size of the goal itself. The bigger the goal, the bigger the response.

Results-driven   Refers to *A, ACT on your plan*. Actions are *results-driven* when they achieve positive, tangible, desired progress toward goals being pursued.

Sensory association   The identification of goals through our senses. This heightens our emotional connection and increases our desire. For example, imagine the smell of the interior and the leather seats of the new car you want to purchase. The car becomes real in your mind because of the sensory association.

Six Sigma   The highest standard of performance in respect to quality—it means virtually error free. *Six Sigma Quality* is a program developed by Motorola in 1985 based on the relationship of a product's early field life reliability to the frequency of repair in the manufacturing process. A sigma is the standard deviation in the mathematical model and a six sigma qualification was found to force changes and improvements so great that manufacturing processing and products became near perfect. The basic concept is that the more things are done right the first time, the better the products will be. (See *Stretch goal.*)

Storyboarding   A technique for visual brainstorming or visual planning. It was developed in the entertainment industry for use in creating motion pictures and cartoons. A storyboard is a series of pictures on cards depicting the story line of a planned film, show, or act. A storyboard can be used to develop action plans by writing "must do" action steps on cards and arranging the cards in storyboard fashion to reveal the step-by-step plan.

Stretch goal   A goal that requires that you stretch to achieve it. By definition it is beyond your present capabilities and resources. A stretch goal will cause an individual or firm to become greater than it was before it had the stretch goal. General Electric Company commonly refers to and uses the stretch goal concept as a tactic for growth, and in 1995 the company announced Six Sigma as its stretch target for the year 2000. (See *Six Sigma.*)

Sympathetic response   A principle in physics where the vibration or stimulus of one object causes a similar vibration or stimulus in a similar object. For example, a struck tuning fork will cause the strings on a nearby violin to reverberate with sound. This principle applies in goal-pursuing efforts—the energy, drive, and actions of one individual or group of individuals toward a goal will stimulate the energy, drive, and actions of other individuals toward the goal.

Ten Elements   The ten elements every goal should have to maximize the power and benefits the goal can produce.

Three boxes in life   A metaphor for life used to establish a perspective when selecting goals. You are living in box A if you are doing what you want to be doing. You are living in box B if you are doing something close to what you want to be doing and you have a plan to get to box A. You are living in box C if you are just making a living not doing anything you necessarily want to be doing. If you find yourself in box C, leap to box A. The risk is not in leaping; it is in *not* leaping.

***Thrusting* goals**   New goals requiring special effort, energy, and drive to achieve. An example of a *thrusting* goal is the creation of a new customer service plan. A program like this requires special effort and energy. *Thrusting* goals contrast with *continuing* goals, which are established goals already being pursued.

Thunderbolt   A term coined in this book referring to an action item to be completed on a given day. A *Thunderbolt* list is a list of the one to five most important action items to be completed on a given day.

Vision statement or **vision of success**   A collective "vision" of what a company, organization, or individual will be like after all major goals have been achieved. A famous vision of success is: "We are going to put a man on the moon by the end of the decade," declared by President John F. Kennedy.

Visualization   The formation of visual images in our minds for the purpose of creating a mental blueprint we can work towards in reality.

Vital link   Refers to alignment and linkage throughout an organization among missions, visions, philosophies, goals, and actions—at both a company level and an individual level. When alignment and linkage exist, companies are optimizing the power they can derive from goals.

What's possible approach   An approach used by Mr. Douglas Ivester, President and Chief Operating Officer at the Coca-Cola® Company, and by other individuals and firms for selecting goals. The process begins by asking the question: "What's possible?"

Index

Mission of The Goals Institute, Inc.

Our mission is to help businesses, organizations, and individuals see what they can become and then become it through the establishment, pursuit, and realization of goals.

We pursue our mission through research, publication of books, audio, video, and electronic works, and the creation, delivery, and distribution of instructional materials and educational programs.

If you would like to receive information about our executive seminars and products or learn about the experiences others have had in applying the *DNA Leadership* approach and setting and achieving goals using *MOSAIC* and *GOAL-DRIVEN MANAGEMENT*, please contact us.

Also, please let us know of your experiences applying the methods in this book that you would be willing to share in future editions or other materials. Proper credit will be given for your contribution.

The Goals Institute, Inc.
Post Office Box 3736
Reston, VA 20195-1736

www.goalsinstitute.com

email: info@goalsinstitute.com

417

About the author

James R. Ball is co-founder and president of The Goals Institute, Inc., a company created to help businesses, organizations, and individuals fulfill their potential through goal achievement.

He is the creator of the *DNA Leadership* model and the two related methods, *MOSAIC* and *GOAL-DRIVEN MANAGEMENT*.

Leadership and executive programs

Mr. Ball has provided executive development programs and keynote speeches for corporate clients including: AT&T, Bell Atlantic, BellSouth Business Systems, Inc., Coopers & Lybrand, L.L.P., Domino's Pizza Distribution, Freddie Mac, Landstar System, Inc., Legg Mason Wood Walker, Incorporated, Mobil Oil Corporation, Ryland Homes, Texaco Refining and Marketing Inc., and The Franklin Life Insurance Company.

Association clients include: American Bankers Association, American Institute of Certified Public Accountants, Institute of Real Estate Management, National Association of Insurance Women, Printing Industries of America, Inc., Society for Human Resource Management, and The Business Products Industry Association.

Venture capitalist

Previously, Mr. Ball was co-founder and managing partner of Venture America, a seed-stage venture capital firm.

Through Venture America he helped finance, launch, and grow over twenty businesses during a twelve-year period. These include: Adaptive Technologies, Inc., Automation Partners International, Inc., Binary Arts Corporation, Clustron Sciences Corporation, Digene Corporation, SSE Telecom, Inc., Universal Power Systems, Inc., Voice Processing Corporation, and The Discovery Channel.

Arthur Andersen

Mr. Ball was at Arthur Andersen for sixteen years where his last position was partner in charge of Andersen's office in Northern Virginia that targeted high technology and rapid growth firms. He served over one hundred clients during his career including Mars, Incorporated, Marriott Corporation, Digital Switch Corporation, Flow General Laboratories, ONCOR Incorporated, Orbital Sciences Incorporated, Sage Software, Inc., and fourteen companies while he was in Hong Kong.

Mr. Ball was in charge of Andersen's Professional Education Division for the Washington, D.C. metropolitan area and he helped develop several practice methodologies.

University affiliations

As an adjunct faculty member at George Mason University, Mr. Ball taught the course he created entitled *Developing an entrepreneurial mindset*. He was co-founder and the first president of the George Mason University Entrepreneurial Institute, Inc., an organization that advances entrepreneurship and business and university relations.

Mr. Ball has presented many broadcasts over the National Technological University satellite network.

He also has provided programs for the Michigan Small Business Development Center at Wayne State University and the Small Business Institute at California State University, Fullerton.

Authorship and additional information

Mr. Ball is the author of *Soar . . . If You Dare*® and *The Entrepreneur's Tool Kit*, a guide for planning businesses. He has a B.S. degree in accounting from Youngstown State University and is a member of the American Institute of Certified Public Accountants.

He and his wife Dolly live in Virginia. They have two daughters, Jennifer and Stephanie.

"Without a method to the madness,
there is only the madness."

—Jim Ball